Ethics in Light of Childhood

Ethics in Light of Childhood

John Wall

Georgetown University Press ⚱ Washington, D.C.

Georgetown University Press, Washington, D.C.
www.press.georgetown.edu

The lines from "somewhere i have never travelled,gladly
beyond," © 1931, 1959, 1991 by the Trustees for the E. E.
Cummings Trust. © 1979 by George James Firmage, from
Complete Poems: 1904–1962 by e. e. cummings, edited
by George J. Firmage. Used by permission of the Liveright
Publishing Corporation.

Library of Congress Cataloging-in-Publication Data

Wall, John, 1965-
  Ethics in light of childhood / John Wall.
    p. cm.
  Includes bibliographical references (p.   ) and index.
  ISBN 978-1-58901-692-7 (pbk. : alk. paper)
  1. Ethics. 2. Children. 3. Moral development. 4.
Child welfare--Moral and ethical aspects. I. Title.
  BJ51.W35 2010
  170.83--dc22
                              2009038712

∞ This book is printed on acid-free paper meeting the
requirements of the American National Standard for
Permanence in Paper for Printed Library Materials.
15 14 13 12 11 10   9 8 7 6 5 4 3 2
First printing

Printed in the United States of America

Change is the nursery
Of music, joy, life and eternity.

—from "Change" by John Donne

nothing which we are to perceive in this world equals
the power of your intense fragility:whose texture
compels me with the colour of its countries,
rendering death and forever with each breathing
…
nobody,not even the rain,has such small hands

—from "somewhere i have never travelled, gladly beyond"
by e.e. cummings

Contents

Acknowledgments

I AM GRATEFUL for support and insight while writing this book from many colleagues and friends, including Don Browning, Marcia Bunge, Bonnie Miller-McLemore, Adrian Thatcher, Trygve Wyller, Pamela Couture, William Schweiker, Myra Bluebond-Langner, Daniel Hart, Daniel Cook, Lynne Vallone, Jane Siegel, Janet Golden, Carol Singley, Stuart Charmé, Charles Jarrett, Margaret Marsh, Barbara Bennett Woodhouse, Annemie Dillen, Bruno Vanobbergen, Keith White, Jerome Berryman, Catherine Bernard, Ian Evison, Elizabeth Marquardt, David Clairmont, Joe Pettit, Anandini Dar, Nyeema Watson, Ines Meier, Dianne Fabii, Brian Gallagher, Christine Evans, Rebecca Winterer, the seventh-grade class of Haddonfield Middle School, and the students in my courses on children. Thanks also to Richard Brown and the staff at Georgetown University Press. My greatest teachers are my parents, Geraldine and Tony Wall, and my wife Clare Leinweber and daughter Isabel Wall.

Introduction

CHILDHOOD FACES HUMANITY with its own deepest and most perplexing questions. What does it mean to be human? What should relations and societies strive for? What is ultimately owed to one another?

Children are a third of all humanity. Yet all too often children are considered merely undeveloped adults, passive recipients of care, occupying a separate innocence, or, perhaps, in need of being civilized. Across diverse societies and cultures, and throughout history and today, serious questions of human being, purposes, and responsibilities have usually been considered chiefly from the point of view of adulthood. Childhood has had to borrow its senses of meaning and humanity from those thought to embody them in some fuller, more advanced, or more important way.

This book turns the tables, specifically around ethical life, and argues that considerations of childhood should not only have greater importance but fundamentally transform how morality is understood and practiced. Beliefs about human nature, relations, and societies should not just be applied to the young as their objects. Childhood requires such beliefs to be systematically rethought. The experiences of children need to become new lenses for interpreting what it means to exist, to live good lives, and to form just communities—for the sake of children and adults both.

This kind of questioning, as we will see, is far from unprecedented. In fact, some of the most influential ethical thinkers and actors in history have reimagined relations and obligations in response to the concerns of children. They have also come to diverse, contested, and conflicting conclusions. Children are arguably the most marginalized group in all of history. Nevertheless, philosophers and theologians, as well as social leaders and parents, have seen in childhood different ways in which to expand the sense of human possibility. Such efforts, while never sufficient, have been integral over time to societies' imaginations of a fuller humanity.

New thinking in light of childhood is needed again today. This is the case for both theoretical and practical reasons. Let us leave the more abstract issues aside for the moment and consider the problematic actual situation of childhood—or rather childhoods—in the contemporary world. For childhood raises unsettling questions in an era of rapid globalization, social instability, and hyper-individualism for both rich and poor countries and across diverse cultural landscapes.

What assumptions, for example, make invisible the ten million children around the planet who die every year of easily preventable diseases and malnutrition?[1] This number is equivalent to almost two Nazi Holocausts every year, or ten 9/11 terrorist attacks every day. Similarly, what systems of belief permit the worldwide growth in recent decades of children's sex trafficking, sweat shops, and soldiering? Why do children everywhere enjoy narrower human rights than adults? Why, despite greater awareness, does gender discrimination in every society continue to distort children's cultures, educations, and families? What structures of social understanding enable global mass media to manipulate children's lives and thinking in a more invasive way than ever before?

Or take the example of my own country, the United States: Why did children overtake the elderly in the mid-twentieth century as the poorest age group in society, so that a quarter of children now live in poverty, and the poorer the younger the child? What makes universal access to adequate health insurance for children such an intractable social conundrum? Why have families—so important especially for children—become privatized, fragmented, and isolated? What social constructions underpin children's unprecedented levels of depression, anxiety, and obesity?

These and many other practical concerns suggest that there is something profoundly distorted in ethical constructions of childhood today and more broadly of human being and relations.

The solution to such problems is not simply to pay children more attention. Nor is it only to provide children more of the kinds of provisions, protections, freedoms, responsibilities, and rights that are already enjoyed to a greater extent by adults. Such solutions are helpful but not finally sufficient. A truly child-inclusive society would be one that not only made children equal to adults but, more radically, transformed its foundations in response to what makes children distinct. It would reform its fundamental presuppositions about what makes for good lives and relations in the first place. The question is not just of practical implementation but also of changing underlying assumptions.

Because children are full human beings, neglecting children diminishes the humanity of us all. It impoverishes the complex webs of social relations in which human beings live and find meaning. Child-centered critiques of society have often arisen in times of great social upheaval. They have coincided with the rise of Greco-Roman city-states, the dawn of feudalism, the emergence of nation states, and the onset of industrialization. Such critiques have been made by the greatest philosophical and theological minds from Plato to Augustine, Aquinas to Calvin, and Locke to Kant, as well as through all manner of sacred, poetic, and narrative literature and collective and individual actions. We are in a time of tremendous global change once again. Without rising to the challenge of rethinking ethical norms in light of childhood, children themselves will be increasingly marginalized and societies increasingly dehumanized.

I call this kind of self-critique "childism." Childism is the effort to respond to the experiences of children by transforming understanding and practices for all. "Isms" can be blunt ideological tools. But they can also help change structures, cultures, and possibilities. Feminism, for example, has effectively challenged ethicists and others to reimagine human life in terms such as care, relationality, embodiment, and power. It is not only by and for women but also for the sake of a changed society overall. Womanism has raised basic questions about gender in relation to race. Environmentalism has called upon humanity to reflect anew on its meaning and actions as part of a larger ecosystem. And from further back in history, humanism itself profoundly challenged, and continues to challenge, long-held perceptions of moral life through concepts like dignity, freedom, and rights. Each of these has expanded human horizons in new ways.

Childism calls for the same kind of profound ethical restructuring. Children are far from homogeneous, but they do form a distinctive social group. Consideration of their experiences and challenges should open up individuals and societies to previously unimagined moral possibilities. Thinking and acting in light of children, whether one happens to be a child or adult, should respond not only to what makes children and adults alike, but also and more self-critically to what makes them different. And it should do so not only from an empirical or historical point of view but also from a constructive or philosophical, religious, and ethical one. Children, like women and men, are absolutely full human beings while also, again like women and men, not entirely reducible to the other human groups with which they live their lives. Children expose suppressed dimensions of human meaning and relations that only they clearly reveal.

This book explores childism as an essential moral question and creates new theoretical and practical responses to it. Part I deconstructs the deep historical archeology of primarily Western assumptions about children—assumptions that continue, for good and for ill, to ground ethical life today. It distinguishes three major forms of childist ethical understanding that I call top-down, bottom-up, and developmental. Part II constructs a more fully child-responsive moral theory. It uses the strengths and resists the weaknesses of inherited historical perspectives. But it also reinterprets contemporary ethical resources to advance a fresh vision of human being, possibility, and obligation. I call this new vision an ethical poetics, since it reimagines moral relations as sites of expanding moral creativity. Part III further refines this ethical vision by considering three specific areas of social practice: human rights, families, and ethical thinking. In each case, the point of view of children is shown to expand what it means to be human in social relations beyond the white noise of adult-centrism.

This hermeneutical circle of reflection—from historical assumptions to new ideas to the rethinking of practices—is intended to help critique and transform some of contemporary societies' most deeply held moral beliefs. I understand that moral norms are diverse and contested and that no one can presume a total perspective on them. Nevertheless, for the sake at least of children, who on some level call for responses from all, I hope to open up creative new moral horizons. The following pages are not intended as an end but rather as a beginning. They hope to disrupt and expand existing senses of the moral being of humanity. The idea is not to toss out adults' experiences of moral life but to widen them to also include children's.

THREE STORIES

There is no better place to begin to destabilize settled thinking than by listening to the complexity of experience. We will start with three brief glimpses into children's lives, or rather into storied constructions of them. Narratives can help in imagining not only the realities of human relations but also how those relations are formed into meaning. Our responsibility is not just to receive information—much less to impose preconceptions—but to enter into a creative circle of listening and response. Children's stories, like those touched on here, are created in part by children themselves and in part by the adults and societies around them, including, finally, you and me as we read about and ponder them. It is this circle of human relations that needs to be traveled—and unraveled—if ethical understanding is to be enriched and broadened.

Annabelle Jones is a small, talkative, and sparkling eleven-year-old girl growing up in the South Bronx in New York City. She makes friends easily with the writer Jonathan Kozol, who reports his conversations with her in his popular book, *Amazing Grace*, which documents some of the lives of poor children in the United States.[2] Jones (I have made up her last name, since it is not given) likes double dutch jump rope, pineapple icies, and her several pets, especially a mouse. "Can a mouse go to heaven too?" Kozol asks her. "I don't know about a mouse," she replies. "He's quite small."

Jones lives with her mother across the street from an abandoned building whose windows are covered in plywood. The small park down the road in her predominantly African American neighborhood is missing its swings, filled with trash, and frequented at various hours by drug dealers. Nighttime is occasionally punctuated by gun shots. Many of the fathers in the neighborhood lack jobs, are in jail, or, like Jones's, have disappeared, and many mothers and grandmothers struggle to provide for their families with few economic or societal resources. Disproportionate numbers of children here have asthma, tuberculosis, or AIDS, and most receive only minimal health care at the local hospital emergency room. Like a quarter of all children in the United States—and at least half of children worldwide—she lives in daily abject poverty, children being the poorest age group in rich and poor countries alike.

While deeply victimized, Jones is not her society's victim simply. In some ways, her own experience of her world is much like that of any other child her age, filled with concerns for mice, candy, school, and games. She lives with energy, love, and joy as well as the usual boredoms and frustrations. Whether she stays in school, avoids drugs and teen pregnancy, and gains a measure of economic security in life is in part a matter of her social surroundings but also in part a matter of her own particular agency. Her story as she grows up is not set in stone but open to some level of renewal, both by her and by her world. Neither, however, does this mean that Jones is simply free or has equal opportunities to others. Her options in life are already more limited than those with more resources. She holds increasing responsibility for her own well-being as she grows up and at the same time is the weighty responsibility of others in her immediate and wider worlds. She, like us all, belongs to a complex circle of interdependent relations which she is both shaped by and shapes for herself.

Ying Ying Fry was born in Hunan Province in China and adopted by a middle-class family in San Francisco. She is one of millions of infant girls who have been abandoned by their birth families in China because of its so-called one-child policy, designed to quell the country's exploding population for the sake of economic growth. It was likely a painful decision for her birth family to leave her outside of a police station, and it was undoubtedly painful for Fry herself, though only days old at the time, to lose the only relationships she knew. The smells, sounds, and bonds into which she was born suddenly disappeared. She spent her first months in a large government-run orphanage filled with other abandoned babies and toddlers, older unadopted children, and sick and elderly adults.

Fry herself tells this story of her infancy when she is eight years old in a book for children and adults titled *Kids Like Me in China*.[3] As she explains, Fry wrote the book shortly after revisiting the orphanage with her adoptive parents. It is co-authored by her mother, and some of its photographs are taken by her father. She is clearly a bright and talented child and her vivacious and thoughtful personality shines through on every page. At the same time, her new life—and her ability to write this book—rely on the support and love of her parents and other adults around her. While Fry may not directly remember her infancy, the reader learns from her about what it must have been like in ways that could not be learned from others. "To get people to have small families, the [Chinese] government made some rules, and they're really strict about them," she says. "But the babies didn't do anything wrong! Why do they have to lose their first families? I don't think those rules are fair to babies." Who else could describe this problem so clearly?

It is evident from this example of infant abandonment that even the youngest child under the most difficult of circumstances interprets their own worlds and relations, however much they are also constructed by them. Babies in particular show that each of us is and has been shaped by many layers of surrounding persons, communities, and histories. Fry herself is partly who she is because of her birth parents, her biological ancestors, the Chinese government, global economic systems, those who manage international adoptions, her adoptive parents in the United States, their own ancestors, their larger societies, and so on beyond any conclusive reckoning. But throughout it all—as a baby, an eight-year-old, and thereafter—Fry is also an active constructor of meaning. She invests her complex, dynamic, and powerful world with her own being, ideas, and aspirations.

Ishmael Beah was abducted in 1992 at the age of twelve by the Sierra Leone government army to fight in its country's civil war. According to his own account, written in his mid-twenties, he lost his family—and his childhood—when rebels destroyed his village.[4] After wandering for months with groups of other children, Beah eventually became one of the world's hundreds of thousands of child soldiers. When his compound was surrounded by rebel forces, he had little choice but to join the fighting and help save his own and others' lives. Soon he was addicted to drugs that allowed him to stay awake for days and fight without fear or compunction. For two years as a young teenager he participated in countless killings, executions, murder of innocents, and destruction of entire villages. "My squad was my family, my gun my provider and protector, and my rule was to kill or be killed. The extent of my thoughts didn't go much further beyond that . . . and killing had become a daily activity."[5]

Beah was eventually rescued by UNICEF representatives and taken to a rehabilitation center in the capital city of Freetown. Here, as he puts it, he gradually learned again to be a child and revived his old loves of hip-hop and soccer. "I would always tell people," he later recalls, "that I believe children have the resilience to outlive their sufferings, if given a chance."[6] Indeed, Beah's resilience is remarkable. He soon finds himself speaking before the United Nations on child soldiering, eventually, as a young adult, becoming a member of the Human Rights Watch Children's Rights Division Advisory Council, graduating from Oberlin College, and then writing a bestselling book about his experiences.

Beah's story complicates, among other things, any notion that children are inherently incorruptible or innocent. While he may not be fully responsible for what he did, something within him enabled him to become a willing and eager mass killer. Beah takes responsibility for what was by his own admission a social agency and participation of the ugliest possible kind. But he is also, and at the very same time, profoundly shaped by larger circumstances. Whatever natural connection to the humanity of others he may previously have had was significantly destroyed. The ability even for a child to construct his own world is ethically ambiguous. It is not simply corrupted by outside society or expressive of innate evil. It includes the possibility for most of the horrors of which only humanity seems capable. Beah's book is a testament to moral life's simultaneous fallibility and potential for redemption.

These three childhoods are at once unique and common. Every human life is both singularly other and constructed by shared communities. There are as many childhoods as there are children. Children's stories are as complex as adults'—and in some ways even more so. Children are each absolutely distinct. They face tremendously serious moral difficulties but also meet them with remarkable inner resources. They are participants in not only families and cultures but also entire societies and global systems.

What is more, children are not reducible to social problems to be solved only by adults; they are not merely victimized or needy. Nor do children start out life as a separate species filled only with purity and goodness. The story of childhood cannot be told in one-dimensional formulas of either innocence and vulnerability or unruliness and undevelopment, or indeed any of the other languages of childhood handed down by history. Whatever differences there may be between children and adults, they do not lie in moral experience's level of diversity or complexity. While the stories of children are all too easily ignored, they are not thereby alien. The very different childhoods of the world, like those described here, just like the world's very different adulthoods, can and should inform moral reflection and action. Indeed, how to respond to the narratives of others who are not simply like oneself is one way to describe the larger ethical problem posed by childhood to humanity.

THREE QUESTIONS

The beginnings of a more fully childist or child-inclusive ethics can be made by formulating three basic questions. These questions, as we will see in the next chapter, have persisted in one form or another throughout Western philosophical and religious attempts to think in light of childhood. They also arise out of the lives of actual children like Jones, Fry, and Beah. They are not the only ethical questions that can be asked. They are in part my own creations. But overall they are a way to engage historical wisdom while listening to childhood more closely and therefore move toward new thinking. The questions described here will help to guide us through the ethical history of part I of this book, as well as through the three chapters on moral theory in part II and the more practical considerations of part III.

First question: What does consideration of childhood suggest about what it means most basically to be human? This is a fundamental question of human nature or being. In technical terms, it is a question of "ontology," or the meaning of humanity's *ontos* or being. The constitution of human being takes us into such issues as what makes humankind distinct, what is most original to it, how it stands in relation to nature, what makes it moral in the first place, and to what extent it might be considered spiritual or transcendent. Here it will be asked in relation to the entire course of human being's entry into, passage through, and exit from the world—not just a privileged adult point. Not everyone agrees that there can any longer be called such a thing as human "being." However, if children are to be fully included as members of the human community, some basic sense of "the human" is ultimately required, one that does not silently assume adulthood as its model.

Such a question can be answered both philosophically and religiously: in terms of what constitutes human being as one can know it and how it might be imagined at human life's ultimate boundaries. Although it is not frequently pondered today, the question of human being in light of childhood has animated centuries of highly contentious debate. Is human nature basically ordered or unruly? Is humanity as it enters the world primordially innocent or evil or both? Are we born blank slates or filled with natural potential? Is humanity somehow distinctively rational? What is human agency? Does human being change in fundamental, relative, or no significant ways as it evolves over its lifecycle (or for that matter over history)? Is humanity somehow also divine? How one answers such questions continues to inform contemporary ethical assumptions, however implicitly, about children and adults both. It also deeply impacts the way one responds to other kinds of ethical questions such as those below.

Consider, for example, Ying Ying Fry. Despite having been abandoned at birth under the most difficult of circumstances, she is of course just as fully a human "being" as you or me or anyone else. But what does this suggest about human nature? Does it mean that all we have in common are biological structures of DNA? Does it mean, less visibly, a capability for social participation? Must one ultimately resort to some kind of mysterious gift of inner spirit? Or does such an infant teach that human being is essentially vulnerable? Is she human by virtue of her needs for protection and love? Her demands for care and relationality? These and a multitude of other fundamental questions are pressed to some of their most revealing limits when asked in light of childhood.

A second question is this: What does childhood teach about what human relations and societies should try to aim toward? This may be called a "teleological" question about moral life's *teloi*, its purposes and ends. What is it that human life should hope to accomplish, realize, or bring about? Toward what ideals should it strive? It may seem paradoxical to look back into human beginnings in childhood to learn about human ends. However, it is only in this way that moral aims and purposes might be understood in their fuller complexity and extent. Where one comes from profoundly shapes where one hopes to arrive.

Again, there are a range of possible philosophical and religious answers from history. The human aim in light of children may be a more civilized social order; the preservation of inborn freedoms; a yet unknown justice or kingdom of God; the overcoming of childlike egoism; the recovery of a kind of childlike simplicity; a deepening of the bonds of mutuality and love; a hoped-for liberation of marginalized groups from oppression; and so on. If nothing else, childhood shows that human life does have ends and purposes. These are not secondary moral concerns, as some claim. Humanity always aims, from birth to death, for something more. Moral life is, as I will put it, essentially temporal. It seeks growth over time. But taking into account its beginnings in childhood complicates the picture of what human life should continually strive to become.

Ishmael Beah's story suggests, for example, that moral desires are both easily distorted and capable of tremendous renewal. What can be hoped for humanity when twelve-year-olds can turn into mass murderers? What can be gained by realizing that those same child soldiers can offer adults a measure of social redemption? Do children inject human relations with greater natural goodness or unruly tendencies that require disciplining? What is the nature of human aims considering that they develop and expand over the course of a lifetime? Is the purpose of societies to protect the diversity of chosen pursuits or to forge structures inclusive of the most disempowered? Is Beah's toting a gun only a false sense of human maturity, and if so, how would a true sense contrast with it? These and other such questions come down to a childist inquiry into how selves and societies should understand their ethical aims.

Third and finally: What, in light of childhood, do human beings owe each other? This could be called a "deontological" question dealing with human *deon* or binding obligations. It concerns, above and beyond being and desires, the nature of basic responsibilities and duties owed to each other by necessity. How should people treat one another as different and dignified members of the human community? On what basis does one treat oneself and others with humanity when "humanity" includes old and young alike?

Childhood has functioned at times in history as a powerful lens for providing an answer to this kind of question. For in a sense it is children above all who call individuals and societies to act with the greatest moral responsibility to others. Are the duties owed one another to meet one another's basic needs? Are they defined by traditional roles in larger communities? Or do they consist in protecting and enhancing individual liberty and autonomy? Is the key obligation to resist structures of unjust powers? To be disrupted by one another's irreducible otherness? To respect all persons as metaphorically "children" of God? Does responsibility bring societies face to face with the "strangers, widows, and orphans" pushed aside by the world? Today these questions have become particularly complex regarding children. For since the Enlightenment, human obligations have chiefly been understood as ways to respect reason and autonomy, traits that arguably prioritize a peculiarly adult point of view.

The situation of Annabelle Jones illustrates the complexity of this question. To a certain extent, she herself already holds ethical responsibilities: to herself, for respecting herself and doing as well as she can in school and life; to others, such as parents, siblings, friends, and teachers, for treating them with dignity and care; and to society, for avoiding violence and being a productive contributor and citizen. At the same time, what is owed by Jones is outweighed by what is owed to her. As a child, and particularly as a girl in her situation, she is more easily marginalized by social relations than are most others around her. However little it may be met, she makes a particularly strong moral claim on her world. Could it be that the Joneses of the world are so easily shunted aside because of too narrowly adult-centered conceptions of moral responsibility to begin with? What new vision of human obligation might open up more child-inclusive horizons?

There are, of course, many other ethical questions that can be asked in addition to these three. There are questions of humanity's relation to the natural world, its moral identity, its uses of power, and much else. Such questions will not be completely ignored in what follows. But the three described here provide at least a starting point for challenging basic historical norms. It will turn out, as we see in chapter 1, that there have developed several historical patterns of response to these types of questions that persist today. Each of these patterns has attempted to respond to childhood, but each has succeeded only in part. The situation is much as it has been historically for other groups such as women. Efforts to include children have in one way or another partly dehumanized them—and hence also both humanized and dehumanized humanity. Our task is to take advantage of a diversity of historical possibilities while overcoming their entrenched shortcomings.

ETHICAL GROWTH

My answers to these questions make use of historical and contemporary ethical resources but also reconstruct them in new ways. I do so because history is finally not a sufficient guide, either in its premodern or in its modern (roughly Enlightenment) manifestations. I do it also because, despite not addressing childhood in much depth, recent developments in what can loosely be termed "postmodern" ethical theory offer freshly helpful resources. Such ideas, broadly speaking, try to overcome problems in modernity without reverting to the problems of premodernity. They are various and subject to much legitimate criticism. And they will need further revision in light of childhood. But new resources are needed for including children in more diverse, differentiated, and dynamic ways. I also draw upon a range of social scientific, psychological, and other empirical investigations, and upon the relatively recent field of childhood studies.

The result is a childist reworking of moral thinking and practices that I call an ethical poetics. It is poetic in the sense that it reimagines moral life as based, not on individual autonomy or on the authority of traditions, but on expanding interdependent creativity. The moral ground of all human relations is creative and expansive growth. What children teach above all else is that selves belong to already constructed social worlds which they are in turn responsible for reconstructing over time in response to each other. Each human being, starting as a child, is a new center of moral creativity in what should be a growing rather than shrinking circle of mutually creative relations.

The ethics I develop in this book is mirrored in its methods. Both are about reconstructing already constructed historical worlds toward more expansive moral horizons. Both respond to children's own voices and experiences in order to reshape ethical understanding. Adults may generally have more experience traversing life's moral terrain, but children more clearly reveal its socially creative dynamism. While it is easy to suppress children's experiences and stories in the give and take of the world, and even easier to ignore what children teach about moral life, the effort to think in response to childhood also promises a kind of social renewal. Childhood is morality's most profound test. Children may be the most important reasons for moral reflection and practice in the first place. The purpose of thinking in light of children is to imagine a more expansively shared humanity.

PART I

HISTORY

Chapter 1

Three Enduring Models

HUMAN BEINGS are historical creatures. We not only live within time, like all things, but we also construct the meaning *of* time through stories, rituals, traditions, and cultures. Present experience aims toward anticipated futures and is interpreted through the lenses of understandings and beliefs from the past. Children demonstrate this historicity of human life acutely. No child chooses the inherited languages and mores that already shape the structures of their lives and thinking from birth. But every child interprets these conditions in new ways for themselves and in relation to their own open and unfolding futures. However diverse human histories and cultures may be, it is always both within and beyond some particular historicity that human beings create senses of meaning, purpose, and obligation.

How one understands the significance of childhood for ethics is likewise fundamentally embedded in histories. This chapter, in contrast with the remainder of the book, pauses to examine the history of childism in depth—the history, that is, of ethical thought that has been conducted explicitly in light of childhood. It is easy to assume that childhood is how one perceives it in the here and now. Empirical and everyday observations tell a great deal about children's and adult's actions, beliefs, and relations. But even the sciences, and particularly the human sciences, begin within horizons of historically structured presuppositions. Every hypothesis is rooted in a received linguistic world, however much it may also challenge and transform it. Even the concept of "childhood" itself is grounded in particular histories, meaning different things in different times and places. As a result, if we wish to question and transform fundamental ethical assumptions through childhood's lens, we must start with a careful archeological excavation of the way childhood has been interpreted, for better and for worse, as significant for moral life in our own histories.

The history of ethical thought in light of childhood involves a long global struggle to humanize children that in the process has also dehumanized them—

and hence also both humanized and dehumanized humanity. Like the history of thought about women, it has proven over time ethically ambiguous. Contra Philippe Ariès, people have always cared deeply about children.[1] But ideas about childhood have not only responded to them imaginatively but also been narrowly simplistic, especially when viewed retrospectively. Unavoidably, in fact, the complexity of actual children could never be matched by the complexity of thought about them. The result has been a long and diverse historical conversation that has often come to sharply opposed conclusions. And it continues to influence children's inclusion and marginalization in diverse societies today. In all its different facets, this conversation needs to be unpacked and critiqued so that we may hope to become less simplistic ourselves, to learn from history's wisdom while overcoming its deficiencies.

This chapter examines the history of ethical childism specifically in the West, from ancient Greek and biblical texts through the Middle Ages and into modernity. The history examined here will prove useful for developing new ways of thinking in the rest of this book. For many it will be a surprise that this intellectual history exists at all. I examine it through the lens of the three basic questions formulated in the previous chapter—questions about humanity's being, aims, and obligations—which have animated moral discussions of childhood and adulthood in one way or another across many different times and places. Others with backgrounds that do not originate around the Mediterranean or Europe would be able to tell different stories. The Western ethical tradition happens to be my own historical starting point, and, for good and ill, it has broadly influenced understandings of moral life over a long period of time and around the world. It contains analogies in other traditions, even if these analogies are not explored here.

What emerges from this history are three major models of child-responsive ethics that I call top-down, bottom-up, and developmental. The differences between these models are not temporal; they do not succeed each other over time. Each model has been present in one form or another for thousands of years, throughout all phases of premodernity and modernity and up to the present moment. Furthermore, there is no straight line leading over time from children's relative neglect to their increasing social and human inclusion, nor from comparatively negative views of children to comparatively positive ones. In both actual practice and theory, various understandings in history have appreciated the significance of children to different degrees and in different ways. And today turns out to be no pinnacle.

The differences between these three models are, rather, conceptual. Each tells a distinct kind of story about the meaning of childhood for the ethics of humanity. Their divergences continue to shape contemporary ideas and help to explain many of today's profound disagreements about children and human relations overall. By unraveling them we expose our own conflicted assumptions and languages, but in the process also open up fresh space for new thinking. It would be hubristic to think one can rise entirely above old prejudices and mistakes. But without understanding history to at least some degree, we render ourselves incapable of improving upon it.

Let it also be noted that none of these three models ever appears in a pure form. They do not represent absolutes but rather tendencies. Some thinkers lean in one direction quite heavily, others relatively lightly. All include in their thinking elements of other models as well. What is striking, however, is how much these models have persisted over time. Despite their complexities and cross-fertilizations, the three models I identify have a certain historical resiliency. They seem to explain important ideas of which childhood is a continual reminder. They are useful today only insofar as they help us understand our own complex ethical presuppositions and possibilities.

We today are children of this history, whether we like it or not. This does not mean that we—and by "we" I mean all who have been influenced by this history—are merely constructed by it. It means that, like children, we are called upon to recreate our inherited understandings into new understandings for ourselves. Each of us is both constructed by history and a new constructor of it, in an unavoidable hermeneutical circle that constitutes the very ability to create meaning at all. One must not only find one's place within history but also reshape and reinvent it. The more profoundly understood one's roots, the more nourishment, freedom, and play may be found for new growth.

THE TOP-DOWN STORY

One persistent and continuing argument about moral life in light of childhood is what I will call the "top-down" story. It suggests that human nature starts out essentially unruly and therefore requires a higher moral purpose and order to be imposed throughout life upon it from above. What childhood demonstrates above all, according to this view, is humanity's original natural state of moral disorder or corruption. Moral life requires, as a result, humanity's careful disciplining into strong moral communities. Human beings begin life in a kind of wild animality or even original sin. The teleological aim or end is to create morally coherent relations and societies based on larger transcending principles, such as moral reason, God's will, traditional values, or the common good. And the basic deontological obligation comes down to each person properly playing his or her social role.

The most influential articulation of this top-down version of childism is found in the fourth-century BCE Greek philosopher Plato. Readers of Plato often forget that children are central to his two great works of social theory, *The Republic* and *The Laws*. In a certain sense, Plato sees in children a great deal of capability, and for his time shows significant interest in not only boys but also girls. But his focus on children arises primarily out of his conviction that they enter the world as irrational animals in need of rigorous ethical training. It is only by educating children in this way that societies have any hope of becoming rational and just. As he puts it: "Of all wild young things a boy is the most difficult to handle. Just because he more than any other has a fount of intelligence in him which has not yet 'run clear,' he is the craftiest, most mischievous, and unruliest of brutes."[2]

The notion that humanity starts out uncivilized and barbaric helps to explain Plato's call, furthermore, for a powerful philosopher-king, for a single rational individual who can impose a wise ethical order on otherwise unruly citizens. It also contributes to his view that society should be built on philosophy rather than poetry (as in traditional Homeric and other stories), for, as children demonstrate, stories easily corrupt the mind by appealing to childish passions and fantasies. What is more, Plato's famous "noble lie"—which teaches people to see themselves as born into natural social classes—depends on the view that otherwise children will grow up to seek too much power for themselves and destroy social harmony. While it is true that Plato also affords children a certain moral dignity, what he learns most importantly from childhood is the need to impose a rationally predetermined social order on brute human nature.

Similarly top-down perspectives can also be found in some parts of the Bible.[3] In the Jewish Bible, one can point most obviously to God's fifth commandment given at Mount Sinai through Moses (which is also the first "ethical" as opposed to "spiritual" commandment) for children to "honor your father and your mother."[4] The building block of a new Israel, after the chaos of its exodus from Egypt, is in a way obedience: of children to parents and the community to God. We could also recall the earlier story of God's command to Abraham to sacrifice his son Isaac. Here, the Israelites' first covenant with God is subject to the ultimate test of submission: to a higher order so authoritative that it contravenes natural bonds and children's very rights to exist. The second creation story in Genesis 2–3 can similarly be read to interpret the original "innocence" of Adam and Eve as characterized, not by purity and goodness, but by guileless susceptibility to a serpent's corruption. The fall of humankind is disobedience of God's laws and results in the punitive disciplines of hard labor, pain in childbirth, and awareness of death.

In the Christian New Testament, the letters of Paul (arguably influenced by Platonic ideas) interpret the fifth Sinai commandment as an exhortation to "obey your parents in the Lord."[5] For Paul, all humanity starting at birth is utterly lost to sin without the redeeming grace brought from above by Christ. Paul famously argues that true righteousness and love require one to "put an end to childish ways."[6] What he means is that human beings' inborn passions of the flesh must be rooted out in order that they may submit themselves to a higher life of the spirit. Actual childhood largely signifies for him a bodily and temporal existence that must be transcended through a second birth as true "children of God."

Such views of children have persisted throughout history in various forms. In early medieval Christianity, for example, the North African Neoplatonic theologian Augustine breaks with his contemporaries (below) and uses childhood as the prime example of his new doctrine of "original sin." In his 397–98 CE autobiography, the *Confessions*, Augustine confesses that "in your [God's] sight no man is free from sin, not even a child who has lived only one day on earth."[7] Why? Because children's natural lack of discipline or concern for others is something all of us should hope to outgrow. "Was it a sin to cry when I wanted to feed at the breast?

I am too old now to feed on mother's milk, but if I were to cry for the kind of food suited to my age, others would rightly laugh me to scorn and remonstrate me. . . . We root out these faults and discard them as we grow up, and this is proof enough that they are faults."[8]

In Augustine, "innocence" takes on the Latin meaning of *in-nocens*: "non-harming" or inability to harm. Children *want* to harm, but since they are small and weak they lack the resources to do so. "If babies are innocent, it is not for lack of will to do harm, but for lack of strength."[9] Childhood is the clearest demonstration of Augustine's central theological innovation: that the human will is so ontologically disordered that it can be made just only by the mercy of God. The historian David F. Wright has even argued that "the custom of infant baptism was the single most powerful catalyst of [Augustine's] formulation of doctrines of original sin."[10] If children are originally pure and good, as many at that time believed, then it is hard to explain why infant baptism should be necessary. Rather, Augustine claims, they are the ever renewed seeds of Adam's fall.

A top-down view can also be found in some of the teachings about children in the seventh century CE Muslim Qur'an. Based in part on the ancestry of Abraham, children here sometimes symbolize humanity's need for "submission" ("Islam"). Children are blessings to the household from Allah, it is true. But just as often they are "temptations" or "trials" that threaten parents' seeking the higher rewards of heaven. "Know that your wealth and your children are a trial, and that with God is a mighty wage."[11] Humanity's need for moral and spiritual discipline, even from the very start of life, is emphasized in the requirement that the first sound a newborn should hear at birth is the whispering in its ear of the Islamic call to prayer. Likewise, the circumcision of boys is sometimes interpreted as a ritual of purification to help direct an otherwise wayward sexuality toward higher moral submission.

The sixteenth-century Protestant Reformation often takes a similar view that disciplining children lies at the very heart of a redeemed society. Martin Luther sees in children's education the most powerful basis for addressing humanity's primordial corruption. He claims that God's commandment "that children shall obey their parents is so stern that he [God] would even have rebellious children sentenced to death. Indeed, for what purpose do we older folks exist, other than to care for, instruct, and bring up the young? It is utterly impossible for these foolish young people to instruct and protect themselves." Luther refers children themselves to Deuteronomy 32:7: "Ask your father and he will tell you; your elders, and they will show you."[12]

Similarly, the Protestant Reformer John Calvin emphatically endorses an Augustinian view that children embody original sin. As he bluntly puts it, "their whole nature is a seed of sin."[13] Children's unruliness, as Barbara Pitkin has pointed out, helps to prompt Calvin's rigorous ethics of family and civil order.[14] Children demonstrate how easily sin may grow toward "dominating," "ruling," or "overwhelming" humanity. Family, church, and community must be structured from the top down by strict submission to God's laws.[15] Children's baptism is not so much a means of actual salvation in Calvin as it is a "sign" or "tiny spark" of God's possible future mercy, so that *adults* may be encouraged to rear their children with the necessary moral zeal.[16] A Calvinistic view of children's depravity does not necessarily mean harsh punishment, as often thought, and Calvin can be credited with founding some of the first public schools and children's hospitals. But Calvin does place the imposition of a higher moral education at the center of hope for a better world.

A different kind of top-down perspective is evident in the work of perhaps the most influential moral philosopher of modernity, Immanuel Kant. This can be seen through his little known but last published work, his 1803 *Education*. Given that this book was published after Kant's other philosophical writings, it can hardly be argued that it shaped his larger ideas directly. However, it does provide important insight into his underlying ethical thinking. For here Kant insists, in contrast with Enlightenment predecessors like John Locke and Jean-Jacques Rousseau (although, interestingly enough, somewhat like René Descartes), that children do indeed start out life as irrational and unruly animals.[17] In this, Kant somewhat echoes Plato but also his own pietist Reformed background that shares much of the thinking of Calvin.

Thus: "The greatest and most difficult problem to which man can devote himself is the problem of education," Kant writes, since herein lies the fundamental moral task of "changing animal nature into human nature."[18] Childhood shows that the human will is first and foremost the plaything of want, instinct, and desire. It is merely "heteronomous," meaning that it is ruled without higher moral principle. Humanity must learn over time to rule itself instead by "autonomous" rationality, that is, by an inner commitment to duty and self-rule. Moral behavior requires the will's "discipline" or "culturation" (*Bildung*), not by an ineffable God, but by the "moral law" written by God into humanity's own reason. And so now rationality itself becomes, in light of childhood, humanity's higher moral disciplinarian.

THE PROBLEM OF AGENCY

These are but a few of many possible examples of top-down childism in Western ethics. Obviously there are great differences among them, and a great deal more could be said about each one. Clearly each includes other perspectives on children as well. But what they share is an underlying sense of humanity as starting out life in a state of natural unruliness, and needing therefore to be disciplined from above in order to create moral societies. Moral goodness must be imposed on children and adults if humanity is to rise above itself.

Such a view is currently making a comeback across many parts of the world. An array of family values proponents, religious and secular communitarians, strict disciplinarians, and, at its extreme, fundamentalists and totalitarians have concluded, albeit in different ways, that moral societies are crumbling, individualism has run amok, and children in particular are treated with too much permissiveness. The first line of attack for a better world, on this view, is to instill moral discipline in children. As the contemporary ethicist Stanley Hauerwas has put it, "intimacy and care are indeed important, but equally important is the initiation of children into moral beliefs and institutions which we value."[19] This argument is not confined to the political right, but is found wherever a greater good is felt in need of stricter imposition on the sea of humanity. Across the political, religious, and philosophical spectrum, the argument is made that humanity will naturally spiral into chaos unless it is invested with a higher moral order.

When not taken to extremes, a top-down approach can have a certain merit for children. This is because it clearly recognizes children's full participation in the human moral struggle. To acknowledge children's unruliness or depravity is not necessarily to belittle them. It can also mean refusing to reduce them to an oversimplified neutrality, purity, or sentimentality. It is to take seriously the conflictedness and complexity of children's moral lives, along with the great responsibilities they should begin to take on themselves for helping to make a better world.

What is more, simple observation of even the youngest of children shows a fundamental capability for doing harm. This is not simply taught by society; it is a facet of human nature. There is no magic age at which the capacity for doing wrong suddenly appears in human lives. Human beings do not spring into the world fully ready to put themselves into others' shoes, to treat people and animals with respect, to show consideration for others' toys and belongings, and to willingly embrace social responsibilities. Augustine is in a certain sense right when he says that tantrums are not civilized behavior. Children as full human beings are not born simply and wholly good.

The problem with this approach, however, as we will see particularly in chapter 2, is that it obscures the depths of human moral agency. Moral capability is viewed on this model as something passively received from above. If the will is disordered by nature, then it cannot ultimately be trusted to act and decide competently for itself. It must submit itself to a higher moral order. The most interesting example of this problem is found in Kant, who is generally thought to be a champion of moral agency in his embrace of moral autonomy. However, autonomy or rational self-rule is specifically excluded by Kant from children. It really means, for him, the submission of desire to reason. As his view of childhood clearly demonstrates, human agency is "moral" only insofar as it detaches itself from instinct and need and places itself under the tutelage of the higher law of impersonal duty. I want to follow my animal passions, but I should instead subject myself to universal moral law. This view of "agency" is profoundly adult-centered, requiring one to overcome rather than embrace what is inborn in childhood.

Lost in the top-down effort to create social order is the sense that each human being, starting at birth, brings to the social order something uniquely creative. Each child is a distinctively other moral agent who invests society with new worth and meaning. From this perspective, which I will flesh out later, the top-down view contains a profound contradiction. A sense of moral responsibility must be imposed on creatures who are presumed originally to lack it. Children, however, could not learn to act morally in society if they lacked moral agency to begin with. A binary opposition of broken starting point and ordered maturity denies humanity's deeper capability for acting morally in the concrete world. It measures morality by an always transcending yardstick whose command is obedience. Moral subjectivity must have deeper roots than moral subjection.

THE BOTTOM-UP STORY

A second form of childism makes precisely this kind of criticism. A countervailing "bottom-up" argument throughout history suggests that what children demonstrate above all is humanity's original goodness, which should therefore be appreciated, nurtured, and cultivated in order to redeem historically corrupt societies. Human "being" is first and foremost from birth a good and natural gift. The moral aim is to infuse a fallen world of ambition, greed, and violence with greater human purity and simplicity. And moral obligations are based on recognizing one another's distinctive natural agency for transforming society for the better. This might sound like a modern story, but in fact it has long and generally forgotten ancient roots.

These roots might first be traced, in written terms, to the Jewish Bible. For, as Marcia Bunge has pointed out, "the Bible includes . . . passages *both* about children needing instruction, training, or guidance *and* about children actively ministering to others, prophesying, or modeling faith."[20] For example, in the sixth-century BCE creation story of Genesis 1 (in contrast with the above-mentioned story of Adam and Eve in Genesis 2–3, written four centuries earlier), humankind or *adam* is affirmed by the text's priestly authors as having been created primordially "in the image of God." Whatever else befalls humanity in actual history, a certain faith can be placed in its underlying original goodness. Children may then be affirmed as bringing into the world a sacred gift of moral light and innocence—however much that world may subsequently corrupt it—that remains a fundamental wellspring of purity and humanity throughout life. What is more, the very first commandment given by God to humankind is to "be fruitful and multiply." This can be interpreted to suggest that procreation lies at the very heart of what God wants of humanity, whether literally, in reproducing actual children, or figuratively, in producing works of labor, culture, and community.

A bottom-up view of moral life in light of childhood is also present in parts of the first- and second-century CE Christian New Testament gospels. The gift and goodness of childhood is strongly affirmed in Jesus's birth being described as God's incarnation. It also informs Jesus being called the "son of God" and his followers "children of God." But most important, in all three synoptic gospels (Mark, Matthew, and Luke), Jesus places a child in the midst of his disciples and declares: "Truly I tell you, unless you change and become like children, you will never enter the kingdom of heaven. Whoever becomes humble like this child is the greatest in the kingdom of heaven. Whoever welcomes one such child in my name welcomes me."[21] Children represent a kind of moral purity or humility that is the very model of redemption for all. Judith M. Gundry-Volf has argued that many of Jesus's sayings use children's utterly powerless position in ancient Mediterranean society to announce a counterintuitive ethics of the weak superseding the powerful.[22] Such prophesies are echoed in beatitudes such as "blessed are the meek." Unlike in Paul, childhood tends to be viewed in such passages less as a state of fallenness to be overcome than as a sign of God's grace entering the world.

A similar view largely animates the early church theologians of the third and fourth centuries, prior to the shift seen above in Augustine. As O. M. Bakke has shown, the architects of early Christianity, as it grew and became instituted in the Roman Empire, generally speak of children as humankind's true "image of God."[23] Clement of Alexandria writes in his *Paedagogus* (*The Instructor*), for example, that Jesus's teachings are centrally concerned with "setting before us, for our imitation, the simplicity that is in children." From this starting point, all may hope to become "unyoked to vice, not broken in by wickedness; but simple, and bounding joyously to the Father alone," "gentle, and therefore more tender, delicate, and simple, guileless, and destitute of hypocrisy, straightforward and upright in mind," and able to "lay aside the cares of this life, and depend on the Father alone."[24] Similar ideas pervade the theologies of Origen, Tertullian, Cyprian, and Gregory of Nyssa, who consistently hold up children as models for adult imitation by virtue of their innocence, simplicity, freedom from desire, sexual purity, and indifference toward worldly status and wealth.

Around the same time, the founder of Eastern Orthodox Christianity, John Chrysostom, interprets Jesus's welcoming of children to mean exactly the opposite of the interpretations of Paul and Augustine: not corrupted bodiliness but freedom from the passions. "For this is the height of true wisdom," he writes, "to be simple with understanding; this is angelic life; yes, for the soul of a little child is pure from all the passions. Towards those who have vexed him he bears no resentment, but goes to them as friends, as if nothing had been done."[25] Such fine declarations may to some extent be mere rhetoric. Chrysostom, though he taught children, was an ascetic who did not have to deal with children's day-to-day upbringing. Nevertheless, one finds here at least the ethical ideal that children are not objects to be molded by society but subjects toward which society should mold itself. He enjoins adults especially to recognize in children a deeper moral wisdom, wonder, and openness than adults themselves tend to attain.

A similarly positive view of children's moral being is found also in parts of the Qur'an. Children are a blessing from Allah: "God has appointed for you of yourselves wives, and He has appointed for you of your wives sons and grandsons, and He has provided you of the good things. What, do they believe in vanity, and do they disbelieve in God's blessing?"[26] In addition, as Alfons H. Teipen has argued, "the Qur'an strongly rejects the notion that children may be 'property of their fathers,' an attitude that appears to have been somewhat prevalent in pre-Islamic Arabia."[27] Such affirmations of childhood are also supported by stories of Abraham as a youth already disagreeing with his father and abandoning the polytheistic idol-worship of his family.[28]

In the later Middle Ages, the fourteenth-to-fifteenth-century female mystic Julian of Norwich, thought to be the first woman to publish in English, takes a similarly high view of childhood in describing Christians' spiritual relation to Jesus as to their "Mother": "The mother may give her child suck of her milk, but our precious Mother, Jesus, He may feed us with Himself, and doeth it, full courteously and full tenderly, with the Blessed Sacrament that is precious food of my life; and with all the sweet Sacraments He sustaineth us full mercifully and graciously."[29] Union with God is like being an infant drinking at Jesus's breast. It is a union to be recovered in adulthood from the earliest of childhood experiences. Likewise, the sufferings and sorrows of earthly existence cry out for a divine Mother who offers her gracious love to those who can accept being her children.

The Moravian theologian and educator John Amos Comenius, in his popular 1633 book *The School of Infancy*, also argues for children as models of moral wisdom. Thought to be an early influence on the European Enlightenment, Comenius argues that children "are valuable to God first because being innocent, except for original sin, they are not yet the defaced image of God" and have "not yet defiled themselves with the allures of sin." Thus, "infants are the living images of the living God," and "he who takes little children in his arms may be assured that he takes angels." In the end, Comenius writes, "God thus wills that children be our preceptors," because they "are given us as a mirror in which we may behold humility, gentleness, benign goodness, harmony, and other Christian virtues."[30] It is children who teach adults to be good, not the other way around.

The best known bottom-up thinker today is the eighteenth-century Romantic philosopher Jean-Jacques Rousseau. In his widely influential 1762 treatise *Emile, or On Education*, Rousseau criticizes the then prevailing view of John Locke (which we'll come to shortly) for "always seeking the man in the child without thinking of what he is before being a man."[31] *Emile* was published almost simultaneously with Rousseau's major ethical treatise the *Social Contract*. His argument in both texts is that one finds in childhood humanity's original state of natural goodness, the first "noble savage" not yet corrupted by the greed and avarice of adulthood and society. "Everything is good as it leaves the hands of the Author of things; everything degenerates in the hands of man."[32] Children, according to Rousseau, begin life neither brutish nor blank slates but naturally wise, just, and good. Each child brings to the social order a free and pure inner capability for self-love or self-esteem (*amour de soi*), which should be nurtured and strengthened over a lifetime to resist its degradation into mere "pride" (*amour-propre*) or seeking esteem from others. The social contract that underlies morality and democracy depends on eschewing popular opinion and relying instead on one's own God-given natural inborn freedom.

The most influential Christian modernist on the subject of children is the founder of modern Protestantism, Friedrich Schleiermacher. Schleiermacher's voluminous writings on childhood—his 1806 *Christmas Eve: Dialogues on the Incarnation*, 1813/14 *Aphorisms on Pedagogy*, and 1818 collection of sermons *The Christian Household*—all predate his major theological treatise of 1821–22 (revised in 1830), *The Christian Faith*.[33] Schleiermacher declares children "the pure revelation of the divine," showing humanity its own true inner capabilities for wisdom, joy, and love.[34] Children are the real "gift" of Christmas, the continuing incarnation of God throughout time. Indeed, it is not adults who baptize children but children who baptize adults, their mere presence immersing the adult world in the original experience of "immediate union" with "the sacred sphere of nature."[35] In *The Christian Faith*, Schleiermacher repeatedly refers to childhood as the preeminent model of his central theological notion of "the feeling of absolute dependence" (on God).[36] Only children fully experience what it means to be wholly created in the image of God, since only they are inwardly free, simple, and humble.

THE PROBLEM OF VULNERABILITY

These and other bottom-up childisms invest children with tremendous moral gifts, wisdom, and agency. They clearly avoid the top-down problem of reducing children to merely passive recipients of adult socialization. As a result, they offer a radically different vision of humanity and society. Humanity's original goodness means that it should trust its own natural instincts, feelings, and intuitions over the stultifying accretions of history. Human embodiment in the world is understood in positive rather than negative terms as a source of goodness and wisdom. As a result, social structures are not the solution but the problem. Adult certainties need to be subject to constant suspicion in order to welcome and nurture human life's ever new spontaneity and diversity. Morality is not the imposition of higher principles over unruly desires but the liberation of natural simplicity for the renewal of a broken world.

Such a view has proven increasingly appealing to many over the past century. The German Catholic theologian Karl Rahner—one of the few major ethical thinkers of the twentieth century to write much about childhood—speaks for many when he says that "we do not move away from childhood in any definitive sense, but rather move towards the eternity of this childhood, to its definitive and enduring validity."[37] Much social and political ethics, philosophical and religious, has sought to reclaim children's distinctive gifts and voices. The "childhood studies" movement that arose among social scientists in the late 1970s was largely, though not exclusively, inspired by a bottom-up view of children as distinct and diverse social agents. This movement takes up again Rousseau's criticism of those "always seeking the man in the child." The United Nations 1989 Convention on the Rights of the Child institutes, among other things, new means for children's social freedom, voice, and participation, on the assumption that children should bring their own full moral capabilities into society.

Bottom-up childism is humanizing in a profound way. Children are granted full humanity precisely as children. Adults too are humanized by their encounters with children and by their own childhood pasts. The span of life is placed into its widest context as not just a movement away from birth but also a movement toward a greater temporal wholeness in which the beginnings of life are centrally affirmed. Age is not a problem to be overcome but a constituent of the fullness of existence. If life starts out on some level fundamentally good, then whatever deceptions and violence it may become involved in along the way do not define humanity at its core.

But such a view also contains its own dehumanizing tendencies. Taken alone—or taken to extremes—it obscures what I will later call the reality of human vulnerability. Children and adults are vulnerable both within and without: within to their own less-than-good tendencies, and without to the destructiveness of the world. The word vulnerability comes from the Latin *vulnus*, which means "wound." If children are imagined to be models of goodness, it is difficult ultimately to see what it means for them to be wounded or to be able to wound others. Children's purity can too easily suggest a certain invulnerability. All the blame must be placed on adults and society without explaining where capabilities for harm come from in the first place. Too strong a concept of children's innate goodness also makes it easier to ignore children's and adults' victimization and neediness.

In other words, if children are the ethical models for society, then society itself can in the end owe children little. Since children are there to save adults from themselves, then adults hold only minimal responsibilities for them. Likewise, if humanity overall is naturally good, being corrupted only in its historical relations and structures, then these structures cannot be relied on much for solutions to human struggles. All of us must chiefly rely on ourselves.

This problem turns out to be especially acute for children. Given all the freedom and agency in the world, children would still remain more vulnerable than adults to social marginalization and exploitation. This is simply because children have, on the whole, less time and experience. Agency alone will not solve children's larger social problems. At its extreme, the bottom-up story reduces children to unrealistic sentimentalization—to a separate, pure species. As the feminist theologian Bonnie Miller-McLemore has put it, "children are neither entirely virtuous nor entirely depraved . . . [but] an amalgamation of imperfection and potentiality."[38] As for women in the past, an excessively high view of children's purity and goodness places them on an ethereal pedestal beyond serious worldly concerns.

Paradoxically, then, children's over-valorizing may permit adults to walk past when they find children in trouble. In the United States, children are so often elevated to romantic heights that they can be safely ignored in many social debates. They are imagined to exist in a private sphere beyond messy public realities. The truth is, however, that all people, young and old, are vulnerable to corruption from both without and within. All bring both goodness and harm to others. And all rely on others' and society's active supports.

THE DEVELOPMENTAL STORY

There is still a third form of childism in the West. It would be simpler were there only two and I could propose a third mediating position. However, there is in reality a triangle of options, and its third point turns out to be just as morally ambiguous as the other two.

This third approach is neither top-down nor bottom-up but what could be called "horizontal" or "developmental." By this I mean that it argues for neither an imposed higher moral order nor an original goodness, but rather a gradual and progressive realization of human ethical potential over the course of time. Humanity in light of children starts out neither pure nor unruly, according to this view, but in a state of fundamental ethical neutrality or blankness. The moral aim is for humanity's unformed potential to unfold over the course of personal and historical time in the direction of social progress. And the chief obligation of moral life is to advance human relations through increasingly rational dialogue. Thus, the point of view of childhood does not call so much for vertical human relations, whether from above or from below, as for horizontal relations extended along a developmental axis over time.

The most influential historical champion of this approach is Plato's student Aristotle. Even though Aristotle has relatively little to say about children, what he does say reflects larger currents in ancient Greek culture that have significantly shaped Western thought about childhood and society. What distinguishes Aristotle from Plato in this regard is Aristotle's view of material nature, which he sees, not as irrational or unruly, but as *pre*-rational: that is, as containing its own as-yet-unfulfilled rational potential. It is for this reason that Aristotle criticizes Plato's argument in *The Republic* that children should be raised by whole societies in common rather than by their biological parents. For Aristotle, children can receive the care and nurturance they need only from their parents, who by virtue of their deep natural bonds are more attached to and invested in them than anyone else.[39] Reason does not overcome bodily nature but instead realizes and perfects it.

A child, for Aristotle, is already a "societal animal" (*zoon politikon*) in potential if not yet in full.[40] This means that children receive care but only gradually learn to give it. They cannot yet enjoy full human "happiness," since happiness (*eudaimonia*) consists, for Aristotle, in actively exercising social virtues.[41] Nor are children owed the same level of "proportional justice" as adults, since children by nature (as well, he argues, as women) have fewer rational faculties. According to Aristotle, birth begins a lifelong process of gradual social development that aims toward the fullest possible realization of social reason in maturity. Such a view, as far as I can tell, is largely absent from the Bible and the Qur'an. Perhaps this points to its chiefly Greek origins.

However, the twelfth-century Sufi Muslim abu Hamid al-Ghazali also comes to a distinctly developmental conclusion. He combines Aristotelianism with Islam to formulate a complex schema of human development along a variety of moral, spiritual, and social axes. Childhood begins the lifelong human journey toward union with the one true Allah. Children are born "soft like the soft clay in which any seed can grow," or like "a precious uncut jewel devoid of any form of carving, which will accept being cut into any shape."[42] This growth is not imposed from above; nor does it arise spontaneously from within. Rather, good character and relations must be guided and nourished dialectically in the same way that a farmer "puts water and fertilizers in the crop so that the crop grows and develops a good quality."[43] Allah's gift of natural reason to each human being at birth may be either cultivated or squandered over time. Long before today's theories of moral development, al-Ghazali argued for three successively more rational moral "stages": from helping others in want, to treating others as equals, to placing the needs of others above one's own.[44]

A similar approach is found in the thirteenth-century theologian Thomas Aquinas, later to become the key ethicist for modern Catholicism, who synthesizes an Aristotelian view of childhood with Christianity. It is difficult to see Thomas's view of children directly influencing his larger ethics and theology. However, it does provide a vivid illustration of his ethics of "natural law," in which humanity's God-given rational potential may gradually develop in actual societies.

For Thomas, children's development again begins within the natural contexts of families, where the biological attachments of parental love may gradually elicit children's growing capabilities for moral love themselves. Ethical reason evolves in four seven-year phases: Up to the age of seven, the young child is a wholly "irrational animal . . . [who] neither understands by himself nor is able to learn from another" ("irrational" here does not mean unruly, but rather without understanding); between seven and fourteen, the child becomes able to learn from others but not to think independently for herself; in the next seven years, up to the age of twenty-one, the adolescent develops the ability to learn from others *and* to think for herself; and finally, only starting at age twenty-one does the full "use of reason" emerge, so that the individual can properly understand not only "things concerning his person" but also "things outside his person" (such as, presumably, nature and society).[45] Again, goodness is not imposed by transcending principles; nor does it bubble up spontaneously from within. Rather, it gradually unfolds under the proper social conditions and over the developing course of a lifetime.

In a similar fashion, the fifteenth-century theologian Christine de Pizan argues in *Treasure of the City of Ladies* that childhood is that stage of life when one cultivates natural "virtue" in the Aristotelian sense of social reason or excellence. Interestingly, and true to her time, the most influential female thinker of the Middle Ages insists on the subordination of mothers' authority over boys and girls to fathers'. Ultimately, in her view, fathers are endowed by nature and God with greater rational capabilities; hence they hold greater responsibilities for investing moral rationality in children. Nevertheless, "the wise lady who loves her children dearly will be diligent about their education . . . [and] will want them to be told and shown all the precepts of virtue and taught the way to avoid vices."[46] A good home and society are defined by the degree to which moral capabilities are formed in their members over time.

A more modern kind of developmentalism begins to emerge in the Catholic sixteenth-century humanist Desiderius Erasmus. Erasmus insists that childhood is the beginning of what distinguishes humanity from the animals: namely, the faculty of moral reason. He argues for "how important it is for one's whole life that one should be initiated into excellence from the very cradle onwards."[47] Unlike animals, human beings start out with tremendous rational and moral potential. "Consider the agility of a child's mind for absorbing every kind of teaching, and the flexibility of the human mind in general. Remember how easily anything that is good and congenial to nature may be learned."[48] At the same time, Erasmus claims, this potential can be corrupted over time by ignorance and neglect. "The beginning and the end, indeed the total sum of man's happiness, are founded upon a good upbringing and education."[49] Childhood shows that happiness and goodness depend on the increasing socialization of humanity's unique rational potential.

Perhaps the most influential view of this sort in modernity, however, is found a century later in the writings of John Locke, arguably the founder of the European Enlightenment. Like Aristotle, about whom he wrote a great deal, Locke sees in childhood the beginnings of the unfolding of natural reason. But unlike Aristotle, Locke locates this, not in social roles, but in the growth of individual liberty. In his widely influential 1693 *Some Thoughts concerning Education*, he argues that children are not unruly animals—as in the prevailing Reformation view of his day—but "white pages" or "wax" (not blank slates, as often thought), ready to be written upon or molded with all the skills and discoveries of the human and natural sciences. Whether reason is ultimately harnessed for good or for ill, children epitomize humanity's potential for increasing rational progress. Locke's language is similar to that of Erasmus: "Nine parts of Ten are what they [children] are, Good or Evil, useful or not, by their Education."[50] The job of society, educators, and parents is not to force children into authoritatively imposed values, but to educate each child to "submit to his own Reason, when he is of an Age to make use of it."[51]

In his *Essay concerning Human Understanding*, furthermore, Locke formulates a loose developmental schema of children's increasing rational freedom: from infant (indeed late fetal) understanding by direct sensory experience; to the increasingly complex "association" of raw experiences into higher-order ideas; and eventually to "reflection" on these processes and ideas for oneself and in dialogue with others.[52] At the same time, in his *Two Treatises on Government*, a founding text of modern human rights theory, Locke argues that social rights do not belong to children per se, since children are not yet rationally developed enough to exercise them. In his view, children's lack of fully formed moral reason makes them unable to participate in the liberties of the social contract without doing themselves and others harm.[53] (We will discuss Locke's, as well as Rousseau's and Kant's, views of children's rights in chapter 5.) Nevertheless, childhood remains, for Locke, the origin of the possibility that a free, just, and rights-based society can ultimately be formed, and that societies themselves may develop in rationality over time.

Johann Gottfried von Herder, the eighteenth-century Protestant theologian and educator, extends this view into the very meaning of "humanity." Childhood, for him, is the temporal starting point of humanity's education into its own humanity. As he puts it, "we *are* not yet human beings, but are daily *becoming* so. . . . The purpose of human nature is humanity [*Humanität*]; and with this purpose God has put the fate of our race in our own hands."[54] Human life at birth is neither good nor evil but in a state of neutral potential. "We are born almost without instinct, we become what we should and can be only through lifelong training toward humanity, and this is the reason our species is both perfectible and corruptible."[55]

Finally, we could point to another well-known educationalist, the nineteenth-century social philosopher John Stuart Mill, who sees in children's development the hope for a free, just, and liberal polity. Among other things, it is Mill who extends the logic of children's unformed rational capabilities into an argument for universal public education.[56] If boys and girls, rich and poor, gifted and ordinary alike are corrupted over time by ignorance, then education is not only a right of all children but required for a progressive society. This again does not mean that children themselves should have the liberty of full social citizens, for "those who are still in a state to require being taken care of by others, must be protected against their own actions."[57] Nevertheless, it is because of reason's innateness from birth that societies can be organized on an increasingly rational basis at all (in Mill's case, the utilitarian basis of "the greatest good for the greatest number"). For each human being brings to the world the promise of increasing the world's rationality still further.

THE PROBLEM OF DIVERSITY

The chief advantage of this developmental perspective over the other two forms of childism is its temporality and realism. It refuses to either demonize or sentimentalize childhood but instead assumes a starting position of ethical neutrality. This allows it to recognize children's dual goodness and potential for harm. It also complicates the question of the relation between children's likenesses to adults and their differences as these diminish over time. Childhood is a distinctive stage in the overall human lifecycle, with its own unique but not entirely separate characteristics. A developmental view, whatever its particulars, sees in humanity its unfolding potential over time.

For these and other reasons, developmentalism has enjoyed a great resurgence over the past century, particularly through the field of academic and popular psychology. We will examine this trend in chapter 3. It includes, of course, Sigmund Freud's developing stages of the young child's psyche, Jean Piaget's phases of children's moral reason, Erik Erikson's eight divisions of the human lifecycle, and a wide range of other perspectives. Although there is much dispute about the specifics, many accept that in some way social and moral capabilities arise over time starting at birth in gradual and definable phases. Each human being must pass through many years—perhaps an entire lifetime—of increasing moral development. More broadly, human societies can be said to pursue "development" economically, politically, and perhaps even morally.

What is also distinct in this approach is its respect for the concrete processes of human nature. Top-down ethicists tend to see "nature" as the problem, so that children bring into the world a mass of passions and appetites that need to be controlled by society. Bottom-up ethicists tend to see "nature" as the fount of goodness and wisdom, so that social relations should be returned as much as possible to it. Developmental ethicists are free, in contrast, to view human "nature" as morally complex, able to distort and to ennoble relations at once.

What is dehumanizing here, however, is that humanity—and especially childhood—is stripped of genuine moral diversity. This is the case in at least two respects. First, while there is of course a diversity of stages of development, there is not a deeper *ethical* diversity of developmental paths. Insofar as human goodness is defined through a developmental lens, whether in discrete stages or more fluidly, it is necessarily oriented toward a single developmental goal. Locke may disagree with Thomas, and al-Ghazali with Aristotle, about in the goal itself, just as Carl Jung may disagree with Freud and Lawrence Kohlberg with Piaget. But once one is committed to a developmental paradigm, one has to choose one or another image of exactly what is to be developed into in order to be able to chart a coherent trajectory of developmental growth. This means that there cannot be a real diversity of moral paths within any one particular developmental schema.

Second, the problem of ethical diversity is especially acute from the point of view of childhood. For the developmental model subordinates, in moral terms, its starting point to its hoped-for aim. Childhood, as Rousseau complained, is given value chiefly as a means to adulthood. Childhood is interpreted through the lens of what children *are not yet*, namely, developed adults. What it means to be a child is paradoxically secondary, for children, to becoming an adult. Childhood is to be understood as a path or passageway to something other than childhood. Adulthood, in contrast, is usually considered somehow complete, or at least more complete. To have developed fully is to have reached some kind of non-childlike humanity.

The truth, however, morally speaking, is that no age in human life, either in childhood or in adulthood, is chiefly a pathway toward something else. Nor is any age in history only significant insofar as it ushers in what is to come. Most adults would feel it dehumanizing to be considered primarily as preparing themselves for a later phase of moral capability. Children are also full human beings who inhabit and create fully meaningful moral worlds for themselves. Children just as much as adults contribute to humanity's remarkable moral diversity. Children are not just undeveloped adults or adults-in-the-making but full participants in the broad sea of human moral experience.

The developmental story does not alone, therefore, offer a sufficiently complex third way. A little bit like in George Orwell's *Animal Farm*, it suggests that while all humans are created equal, some are more equal than others. It is largely for this reason that the dominant language of developmental moral psychology has been challenged in recent years by sociologists, anthropologists, historians, and others who have argued for understanding children as moral agents in and of themselves, and through a diversity of cultural, historical, gender, class, and other kinds of social constructions. We can also look deeper into history. It is no accident that thinkers like Aristotle and Locke, while overcoming problems with other ways of seeing children, do not finally understand children as capable of social rights or citizenship. The point has been made repeatedly by bottom-up critics in particular that children are distinctive moral beings in themselves and not just developing adults.

CHILDISM IN HISTORY

This long detour into intellectual history shows that thinking ethically in light of childhood is more complex and problematic than it might at first appear. It is not that major architects of Western social thought have not deeply concerned themselves with children, for in fact many have. Nor is it that past thinkers have held unenlightened ideas that we can now surpass. It is that the perils of oversimplification and dehumanization are many and diverse and can be found in even the most strenuously child-responsive endeavors. It has taken thousands of years to overcome patriarchal prejudices against women, held by men and women both, and these efforts continue today. How much less sanguine should we be, then, when it comes to ethical assumptions about children! Ethical thought and practice face a history of ingrained adult-centrism—more ingrained than adults may be able to imagine—and so our task of thinking anew must struggle with its own historical depths.

At the same time, if history has constructed such a variety of stories about children's fundamental humanity—and of humanity in light of children—then we can hope ultimately to construct new and better stories still. By recognizing history's diverse strengths and shortcomings, we stand in a position to begin to recreate history in more broadly child-inclusive ways. Humility need not give way to despair.

It would hardly be fair to simplify this past and then accuse it of oversimplification. However, we can keep in mind the larger ethical difficulties—as well as what is helpful in various models—by placing the childist history above into the following table.

Humanity in Light of Childhood			
	Being	Aim	Obligation
Top-down ↓	unruly	social order	fulfilling roles
Bottom-up ↑	good	natural simplicity	respecting gifts
Developmental →	in potential	progressive rationality	engaging in dialogue

And here, for the sake of comparison, is how my own alternative will compare.

Circular ↻	creative	narrative expansion	responding to otherness

My alternative, as we will see, takes certain elements of all three of the historical possibilities. But it crafts their linearity into a new kind of ethical circle that is not finally reducible to any of them.

In sum, allow me to offer an analogy, adapted from the Enlightenment philosopher of science Francis Bacon.[58] A top-down childism tends to interpret human beings as rather like ants: finding a sense of purpose through their roles in a larger social order. A bottom-up view sees people as more like spiders: spinning from within themselves strong silken threads against the winds of the world. Developmentalists view humanity along the lines of flies: passing through stages of metamorphosis to eventually swarm into flight. My own view, in contrast, is that human beings in light of childhood are more like bees: circling widely in diverse fields to create a rich honey for the hive.

Let me repeat that in these models we are speaking only of tendencies. The thinkers mentioned above are all more complex than our merely illustrative historical analyses can show. What is more, the differences between our three historical forms of childism do not have to do with differences between philosophy and religion. All three tendencies persist in one way or another throughout Judaism, Christianity, Islam, and secularism. The view that religion holds a dim view of children is an old Enlightenment myth, propagated in response to one particular Reformation worldview dominant in Europe at the time. This myth needs to be dispelled in order to move beyond binary thinking and toward more complex ethical possibilities for today.

Furthermore, there is no great dividing line between pre-modernity and modernity. If there is a difference introduced in modernity, it is a greater sense for the moral worth of the individual. But this sense can be interpreted, it turns out, in any number of top-down, bottom-up, and developmental ways. The individual can be either an autonomous ruler over their own desires, an instinctual social redeemer, or a progressively more rational social contributor. The more fundamental ethical differences in history, at least in light of childhood, are more historically deep-rooted.

Each of the three major historical tendencies charted here remains both profoundly influential today and finally insufficient. The question for us is not—or at least need not be—which one we should pick. The more helpful and hopeful question is how to avoid history's various drawbacks while taking into account its various kinds of wisdom, in order to construct a new and even more fully child-responsive ethics. Our task is not restorative but creative. Historically ingrained beliefs about children's unruliness, giftedness, and potential need to be reshaped with a deeper appreciation for children's agency, vulnerability, and diversity. Ideas of childhood are not simply going to improve over time. They need to be imaginatively reconstructed.

As in the case of children themselves, past roots of moral life need to be cultivated but in new ways open to what is creatively new. Generally speaking, we do not have as much trouble thinking about adults from a diversity of ethical angles at once as we seem historically to have had about children. This kind of increased complexity needs to be invested in what can be learned about humanity specifically from childhood. In many ways, children are more ethically complex than adults and open up especially broad ethical horizons. Just as each child is a wholly new human being, so also does thought about ethics in light of childhood call for new thought, perhaps without end.

PART II

THEORY

Chapter 2

What Is Human Being?

IT MAY SEEM OBVIOUS to say that children are full human beings. But as the history sketched in the previous chapter shows, it is not easy to explain what exactly this means. Leading thinkers' efforts to describe children's full humanity have resulted in one or another form of oversimplification. Of course, such is the case for any person or group. It is to some extent inevitable that talk about humanity is dehumanizing. But for children in particular, the problem is complicated by the fact that they cannot, on the whole—nor should they—be held as responsible as adults for making their own particular experiences of humanity known. Children's ethical complexity is especially readily obscured. Overturning historical biases about childhood will take more than empirical investigation, helpful though this is. It will also require ethical self-critique.

The first step in such an exercise, undertaken in this chapter, is to ask what childhood suggests about the nature of humanity's basic moral "being." How does consideration of children's worlds and experiences challenge what it means to have humanity in the first place? Rather than asking simply what makes children and adults alike, we should ask what makes children and adults alike in light of children rather than adults. Each new child changes everything. The same should be the case in understanding the nature of human being. The humanization of childhood depends on the childization of humanity.

In the previous chapter I argued that Western intellectual history provides three basic answers to what childhood teaches about being human. A top-down view in figures like Plato, Augustine, Calvin, and Kant claims, in essence, that children make clear human being's fundamental moral unruliness, its natural state of uncivilized, undisciplined, even sinful disorder. A bottom-up perspective in figures like Jesus, Chrysostom, Rousseau, and Schleiermacher suggests, in contrast, that children demonstrate humanity's original moral goodness, its natural gift of innocence prior to the corruptions of societies. And a developmental approach in figures like

Aristotle, al-Ghazali, Thomas, and Locke argues that children exemplify human-ity's natural moral neutrality, its inherent potential for good or ill depending on individual and social increases in rationality. Each of these views remains part of the deep archeology of ethical understanding today, provides something useful, but is at the same time finally insufficient.

On top of this archeology, we must also consider new ideas about the being of childhood that have arisen more recently. Some of these come from observa-tions in the human sciences about children's experiences. For example, as sociolo-gists and anthropologists have shown, children have wider capabilities for social agency and voice than history has generally assumed. They may also, as Freud and others have argued, have more complexly conflicted inner psychological lives. Other advances come less from observation than from broad cultural movements. Feminism, for example, deconstructs a pervasive historical patriarchalism toward girls and systematically gendered distortions of power. Environmentalism helps to understand childhood as deeply bound up with nature. Finally, how children are understood by adults has itself been shown to be historically and socially con-structed, the very notion of "childhood" being diversely interpreted throughout the many cultures of the world.

These kinds of historical and contemporary challenges require that we explore human "being" in a more concrete, historical, and culturally constructed way. It requires, I will argue, a kind of phenomenology as imagined by the likes of Ed-mund Husserl, Martin Heidegger, and Paul Ricoeur. That is, it must move beyond abstract analysis to the investigation of human being as lived experience. If moder-nity sees being human as subjectively separate from an objective external world, phenomenology rejects this dichotomy by exploring human being as world-con-stituted: as always experienced through particular languages, relations, materiali-ties, and times. Human being, in other words, is "being-in-the-world." It is not separate from but within the world. Indeed, childhood should remind humanity in the strongest possible terms that its being is embodied, historical, and relational through and through.

My argument in this chapter is that human being in light of childhood is not therefore entirely culturally constructed, but rather consists in a fundamental capability for creating meaning. Human being is simultaneously constructed and constructive. That is its most basic nature. I call this capability *world creativ-ity*. To be human, from birth to death, is to create new worlds of meaning from the worlds of meaning already created by history and others. Each of us is born into a social world whose shape has already been constituted through time, but which each of us cannot help but also reshape over time into meaning for our-selves. Hence what I am calling humanity's circularity: its being as both passively created by and actively creative of its constituting worlds of meaning. Human being-in-the-world is more than mere freedom, reason, historicity, or even oth-erness. Rather, it is the restless and endless play of fashioning and reinventing the world itself.

CHILDREN'S MORAL AGENCY

What must first be noted in a more rounded view of human being is what it means on the basic level of human moral agency. Historically speaking, as we saw in the previous chapter, understanding human being in light of childhood has been centrally concerned with the kind of agency, or lack thereof, that children are born with. Some have tended to minimize children's agency by asserting their need to submit to the more experienced agency of adults and societies. Others argue that children bring into the world a powerful moral agency of their own that adults would do well to emulate. Still others see children as gradually increasing in social agency over time as they grow up. Today, these competing views affect not only how one sees children but also how one sees the nature of being human.

The concept of children's "agency" has been championed most recently in the growing field known as childhood studies. The sociologists, anthropologists, historians, and others who first developed this field fixed upon agency as one of the defining characteristics of children's full humanity.

In this view, agency refers to children's capacities to participate on their own behalf in society. It is also defined along somewhat feminist lines of children being empowered social actors. Children are dehumanized, it is claimed, when they are seen as merely passive recipients of adult socialization or adults-in-the-making. As the groundbreaking scholars Allison James and Alan Prout argue, "children must be seen as actively involved in the construction of their own social lives, the lives of those around them and the societies in which they live. They can no longer be regarded as simply the passive subjects of structural determinations."[1] This also entails, as others have put it, children being understood to have a social "voice," a "commitment to *make known* their own ability to act on their own behalf, whether to ensure their own interests or to modify the world that surrounds them."[2]

As agents with voice, children construct their own worlds of meaning and shape their surrounding social relations. They form responses to poverty, make uses of mass media, give meaning to families, direct their experiences in classrooms, and engage in philosophical and religious thinking—and with as much complexity and diversity as adults.

One striking example is found in studies by the cultural anthropologist Myra Bluebond-Langner of American children who are dying of leukemia. Such children defy usual models of the young as passive and unknowing recipients of adult care. Rather, even at early ages, they are aware of the fact that they are dying and, furthermore, take an active responsibility for the impact of their dying on others, such as parents and medical staff. When five-year-old Jeffrey is asked, for example, "Why do you always yell at your mother?" his reply is: "Then she won't miss me when I'm gone."[3] Other children collude in parents' and providers' silence about their prognosis being terminal. Children are not just recipients of nurturing but also "willful, purposeful individuals capable of creating their own world, as well as acting in the world others create for them."[4]

This notion of children's fundamental moral agency adds something new to the understanding of children's human being that has never fully been articulated before in Western history. It essentially presses a tradition of bottom-up thinking to a more complex conclusion. Figures like Clement and Rousseau tend to see children as moral agents, but primarily only within the limited worlds of families (however much more broadly family itself would have been understood in the past). Perhaps as a result, they tend to elevate children's agency to highly senti-mentalized proportions. Indeed, Rousseau explicitly argues for protecting chil-dren's agency from public society for as long as possible on account of the latter's power to corrupt it.

In today's postindustrial era, however, when private family and public life may be more sharply divided than ever, the childhood studies movement emphasizes children's agency and voice in all realms of experience. Just because children now find themselves rather sequestered in the home—which was Rousseau's dream—it may be more important than ever to recognize how they do and can act in com-munities and institutions (such as hospitals), consume mass media, add to the economy, create culture, speak up for themselves, participate in research, organize politically, and exercise rights.

The notion of children's agency, voice, and social constructiveness faces, how-ever, a basic philosophical dilemma. This dilemma is similar to the problem rec-ognized not long ago for women by some so-called "third wave" feminists. While "first wave" feminists fought for the right to vote, and "second wave" feminists, be-ginning in the 1950s, demanded equal participation in work and society, more re-cently some feminists have argued that, beyond simple equality, change is required in the very structures of male-dominated society in response to what is distinctive about women and womanhood.

So far, the childhood studies movement has chiefly embraced what could be called a "second wave" form of childism. It focuses on asserting children's equal agency and voice, the ways in which children participate in society as much as adults. However, as third-wave feminism has shown, this strategy could end up asking those who are historically oppressed to conform to the longstanding moral structures imposed on them by their oppressors. Instead, those very historical constructions should be radically reconfigured. Childism will become fully re-sponsive to childhood only when it insists on a child-inclusive view of human being for all.

Such a shift especially means rethinking conceptions of human agency, for these have tended since modernity to be defined in strongly adult terms of freedom, au-tonomy, and independence. On such terms, no matter how much agency children have, they are likely still to remain disproportionately socially marginalized. For example, rich and poor children today are exposed like never before to the tre-mendous influence of mass media. Advertisers, in fact, quite explicitly argue that in selling products to children it is they who, more than nay-saying parents, are respecting children's agency and voices.[5] While it is true that children's autonomy is in a sense being encouraged, it is also true that the more powerful "agency" here is corporations run by adults for their own profit. What children show is that the notion of human agency can be paradoxical and even self-defeating.

BETWEEN AGENCY AND VULNERABILITY

What is needed in light of childhood is a deeper sense of the connection between human agency and human vulnerability. These should be understood, not as polar opposites, but as intertwined for all human beings in a dynamic and creative tension. As we saw in the previous chapter, the term "vulnerability" comes from the Latin *vulnus*, meaning susceptibility to wound or harm. It does not occur with particular frequency in the history of thought about childhood. However, this history does provide the term with at least three possible meanings: being overwhelmed by one's own disordered animality; having one's inner gifts and talents squashed by a larger corrupted society; or remaining captive to an undeveloped or uneducated ignorance. To these we may add a further (feminist) possibility: vulnerability as the potential to be excluded from the levers of social power. Adrian Thatcher has described children in this last sense as "often the ones with no voice, the unconsulted and sometimes undeserving victims of oppression."[6]

What childhood suggests, in part, is not only that humanity contains vulnerability at its core, but also that whatever vulnerability it contains is not simply opposed to the freedom of self-empowering agency. When agency and vulnerability are dichotomized—as for example in the remarkably adult-centered rational individualism of much of modernity—vulnerability devolves into the mere absence of a human ideal: absence of self-control, of reason, of freedom, or of power. As Martha Nussbaum has shown, this hierarchization of agency over vulnerability can be traced ultimately to the origins of philosophy in the ambitions of Plato.[7] For Plato (as his view of childhood also shows) founded understanding and goodness on the overcoming of the mind's captivity to mere desire, fortune, and chance, and particularly to the greatest site of human vulnerability: the body. Since then, many Western philosophers and theologians have assumed that the slings and arrows of outrageous fortune are best opposed by the assertion of a more forceful will or agency. This prejudice against vulnerability is not only (arguably) male-centered but (even more profoundly) adult-centered.

The deeper meaning of vulnerability has to do, not with lack of agency, but with openness and relationality to the world. The self as an invulnerable island is not a self but an empty shell. As the theologian David Jensen has suggested, vulnerability is better understood as an expression of human difference: "A baby is open to any human being who will assuage that gift of otherness. . . . The vulnerability of children . . . is a fact of the God-given relatedness into which persons are born: though most visibly in infancy, we never outgrow it."[8] To live in relation to others and societies is never simply to act upon them. It is always also to make oneself vulnerable or open to being shaped by them.

All human beings from birth to death must negotiate a lifelong dynamics of agency and vulnerability in relation to one another. Being-in-the-world is from the very beginning both passively constructed by others and societies and actively constructed by a self. The world has already imposed on each of us a fortune, fate, language, historicity, biology, gender, relations, politics, and much else. No one chooses the world that they are born and socialized into, however oppressive or supportive that world may be. At the same time, however, the world does not reduce anyone to its purely passive victim. As the phenomenologist Paul Ricoeur has put it: "Freedom is not a pure act, it is, in each of its moments, activity and receptivity. It constitutes itself in receiving what it does not produce: values, capacities, and sheer nature."[9] Agency is always conditioned by vulnerability and vulnerability in turn shaped by agency.

Consider some of the most vulnerable children in the world: those orphaned by the AIDS epidemic. Such children are profoundly shaped by circumstances far beyond their control: a disease propagated largely by adults and by poverty, culture, ineffective politics, and so on. At the same time, they are not thereby robbed of the capability for responding and creating meaning. Some children in India, for example, formed a theater group that writes plays and travels around promoting AIDS prevention. "I plead with all so that such people may live," says ten-year-old Kunda Deepthi.[10] I was at a conference in India where the child participants were deeply aware of the many problems facing their societies and provided among the most creative solutions to them.[11]

At birth, each human being begins a lifelong process, however difficult, of shaping his or her worlds in passive-active tension with the very worlds themselves by which he or she is shaped. One's body, relations, society, culture, and history are always both passively received and actively reshaped. They are throughout life both already interpreted for you and taken up into your own interpretations of them. History is at once *already* there and yet *someone's* history, both objective and subjective, both given and receiving new meaning.

Being human, especially in light of childhood, involves neither pure agency nor pure vulnerability but, more fundamentally, the experience of creative tension between the two. Adults' worlds are psychologically, socially, culturally, and historically preconstructed just as much as are children's. In a sense they are *more* preconstructed because of increased accretions of language, culture, experiences, and responsibilities. Adults are vulnerable to powers and fortunes (including finally death) at the very core of their being. Likewise, adults, like children, have a certain agency allowing them to respond to their multiple passivities and vulnerabilities in ever distinctive new ways.

Children teach in the starkest possible terms that human agency and vulnerability coexist in a lively tension. While this tension may become relatively obscured in adulthood by habit and routine, in childhood it is likely to be relatively visible and dynamic. The word "tension" comes from *tensus*, meaning *to stretch*. Children are likely to be more able than adults, on the whole, to stretch out their own existing worlds of meaning. They are simultaneously more energetically free agents and more profoundly vulnerable to circumstances. The tension or stretch of existence tends to be especially vibrant and alive.

An infant stands before the world full of untold possibility, ceaselessly exploring, playing, taking in new sounds and smells, opening up previously unknown potentials. Adults may not be so lucky as they face hardening habits and viewpoints and diminishing possibilities, becoming more likely set in their ways. Yet, at the same time, an infant is more profoundly vulnerable to others' and society's shaping and marginalization of them, to the point where without others they would simply die. The vulnerability of adults, in contrast, may be more fully mediated by experience, resources, and knowledge. What children show, however, is that agency and vulnerability cannot finally be separated. They stand in living relation to one another.

This tension of vulnerability and agency begins to suggest, in a very basic way, how human being-in-the-world with others involves a circle of world creativity. Being-in-the-world is not just passively received, actively constructed, or forged gradually over a lifetime. Rather, it involves all three at once. It is the perpetual creation of given worlds of meaning into new worlds of meaning over time. Rather than imposing agency or receiving conditions, it is dynamic and reconstituting. The truly wonderful and strange capability that humanity is born with is that of making anew what already is. Human being is self-creative and world-transforming. Like bees, each of us endlessly sets out on a lifelong circle between the already constructed social hive and the new nectar of experiences from the field.

FROM GIFT TO GIFTEDNESS

To understand what makes this tension possible, we can turn to the old historical notion of human being as gift. For in a certain sense to act or even to be in the world is a "gift" simply given to each of us at birth. But traditional notions of humanity as a gift given at childhood will need to be rethought. For they are each too simple: the gift *of* goodness given through the child to the world; the gift *to* parents and society of the child as their property; or the gift *for* developing one's own potential. What fuller sense might be given to humanity as a gift that learns from the profound circularity of children's agency and vulnerability?

Here I would like to take a quick detour into recent phenomenological discussions of "gift" that examine it in terms of passive-active moral exchange. In fact, gifts in general are much more complex and strange phenomena than Westerners, at least, have historically been used to imagining.

According to Jacques Derrida, a gift in the ordinary sense is strictly speaking "impossible": "As soon as the donee knows it is a gift, he already thanks the donator, and cancels the gift. As soon as the donor is conscious of giving, he himself thanks himself and again cancels the gift by re-inscribing it into a circle, an economic circle."[12] No gift is ever given without strings attached, so to speak. It is in some way always automatically returned and not simply "free." Much as the anthropologist Marcel Mauss has shown is the case among potlatch societies, an "economy of gift" gives protections and support by those in power in return for their subjects' gifts of loyalty and work. Broadly speaking, giving a gift always involves on some level receiving something in return. It involves both agential and vulnerable circulatory dynamics.

All of this becomes even more complicated when one considers childhood—and therefore humanity—as itself the gift. This *human* gift—this gift of humanity—is even stranger and more paradoxical than Derrida's and Mauss's gifts between human beings. To say that a child herself is a gift is to imply that the child is not only given and received but also herself simultaneously gives and receives. She has a full circulatory system, a blood flow, a life. The child comes into the world both giving something previously unknown to that world—her presence, if you will—and at the same time is given by that world as a gift from parents, society, natural evolution, and possibly the gods. Likewise, parents and society, in turn, both passively are given the gift of a child and actively give this child gifts of such things as existence and survival.

In other words, no child simply gives herself to others or the world, and no child is simply given by them. A child is a "gift" in the complex sense of both being passively given her being by the world and actively giving being to the world. She comes from us yet also comes to us. She is a "being" in both the active and the passive senses of that word.

Trygve Wyller has explored the notion of childhood as a gift using a slightly different phenomenology than Derrida's, one that arguably better captures the sense of gift in children. A child's givenness, according to Wyller, is in one sense a matter of simple perception: "Since givenness is there before any cognitive reflection, any child has a right to be treated according to this givenness," including the perception that "children are not gifts to anyone."[13] Children are their own gift and not anyone else's property. At the same time, children must be "given" aid and support. As Wyller puts it: "Children do not owe us anything. Grown-ups and grown-up society owe them a lot."[14] (I will argue later that children do, however, owe others something.) Children are gifts in the dynamic sense that in simply giving something to the world they also engender an obligation in the world to give something to them in return. This makes children, from the day they are born, participants in an "economy of the gift" by already engaging in the give-and-take of entire social systems.

This strange circularity can be pressed even further by translating gift into the language of *giftedness*. Each human being is *gifted* in the sense of passively being given meaning by a world to which he or she actively gives meaning anew. Everyone, in this sense, is a "gifted" child. Giftedness is both concretely situated in the world as it already is, and—unexpectedly, irreducibly, even mysteriously—reshapes that world in previously unforeseen ways. Each of us has a kind of concretely embodied genius, as one might call it, that allows us, not to float free of the world, but to reinterpret and refashion it from within. This is not a Romantic genius found purely within, but an embodied genius found in all experience.

Each human being at birth simply appears in the world, physically and otherwise, as a new gift to that world. But each also, in this very appearing, is vulnerable to that world's given relations and constructions. What makes humanity peculiarly gifted is the capacity not just to repeat its world, as to a large extent is the case for other forms of life, but to create the world into new worlds of meaning and possibility. One might think of Jacques Lusseyran, the blind teenager who directed a massive French resistance movement during World War II through his special gift for sensing compatriots as opposed to infiltrators.[15] His vulnerability in the form of his blindness—and his facing hostile political powers—also made him able to give the world something new. One's conditions help to draw out one's unique capabilities, which in turn change one's conditions.

The giftedness of each new child in the world begins a dynamic circle of agency and vulnerability that is the very foundation of human relations and society. A child appears in society open or vulnerable to being shaped by others and history. But society itself—from parents to cultures and whole communities—is vulnerable also to that child's disruption of its meanings and habits. A tension runs back and forth in both directions between child and world. Humanity exists in between subjectivity and world. It may then give changing meanings to the worlds into which it is already born. Without a relation to a world, there is no such thing as a gift for bringing to the world something new. Without childhood, there is nothing new to bring, no original giftedness. Childhood is the origin of both human givenness in society (it is when we first appear, both to ourselves and to others) and human giving to society (it is when we first subject ourselves and others to interpretation and shaping).

What makes our relations with one another truly human is that we are neither mere objects to one another nor utterly isolated subjects. Rather, we cross over into one another's worlds by giving and receiving new meaning. The true economy of the gift is the cycle of exchange between persons. No one begins this cycle and no one stands at its completion. Rather, at birth each human being joins into human relations' give and take until death.

By "giftedness" I mean, therefore, the capability for joining this circle of human meaning at all. It is the ability to give one's own new meaning to an already meaning-saturated world. It imposes itself on social relations even as it opens the self in social vulnerability. It is both constructive and deconstructive, making and unmaking of meaning.

With Schleiermacher we may say that each child is a wondrous gift—only now without romanticizing childhood as somehow invulnerable and pure. A child as gift is not just a gift *to* society but a gift *of* a new and living social relation. Gabriel Marcel has said that there is no I without a body and world in which the I is incarnated.[16] We may now say, more broadly, that there is no gift of the I without a world and society that does not both receive it and give back to it. The true giftedness revealed by childhood is the capability for being in the world. This capability is for the give-and-take of creating worlds of meaning. To be human is not to stand apart from the world as a self-contained rational ego; nor is it simply to play a role in a larger society. It is to join in the whole circle of constructing and being constructed that constitutes meaningful relations as such.

BEING DEPRAVED

This refashioning of what it means to be human in light of childhood can be taken another step forward in terms of ethics. The passive-active gift for meaning everywhere falls sort. Creating worlds with others also inevitably turns empty and destructive. This brings us to the Kantian question of why humanity is capable of defeating its own fundamental humanity. As we have seen, history has often used childhood as a powerful lens for responding to such a question and, therefore, for understanding what is not only good but also broken about human being.

In an interview about his famous novel *Lord of the Flies*, William Golding was asked why the boys in it, deserted on an island after a plane crash with no surviving grownups, turn to savagery, violence, and finally murder. Can there be any sense left of childhood innocence? His response is that the children are "innocent of their own natures. . . . [since] they don't understand what beasts there are in the human psyche which have to be curbed. They're too young to look ahead and really put curbs on their own nature and implement them, because giving way to these beasts is always a pleasure, in some ways, and so their society breaks down."[17]

The title of Golding's novel comes from the Bible (2 Kings 1–2), where the prophet Elijah mocks the enemy god Baal by distorting his name from *ba'al zebul*, or "lord of the high abode," into *ba'al zebub*, or "lord of the flies." This term also appears later in the New Testament as a name for Satan. Importantly, however, Elijah himself is soon mocked and jeered in turn by a band of small boys, whom he curses in the name of his own God, YHWH, to be mauled by two bears.[18] Golding's children, like these boys, have been captivated by some kind of devilish "beasts that are in the human psyche." So also, in a way, has Elijah. Yet in a strange sense each is also this beast's vulnerable or innocent victim—innocent in the sense of not exactly knowing what they are doing or deserving the suffering that befalls them.

While many today do not like to think of children as possibly evil, sinful, or bad, in fact it would be strange and dehumanizing not to admit for children what seems so evidently the case for humanity overall: namely, its capability not only for meaning and goodness but also for destruction and harm. If children truly are full human beings—or, at least, if they are to teach us something about the nature of full humanity—then it would be unwise to rule out from the outset their capability for doing wrong. Such is especially the case if we do not cling to modern notions of evil as purely rational or individual. The deeper question, pondered intermittently throughout the history above, is in what sense humanity's capability for *not* being human—for being inhuman—might be said to grow out of childhood, however much it may grow worse in adulthood.

Thinkers from Plato to Augustine and Calvin to Kant have insisted that human capabilities for self-destruction and violence are not simply acquired as we age. There is no particular age at which the capacity to hurt oneself and others suddenly appears. Nor are evil sensibilities merely adopted from external society, which after all is itself made up of human beings who all began life as children. Rather, human depravity, while arguably less to blame in childhood, must be present in some sense from birth. Theologians such as Augustine speak in this regard of childhood's "fallenness" or participation in "original sin"; philosophers such as Kant of childhood's "natural disorder" or "unruliness." Is there a sense in which the gift for meaning and relations from childhood is also a curse?

Children are not in actuality the most depraved of human beings, but they are surely among the most susceptible or vulnerable to depravation. Indeed, as Golding's novel suggests, they are in a sense *more* susceptible to joining in with the violence of humanity because their innocence, in the sense of newness to the world, provides them with fewer resources and experience to overcome it. The child soldier Ishmael Beah, for example, is not as responsible for his acts as are the adults around him, but he does prove easily capable of horrendous violence and mass murder. Indeed, this vulnerability is precisely why child soldiers are recruited. Or think of the harassment by their peers that is often suffered by gay children in American schools—abuse that is casually and purposely traumatic.[19]

Kant describes this inner human capability for wrong as "radical" or "inscrutable."[20] What he means is that there can finally be no explanation for why human beings turn against their own humanity. The destruction of humanity within oneself or others is paradoxically a capability belonging to humanity. Evil involves the defeat of what one's own deeper humanity demands, a privation of one's own truer being. For all his vulnerability, and for all his legal and moral nonblameworthiness, the child soldier is still capable of performing evil acts and sensing on some level that they are wrong. A toddler may snatch another toddler's toys, a five-year-old punch her friend, a ten-year-old bully her classmates. If these behaviors are merely learned from adults, then children are some kind of strange separate species, altogether morally passive.

Children stand at the very point in life when doing wrong to others (and oneself) begins to form itself into something to embrace and enjoy. If one can speak of a habit of violence or marginalization, it is in the earliest years that it begins to take hold. It is able to grow in the young because it satisfies something deep within human being while, at the same time, taking advantage of a deep human vulnerability to it. It may possess less strength and self-consciousness than is able to be achieved in adulthood, and it may not rightly be as prosecutable by law, but this does not make its presence in children of an entirely different order of being. Even Hitler started out life as a fresh-faced baby. What he grew up to become cannot be blamed solely on the adults or society around him or on his own future adult choices. He did not suddenly become twisted and hateful when he turned eighteen. The children who committed mass murder at Columbine High School were both shaped by circumstances and, on some level, willing and culpable agents.

What children show is that human depravity is neither purely autonomous nor purely received from society. It belongs to a full circle of social relations, both already constructed and reconstructed by each person anew. Depravity, one might say, is both depraved and deprived. It is both imposed on social worlds by selves and the robbing of selfhood by social worlds. It is both given by and given to humanity: the self-defeat of its giftedness for creating meaning. Violence is committed within an already violent and unjust environment and in some way also adds to it. To do wrong is both to fall into temptation and to choose to let temptation happen. Childism will have to insist on evil's simultaneous agency and vulnerability, its arising from both within and without, its origination in both self and world. It is part of the circular nature of human being-in-the-world.

From this angle, the cure for a corrupt world is not the innocence of childhood. Nor, on the contrary, is it children's initiation into the values of adults. Children are not as free of destructive capabilities as one might hope, nor is society as wise in comparison as adults might flatter themselves to believe. Something essential is missing from the very being of humanity all the way from birth to death. There is an important sense in which human being is lacking in full humanity.

HUMAN BEING AS TRAGIC

If it begins already at birth, this kind of self-defeat of human being can be called tragic. Being human means being bound up throughout life with already meaningless and unfair relations and compounding them further through one's own participation. Other scholars and I have examined this tragic dimension of moral life through the eyes of Sophocles's ancient Greek tragic play *Antigone*.[21] However, before I tried to think in light of childhood, I barely noticed that Antigone is in fact a child. Nor to my knowledge has anyone else noticed this in a long history of ethical commentary. I would like, therefore, to examine this play a little more deeply as an illustration of how humanity defeats its own humanity. The fact that Antigone is a child—or an adolescent, if that term can be applied to those times—turns out to make a difference in how one reads the moral of the story.

The story is that the girl Antigone defies the order of her uncle, the king Creon, by providing burial rites to her brother Polyneices, who had died fighting as a traitor to the city. Creon's decree is unwavering, and Antigone is prosecuted for her crime by being buried alive in a cave. Before the king finally relents and changes his mind, Antigone commits suicide, and so in quick succession do Creon's son, Haemon, who is engaged to marry her, and in grief Creon's wife, Eurydice.[22]

Recent feminist phenomenologists have shown that the tragedy of this play is not simply that there is a conflict of irreconcilable goods: the good of families burying their kin versus the good of cities punishing traitors. This is the argument of G. W. F. Hegel, who claims that Antigone and Creon "both are one-sided, though at the same time both obtain justice too."[23] Rather, the problem is a larger patriarchal imbalance of power, whereby Antigone's right to assert her own voice in society is already silenced because she is female. As Luce Irigaray notes, Antigone loses out, not because her argument is weaker, but because her socially constructed femininity prevents her from standing up for her convictions in the public sphere. "Creon, the king," Irigaray concludes, "will, in the end, endure a fate as cruel as Antigone's. But he will be master of that destiny. Antigone is silenced in her action. Locked up—paralyzed, on the edge of the city."[24]

Antigone's problem is compounded in that not only is she female but she has also not yet reached the Greek age of maturity. For a child she surely is, being variously termed *pais* ("child"), *neanis* ("young girl"), *kore* ("maiden"), and *parthenos* ("girl" or "virgin"). One of the most important facts about her is that she has yet to pass into full adulthood through the rite of marriage (to Creon's son).[25] Indeed, it is precisely adulthood that Creon aims to deny her. Antigone is further trapped in childhood by the facts of her birth: she is haunted by having been fathered by Oedipus through incest with his (and therefore also her) mother.

If it is unwomanly in this situation for Antigone to assert her rights, it is even more unchildly. A child can less easily make a claim upon the laws of society without that society also being willing to hear it. Even if Thebes were completely nonsexist and fully open to the agency and voices of all—including both women and children—Antigone would still have less power than fully adult women and men because she would have less experience in exercising it. Even were she male, as a youth she would remain profoundly vulnerable to the actions of the adults around her, on whom she relies for public inclusion.

A childist analysis suggests that any person or group of people can be deprived of humanity, not only (as feminists rightly argue) by being robbed of social agency, but also, and just as profoundly, by not being acknowledged in one's social vulnerability. The tragedy of human relations is not just that social agency is routinely denied. It is more profoundly that social agency is always and everywhere separated or abstracted from the realities of social passivity. Human passivity is what the ancient Greeks called fate, or susceptibility to surrounding powers. Antigone has a kind of free agency, but it is reduced to taking her own life. It does not find wider expression in the social circumstances imposed on her by her world. Creon also struggles for meaning, but in a way less disconnected from social conditions.

The tension of human agency and passivity can lead moral relations to become either creative or destructive. If the problem were only the lack of inclusion of Antigone's voice, Creon could continue to assert his own voice quite legitimately; the solution would be for both to speak and act equally. But Creon is to be condemned in part because he fails to account for Antigone's deeper susceptibility to social marginalization as a girl. His agency is used coldly and blindly and without wisdom about life's vulnerability—both Antigone's and, in the end, his own. The moral connection is lost as his greater power is used to destroy rather than enrich the complex circle to which he belongs of human interdependency.

This circle is indeed wide and deep. Since every human being is born into a particular historical lifeworld, each is also faced with the inexhaustible challenge of its already distorted structures. No one can claim to reach society's full depths or to overcome its hidden or revealed violence completely. No one, from newborn to king, is that invulnerable.

Acts of depravity dance a strange and everlasting duet with inherited deprivations. The inhumanity of actively doing harm is compounded by the inhumanity of passively received history. There would be little or no social marginalization were it not so easily able to take root in humanity's most formative years. From birth onwards, selves simultaneously become distorted by societies and add to the distortions themselves. The tragedy is that this cycle begins before anyone realizes it or has much power to change it. No one ever plumbs the full depths of the damage.

If children are less destructive in this sense than adults, it is not because they exist in a separate, pure sphere, but because their circle of relations is on the whole relatively smaller. The younger one is, the less is likely to be one's scope for either hurting others or perpetuating the already existing violence of history. Childhood innocence lies in a relative lack of experience in dealing with the tragic cycles of the world.

This means that children are less responsible for the wrongs they commit but also more susceptible to wrong's power within and over them. It means that children generally commit smaller acts of violence than societies impose on them. Like Adam and Eve in the Garden of Eden, the fact that they do not know evil's fruits makes them vulnerable to the serpent's temptation. In contrast, adults' greater experience in the world means they have more power to create a better one. The structure of nonbeing in children and adults is a matter of degree rather than kind. It is the extent to which the human gift for creating worlds turns instead to destroying them.

THE ONTOLOGY OF PLAY

The problem of humanity's inhumanity will be examined in more specific terms in the next two chapters, focusing on the destruction first of selfhood and then of otherness. Here, however, on the level of basic human being, we can begin to trace the outlines of how it may be possible to respond to it. For hope can be found in a deeper capability from birth onwards for being human as such. This capability, I have argued, is for creating already created worlds into meaning. It must now be considered a little more profoundly in the face of the tragic reality that it always in part defeats itself. Does childhood offer any lessons that can save our account from ontological despair?

What childhood ultimately shows is that moral creativity remains possible because of an inexhaustible human capability for play. I define play, in this fundamental sense, as the gift in all persons from birth to death for opening themselves up to more expansive experiences of being and relations. Empirically speaking, play is just one kind of experience among others: children's and adults' games, imagination, pretending, sports, art, literature, theater, and so on. But on a deeper level, play can also be understood as the very dynamics of human being-in-the-world. On this level, play is the passive-active tension with the world that makes it possible to create meaning at all.

This means that being-in-the-world is not something that plays; rather it *is* play. Play is its primordial experience. Human being is neither what already is nor freedom from it, but the underlying dynamism of play in between. To be human is to be in a state of in-betweeness. It is to be a wanderer in one's own land, to be limbic, liminal, back and forth, closed and opening, hidden and revealed—in a word, playful. It is impossible, in this sense, *not* to play.

Today we like to think of ourselves as more open to play than were people in the stodgy historical past. However, what we mean by play tends to be rather narrow, a kind of childish pastime or sentimentality. Play is only historically new in the degree to which it has been romanticized.[26] A more fully childist view will refuse to sequester either children or play into a separate private and unserious realm. It will discover instead from children what constitutes the playfulness of being human. The challenge today, at least in the West, is to move past an exaggeratedly bottom-up picture of play as pure, joyful spontaneity unsullied by worldly care. This is a purely comic view lacking any sense of the tragic. As a result, it does not capture the deeper complexity of creative being. Comedy and tragedy need to be connected.

It must also be noted that human play is not the opposite of a supposedly adult seriousness. Just watch a child drawing. From the point of view of the child herself, play is the epitome of seriousness. It is generally taken more seriously by children than is work by adults. Play is not only serious but capable of turning nasty and mean. Few get into more frequent fights than children playing a game. Play is a kind of work. As Freud rightly says, play is a condition for the possibility of healthy work in life. However, this is not because children later develop separate capabilities for work; rather, it is because play *is* work, the very same activity. For children, there is not a sharp dividing line between play and not-play. Much of children's play is indeed playing at working: being a nurse, teaching, fire-fighting, caring for dolls, and so on. It is considered important and necessary. Likewise, adults too can see how there may be a sense of play in their jobs, relations, culture, and politics, however little this sense is fulfilled.

Play is not, in fact, a specialized childhood activity at all. It is not even the province of adults' "inner children." Rather, more fully understood, it is fundamental to being-in-the-world. If it is more sharply visible in children, this is not because it is only or chiefly children who play. It is because children are new to the game and so take part in its tensions, frustrations, and joys often more visibly.

Apart from romanticizing play, the opposite tendency in Western thought on children has been to instrumentalize it: to view play as a tool for teaching children what values to have or how to grow up. This view is shared widely in history, arguably more widely than the romantic view. Plato, as usual, sets the tone by arguing that play is useful because it makes children especially malleable: "If a boy is to be a good farmer, or again, a good builder, he should play, in the one case at building toy houses. . . . We should seek to use games as a means of directing children's tastes and inclinations toward the station they are themselves to fill when adult."[27] Here, play is tied to what could be called its more tragic dimensions. Playfulness can lead to wrong and antisocial habits; therefore, adults need to step in and direct it toward something better, indeed away from play itself toward eventual adult work and the good of society. But the dangers of play are taken so far as to rob human play, for children and adults both, of its agency and spontaneity, its comedic undoing of structure.

Such a view can go so far as to deny a connection between play and goodness. Augustine's autobiography regrets that he played too much: "I was disobedient [to my parents and teachers], not because I chose something better than they proposed to me, but simply from the love of games."[28] John Wesley declares of the students in the Kingswood School that he founded in eighteenth-century England: "They ought never to play."[29] Play, according to this logic, must be replaced by work in order to learn social and spiritual discipline. Even John Locke, that great architect of the Enlightenment, argues that "all the plays and diversions of children should be directed towards good and useful habits, or else they will introduce ill ones."[30] Play, in these views, is the basis for a future of frivolousness, irrationality, and immorality, unless refashioned by adults.

PLAY AS CREATIVITY

A way beyond either sentimentalizing or instrumentalizing play begins to suggest itself in some of the ideas of play that have been developed in phenomenology. (I will turn to conceptions of play in contemporary developmental psychology in the next chapter.) These philosophical views are generally not attentive to childhood, in that they learn little from children themselves. But they do help us see play as fundamental in a different kind of way: not as belonging to only part of humanity or some human activities, but as a definitive element within being-in-the-world. There are three somewhat different such perspectives here that are useful for us to draw upon. Ultimately, though, they will have to be played around with some more.

One perspective is that human being-in-the-world involves play through selves' involvement in the endless transformations of meaning in history. This view is developed by the hermeneutical phenomenologist Hans-Georg Gadamer, who opposes a long "subjectivization" of play in the aesthetics of Kant and his followers (who include, among others, the Romantics) in which play is viewed simply as freedom—that is, freely chosen activity. Instead, Gadamer highlights what he calls "the primacy of play over the consciousness of the player."[31] As illustrated in games, play is less "something a person does" than something that "absorbs the player into itself."[32] In playing chess, for example, you experience yourself as part of the flow of the game rather than simply manipulating the game at will. One "loses oneself" in the play of the game. Only then does one fully play.

Gadamer argues that this kind of absorption into play is characteristic of all human being-in-the-world. Play is the "to-and-fro movement" by which larger history unfolds itself within each and every one of us individually. To be historical creatures is to take part in a historical playing—a playing out of history. Tellingly, Gadamer calls play essentially tragic: the situating of personal choices within what are finally unchosen larger historical effects. For example, Antigone chooses to bury her brother, one might say, but the meaning and consequences of doing so escape her control, for she is caught up in a historical play of social forces. This may be why it is particularly effective to reveal this play in *a* play, a preconstructed world whose outcome the audience knows has already been determined. All people find themselves always already belonging to a greater playing out of languages and traditions into meaning. This "play" Gadamer calls history's "transformation into structure": its emergence into, or rather *as*, human consciousness.[33]

Other phenomenologists, however, take a somewhat opposed view. They argue that play describes the experience of history's deconstruction or undoing. Jacques Derrida, for example, claims that language involves "play" precisely insofar as historical meanings are undermined. What is nondeconstructable amidst the infinite possible disseminations of meaning is precisely "the play of differences." In other words, language and meaning are always in a state of play, in the sense of being unstable and open-ended. New differences of meaning cannot help but bubble up. Human meaning has its "nonfull, nonsimple 'origin'" in "the play of traces" by which it expresses *différance* (difference with an *a*), that is, difference endlessly deferred. "What we note as *différance* will thus be the movement of play that 'produces' . . . these differences."[34] In contrast with Gadamer, Derrida's view of human being as play could be described as essentially comic: based on freedom, invention, accident, puns, undoing, and mischief.

A third phenomenology of play stands somewhere between these two and comes closer to my own. If Gadamer sees play in historical being and Derrida in the interruption that is nonbeing (or absence), Richard Kearney sees play in the dynamics of the relation between the two. Ontologically speaking, play for Kearney is the to-and-fro between being and nonbeing, meaning and lack of meaning, historicity and alterity, construction and deconstruction. It consists in humanity's always unfolding "possibility": its possibility for new meaning in the world.[35] Human being is neither already structured into meaning nor something whose meaning is forever escaping, but rather an endless process of becoming or coming-to-be. In what may be called a tragicomic perspective, the meaning of our lives is forever being reconstructed in new ways over time.

This middle way sees human being as neither given nor impossible but rather poetic and creative. Kearney names life's possibility for meaning as "narrative," meaning an "identity woven from [one's] own histories and those of others."[36] We will come back to the concept of narrativity in the next chapter, where we consider the creation of worlds in time. But as Kearney notes, "There is narrative and there is narrative. For while some stories congeal and incarcerate, others loosen and emancipate."[37] The play of human being turns history toward either greater or lesser possibilities for meaning. It is neither already played out nor playfully destructive but open-endedly self-creative.

Interestingly, Kearney also names this possibility as God—God in the sense of "a player rather than emperor of Creation."[38] God as Creator is not removed from the historical world but lies within the world itself as "the play of ongoing genesis, transfiguring the earth." She is immanent. "The play of Being and the play of God" invite humanity "to join the dance-play of the possible that began in Genesis, before we even came to be, and that continues on beyond our death until the kingdom comes." Play in this symbolic or liminal register is what makes possible the world's hopeful renewal. "The virtue of play . . . is when we do not take ourselves, or our world, or our God *literally*. When we learn the humility and humor of participating in a game without emperors. Like a child playing in sand by the edge of the sea. Not idle play. Sacred play upon which the future of our world reposes." To play is, paradoxically, to belong to history by transforming it ever anew.

Can we go further, however, in what we learn about human being as play through our thinking so far in light of childhood? All people play. Nevertheless, do children reveal something distinctive about play across humanity?

Play is part of what makes us human because it is what allows us to inhabit the fundamental tensions by which to create worlds of meaning. On the one hand, children enter the play of history with the deepest imaginable vulnerability. They more than others are "played by" history in all its traditional, cultural, family, social, gender, and even biological senses. Witness again Antigone, who even as an adolescent finds herself having to play out an unchosen place and meaning in her world. Children in a certain sense passively join in whatever games are around, however wonderful or ugly, liberating or oppressive.

On the other hand, this passivity highlights the mystery and wonder of children's playful agency: their capability for transforming the world into ever new possibilities. Even in the deepest vulnerability at birth, human beings begin to invest their worlds with productive new shape and meaning. They reach out for communication, attach themselves to loved ones, build up symbolic languages, interpret shapes and sounds and culture. Antigone, constrained as she is, questions the assumptions of her elders and opens up radical new possibilities. Children bring to the world powerful imaginations, capabilities to pretend, and fresh perspectives.

Who I am—my very being-in-the-world—is from birth to death at once historical and free: a circle in which I am both played and player. I both am given to myself and give myself to myself ever anew: a circle of play itself. To be in the world is to play with its possibilities for creating meaning.

An infant like Ying Ying Fry plays in both a tragic and a comic sense at once. She is caught up in powers much greater than herself, including cultures, adoption policies, economics, and family dynamics. Yet she also undoes and reshapes them. Babies and children might cry more desperately and laugh more unreservedly than when they grow up, for they are at once more helpless and more free. The dance of being and nonbeing is only just beginning, as yet relatively stark, and so perhaps both more bitter and more joyful. The imposing play of historical powers meets the liberating play of endless difference in each life's new possibility.

Play is the condition for the possibility of new possibility itself. To be human is to inhabit a dynamic world of not only what is but also what could be. No one creates meaning out of whole cloth apart from history, society, family, and culture; at the same time, no one is utterly created or defined by them. Humanity's being-in-the-world is both limited and limitless, constructed and to be constructed, finite and infinite. It is a circle of poetic possibility whose horizons are mapped only by playing in the world itself.

This playfulness brings us back to the in-betweenness of being as tension. *Tensio* literally means stretching. I am already something but I am also always stretching toward something else, some unknown possibility. Play is tension turned toward new possibility. The playful tension of being-in-the-world can devolve into nostalgia for the past, the false freedom of nihilism, or rigidly utilitarian goals. It can run into the tragedy of social oppression or the comedy of disconnected meaninglessness. But in the end, play is the heartbeat from birth to death of the creation of the world into meaning. No one escapes the tension of having to create meaning into fuller possibilities. Without the gift of play, there would be no world of meaning at all. Being-in-the-world is playing-in-the-world. It is the play of world creativity.

BEING AS MYSTERY

If so, then being as creation can be pressed still one step further to the ultimate experience of being as a mystery. At the center of the circle of world creativity lies an invisible darkness, a vanishing point. The mysteriousness of the gift of play does not lie in its sentimental spontaneity. The mystery is that humanity can play with its world of meaning at all. Creativity cannot ultimately create an explanation for itself. There is nothing knowable prior to each new human being's strange ability to create its own being in the world.

An infant's bonding with a parent introduces a uniquely formed world never before experienced by humankind and never again to be repeated. As I write this I form a sense of meaning wholly unique to me now, and as you read it so also do you. Rather than being trapped in the way things are, but without leaving them behind either, each of us plays within the tensions of meaning that surround us, and we do so in ways that stretch meaning always toward something new. No single human experience, relation, or idea is exactly like any other. I can no more anticipate what meaning you or I will make of our lives than I can foresee the next page of a story.

But most mysterious of all is not just what can be created but the very fact itself of world creativity. Play is ultimately impossible to explain because it is not *a* meaning but, rather, the very condition for the possibility of meaning as such. It could be called an impossible possibility: able to be experienced, evoked, even symbolized, but not finally containable within the playground of play itself. Life is indeed a tale told by idiots: no one knows, in an ultimate sense, the meaning of their autobiography, or why they are able to have an autobiography at all.

Childhood helps illuminate humanity's strange creative possibility because it lies at its most visible worldly origins. The Bible at one point juxtaposes two claims: "For mortals it is impossible, but for God all things are possible"; and "it is to such as these [little children] that the kingdom of heaven belongs."[39] Children represent humanity's ultimate creative possibility, not in the sense that children secretly know the answer to the meaning of life, but in that they may be more open, on the whole, to the apparent impossibility of creating unknown meaning. Children are simply the newest to the world, and so can play in the world in relatively more creative ways. They may not so easily take comfort in metaphysical or literal explanations or, on the contrary, world-denying cynicism. Rather, they are generally more likely to let themselves be vulnerable to the possibility for possibility itself: the possibility that what seems impossible is not therefore without meaning, the possibility for inventing worlds of meaning at the limits of imagination.

If childhood brings us into touch with religion, it does not do so in the first place through theological speculation or sacred romanticism. A child does not offer proof of God's existence or some direct access to the beyond. Nor does a child reduce the mystery of being human to a blind leap of faith. The deadeningly top-down fundamentalists who think they have special knowledge of the divine have nothing to learn about the mystery of life from childhood. Prior to any such theorized divinity is a child's or adult's experience of the mystery of creating meaning at all, of being in the world but also being able to remake that world anew. It is this original depth of experience itself that takes us to the real boundaries of what can actually be known.

The phenomenologist Jean-Luc Marion identifies this mystery—which he calls God—with the "givenness" of meaningful experience as such. God is a name for the possibility of experiencing phenomena in the world at all. Such a God can be represented or symbolized only through an "icon," Marion says, which explicitly claims not to be able to represent what it represents, only to open the imagination up toward it. An icon first of all gazes at me through its own face, before I can interpret it. Were this mystery actually representable, it would no longer be God but an idol, something reduced to the world's own limitations. The mystery of givenness is the gift of the possibility for meaning. But this possibility itself, this strange inner divinity, "unbalances human sight in order to engulf it in infinite depth."[40]

Childism presses the possibility for such an unbalancing gift along more fully circular lines. It suggests that the gaze of such a mystery is not straight but bent, that it curves back around to itself. That is, the mystery of a meaningful world is not ultimately given from some iconically self-transcending beyond. It is humanity's creative giftedness itself. We can catch a glimpse of it, however dimly, because it reflects our own experiences of world creation from birth onwards. The gift is not, in other words, merely passive, something simply given by a Wholly Other. It is, rather, a passive-active giftedness or capability for giving the given world meaning. It is not just givenness but giftedness. What must remain the deepest mystery is why human beings can recreate their worlds at all, why they can create icons, idols, images, and any other kind of meaning in the first place.

THE IMAGE OF IMAGES

Creation and creativity are in fact central images in many religions. Some argue that the world's Creator is a wholly self-sufficient Being, in contrast with mere beings like us. But the experience of childhood presses us to consider a Creator as one symbol for the mystery of human world-creativeness. From this angle, humanity is an image of this image, an image of a Creator of worlds. When one makes meaning in the world, one is imitating, in a sense, an imagined creation of the world itself. What childhood teaches is that human beings play integral parts in the creative forces of the world, whether ancestors, nature, culture, or gods. Symbolically speaking, humanity is both part of something larger than itself and capable of its own further enlargement beyond reckoning. The Creator may be used to symbolize the mystery of my experience from birth of contributing toward an infinite and unfathomable world creativity.

Take, for example, the childhood innocence of humankind (*adam*) in Genesis 1. Here, humankind is affirmed to have been primordially created as uniquely its own Creator's "image" (*tselem*). The earth, skies, plants, and animals are merely created; humanity is gifted as being also an image of its Creator. Thus, in Genesis 1:27, it is claimed that "God created humankind in his image, in the image of God he created them; male and female he created them." Read literally, God here is reduced to an idol: an image in which the divine is directly represented in one of its visible creatures. But as an icon, the Creator is an image of the mystery of world creativity, a mystery in which human beings share as part of their purpose in being in the world.

God creates here in a distinctively circular way: as both the subject who creates (in this case, humankind) and the object in the image of which he does so (himself). Likewise, humankind as this God's "image" appears circular too: as both a subject capable of creating (in the image of God) and the object to be created (its own being-in-the-world). The original innocence of *adam* is not a simple pouring forth of goodness; it is a complex circle of self- and world-making on the basis of a world already made. As W. Sibley Towner has interpreted this passage, children "are God's creatures and chosen partners in the world of creation."[41] Like a Creator endlessly creating an image of itself, humanity from birth onwards endlessly creates its own images of its humanity.

This worldliness of human innocence is also affirmed in the very next line of the myth, Genesis 1:28, the first command of the Bible: "God blessed them, and God said to them, 'Be fruitful and multiply, and fill the earth and subdue it.'"

Human innocence is not to be ethereal or otherworldly but rather engaged with the earth and other people in a fruitful and dynamic way. Read literally, the command here is for human pro-creation, the generation of offspring, that is, children as its objects. But read symbolically, it is to generate new worlds, something in which children themselves share. The affirmation of *adam* as an image of its Creator means that *adam* is fundamentally in existence to create. Amid the waters, earth, and chaos of life is a call toward endless "fruitfulness" in order to "multiply" human possibilities. The ancient rabbis and church theologians call this the *imitatio Dei*, "the imitation of God."[42] In light of childhood it is the *imitatio Creatoris*, the imitation of the Creator.

Childism encourages such a poetic rather than merely metaphysical interpretation of the divine. The Creator can be read as a symbol, among other things, for the strange primal human experience of creativity in the world. From the point of view of childhood, this creativity does not depend on a prior theological argument for God but arises first of all out of an inner experience of mystery, one that the symbolism of God is one way to evoke. If this symbol of the Creator is itself a creation, by human beings in a particular time and place and not in other times and places, this does not render it meaningless. Rather, it is important because it is one way, though far from the only way, of describing the depths of humankind's own world-creative giftedness.

Such is the case most visibly of all in humankind's beginnings in childhood. Children are not just marble or wax to be formed into something new by others. Rather, however strange it may seem, they are both created and creators at once. At the most vulnerable moment of birth, the mother's breast, the father's touch, the surrounding smells and sensations are never simply given to the child. They are always also, and at the very same time, given meaning by the child. This basic capability can be explained on one level by physical properties like the human infant's brain, the evolution of consciousness, and biological capacities for worldly sensation. But on another level, scientific explanation itself already exercises, and hence presupposes, the very same human capability for creating new meaning. William Schweiker has called such a capacity for meaning "radical interpretation," meaning that on some level self-understanding "strikes at the root of who we are."[43] What is radical is that it is possible to create meaningful worlds at all, whether through science, religion, poetry, or relations. As for children, no one can create an explanation of the origins of this explanatory creativity within them. It simply exists as part of humanity's way of being.

Children show above all that such a gift is not static but dynamic. John Chrysostom long ago compared parents to the great Artist of everything: "Like the creators of statues do you [parents] give all your leisure to fashioning these wondrous statues for God."[44] But now we can see that children are not just objects of the artistry of adults, but also, in a more fundamental sense, subjects who are artists of themselves and others too. If people are like statues, then they are chiseled from both without and within.

Children are the first creators because they are never merely subsumed into the worlds of meaning into which they are born, as has often been assumed given their relative vulnerability. Rather, they miraculously also remake those worlds for themselves and for those around them. Everyone is born already capable of investing humanity with singular meaning. However much children are molded by history and by others, they also originally and open-endedly mold themselves. The true mystery is that, from the beginning, humanity reconstructs its own already constructed existence.

Hindu Brahmin boys receive a sacred thread at a special ceremony when they turn seven or nine. It is worn over the left shoulder for life as a sign of moral responsibility and to ward off evil spirits.[45] Are we not all, from the moment of birth, clothed in an invisible sacred thread that invests our bodies and lives with meaning, an infinite loop of making and remaking our own lives? Does not everyone, like a Brahmin boy, both receive meaning from surrounding environments and make this meaning anew for themselves? The infinity of symbols, relations, and dreams in which human beings clothe themselves over history is really a vast web of social creativity to which each adds another thread throughout life.

WORLD CREATIVITY

Whether it is mysterious or not, human being in light of childhood involves the gift for world-creativity. Being-in-the-world is creativity-in-the-world. Young and old are the coauthors of the play of life that they find themselves already born into. Human nature is conditioned by everything from molecular makeup, biological evolution, historical forces, power, religion, culture, family, gender, psychology, circumstances, others, and luck. But at the same time, it weaves these conditions through time into one's own worlds of meaning. A childist account suggests that the ongoing formation of meaningful worlds is not just a part of being human but its primordial experience. It is not simply confined to childhood, completed in adulthood, or performed only in certain activities. It is what people are as passive-active, gifted yet broken participants in meaningful lives. To be human is to occupy a particular historical time and place by forming it anew.

This conclusion does not deny—rather, it affirms—the full plurality of human meanings and cultures. Indeed, world creativity is the condition for the possibility of diverse cultures in the first place. When an infant is born among the Beng in the Ivory Coast, she is considered an ancestral reincarnation bringing to the village a full spiritual and cultural life of her own.[46] She cannot yet speak or feed herself, is utterly dependent on the care of those around her, and, today, has among the highest chances in the world of not surviving her first years. Yet, she is still a contributing member of her society, bringing to it what I am calling her own giftedness for meaning. It is this that makes all human beings as fully human as all others.

Being-in-the-world is world creation. In the words of Henri Bergson: "For a conscious being, to exist is to change, to change is to mature, and to mature is to go on creating oneself endlessly."[47] We can now see that, considering children, this self-creation arises out of, and is made possible by, the dynamic world-creativity that constitutes being human. We are like bees rather than like ants or spiders. We are neither workers for a world already fully ordered nor spinners of worlds purely from within. Rather, we are circulators among the diverse fields of experience that enrich life together. There is no pure freedom or total historicity, only the endless creation of meaningful worlds born anew within each new child.

Chapter 3

What Is the Ethical Aim?

SO FAR, we have only considered the abstract question of the nature of human being. Childhood has a surprising amount to teach on this score. However, ethics is not just about being but also about doing, especially by and for children.

This chapter takes up the second question posed in the introduction of what, in light of childhood, selves and societies should strive toward. This is different from the question addressed in the next chapter of what obligations are owed to each other regardless of outcome. First it is necessary to ask what is technically known as a question of teleology: of moral life's aims, ends, purposes, or direction. If humanity from birth is a world creator, then what should it strive to create? And not to create? Given what humanity is, what should it hope to become? Moral relations are filled with desires, aspirations, goals, and dreams. Does the point of view of childhood affect how these are understood?

These questions are complex enough without adding childhood into the mix. Indeed, it is on the face of it rather paradoxical to glance backward into the beginnings of life to learn something about what in the future should be aimed toward. However, it is precisely in this way, I now argue, that we may approach the growth and flow of human life with fuller dynamism and complexity. It is in this way that ethical aims may properly be understood in relation to life's whole. In fact, persons and societies have frequently invested their dreams in children. There is a sense in which children stand for human possibility itself. Considering childhood offers a vital angle of vision for examining life's great unfolding journey.

What childhood teaches, I argue in this chapter, is that the ethical aim must be understood as selves' and societies' *narrative expansion*. By "narrative" I mean the activity of creating a meaningful life in time. The point of view of childhood makes it especially clear that human strivings are inherently temporal: that they arise out of personal and historical pasts and anticipate future hopes and possibilities, and that they bind these into presently evolving stories. By "expanding" I refer to the

possibility that life's complex narratives may achieve an increasingly diverse wholeness. All the many, various, and conflicting parts of one's life story—its multiple
pasts, futures, and presents as a self with others—may be invested with a more
rather than less inclusive narrative unity. There is no such thing in life as an actual
narrative whole; but it can be approached either more or less fully. Like bees in
their making of honey, each of us is called to circle farther and wider in the world
over time in order to create a more richly diverse life story. The human aim is an
expanding narrative wholeness of life.

THE ILLUSION OF TIMELESS REASON

Natalie Babbitt's novel for children and adults, *Tuck Everlasting*, is a narrative dealing explicitly with this kind of unfolding narrativity of time. It challenges what
could be considered the peculiarly adult-centered notion that the aim of ethical life
is to escape time by achieving some kind of fixed goal. Happiness and wisdom do
not lie in overcoming childhood—nor in its opposite, recovering a lost childhood
innocence—but in embracing what childhood more fundamentally demonstrates:
that human being is temporal through and through.

In the novel, a ten-year-old girl, Winnie Foster, meets a family, the Tucks, who
have accidentally drunk from a well that freezes their ages in time, seemingly in-
definitely. Winnie finds out about the well from the Tucks's son, Jesse, who falls
in love with her and urges her to drink too and join them. But she is ultimately
persuaded by the father, Tuck, that this kind of immortality would be no life at all.
"It's a wheel, Winnie. Everything's a wheel, turning and turning, never stopping,"
he explains. "Dying's part of the wheel, right there next to being born. You can't
pick out the pieces you like and leave the rest. Being part of the whole thing, that's
the blessing. . . . If I knowed how to climb back on the wheel, I'd do it in a minute."

By deciding ultimately not to drink from the well, and so to live out her life in
time, Winnie is also, paradoxically, choosing that her own time will end in death.
This choice is a kind of coming of age. Confronted with the dream of timelessness—a dream perhaps shared by us all—she finds that it would be empty and
meaningless, a life devoid of movement and significance. "You can't have living
without dying," Tuck tells her. "So you can't call it living, what we've got. We [the
Tucks] just *are*, we just *be*, like rocks beside the road."[1]

Winnie's growth or maturation here is not the grasping of some eternal truth by
which time can finally be transcended. She neither suddenly becomes a fully wise
adult nor taps into an inborn wisdom of childhood. Rather, what she learns has
to be understood—by her and by the readers—in relation to her own particular
temporal experiences, her own distinctly unfolding story. The deeper wisdom is
a genuine step forward in her understanding of what it means to be human within
the flux and change of her own particular time in the world.

As mere empirical knowledge, it is obvious that every single human being is born
and eventually dies, moving through time in between. But as parts of a person's

own particular life narrative, the movement from birth to death is open-ended and fraught with anxiety. As Winnie learns more fully, the progress of one's life—to oneself and to others—is not just incidentally but fundamentally a narrative. One's time is not simply given but also has to be continuously retold. It is possible to spend one's life in vain attempts to escape concrete temporality, like the huckster in the story who tries to find the well in order to sell its contents for a profit. It is possible to try to live apart from one's real life, as if the personal and historical pasts one shares with others do not influence one's choices. It is possible to lose oneself in empty future dreams, like the idealist who never accomplishes anything. But it is ultimately necessary, as Winnie learns, to try to make sense, however sadly and endlessly, of life's fullness as a complex unfolding story.

Each of the historical childisms examined in chapter 1 contains an element of narrative striving but also a fantasy of getting off time's slowly turning wheel. Each in a more or less subtle way pins human fulfillment on a false adult sense that time can be overcome. They imply that time can be either disciplined, reversed, or predicted.

Much of the problem can be traced to Plato. The grandparent of what I am calling a top-down perspective insists that childhood is the epitome of humanity's failure to inhabit timeless ideas. Education, he argues, should put aside the fantasies of the storytellers and embrace instead "the rightly disciplined state of pleasures and pains whereby a man, from his first beginnings on, will abhor what he should abhor and relish what he should relish."[2] What pleases and pains one over the shifting course of life should be directed from above by eternal ideas. Even Augustine, whose notion of time we'll come back to, claims that "the higher part of our nature aspires after eternal bliss while our lower self is held back by love of temporal pleasure."[3]

In contrast, those historical figures of a more bottom-up bent are not necessarily therefore more temporally minded. Time tends to be obscured here in the opposite direction: in seeking a return to a timeless childhood origin that historical time degrades and corrupts. Thus, for example, the early church theologian Clement of Alexandria speaks for many of his contemporaries when he argues that human maturity is a recovered childlike simplicity that beckons eternally from one's past: "Rightly, then, are those called children who know Him who is God alone as their Father, who are simple, and infants, and guileless, who are lovers of the horns of the unicorns."[4] Likewise, Schleiermacher calls adults to redeem the "kernel of truth" that was originally embedded in each child's soul in his or her "natural inclinations and talents." The child remains true to herself by shedding her merely outward "childish husk" in order to "manifest the workings of the divine Spirit" that incarnate what is eternal within her.[5] The reversal of top-down ideas in this opposing childist tradition only changes the direction in which we should look to escape time: in past origins rather than future order.

Developmentalists, finally, naturally offer more hope. For the aim of human socialization is itself implicitly temporal. However, the "end" of moral development has usually been understood in history as a time when development in time will come to an end. The progress of the self (or society) should aim for a final stage of development, a fully adult maturity, when the developmental task is concluded. Thus, for example, Aristotle sees children as growing toward a kind of "happiness" or "excellence" (*eudaimonia*) that is fixed in the time of adulthood: "A boy is not happy; for he is not yet capable of [virtuous] acts, owing to his age; and boys who are called happy are being congratulated by reason of the hopes we have for them."[6] Similarly, Locke views childhood as a time of learning to govern changing desires with fixed reason: "As the strength of the body lies chiefly in being able to endure hardships, so also does that of the mind. And the great principle and foundation of all virtue and worth is placed in this, that a man is able to deny himself his own desires, cross his own inclinations, and purely follow what reason directs as best."[7] Temporality is confined chiefly to childhood, whose moral aim is to develop into the atemporality of adulthood.

None of these different ways of understanding the ethical aim sufficiently appreciates what Winnie Foster learns about time. They do not understand human striving as temporal in and of itself. Each embraces some kind of timeless ideal— whether in the future, the past, or adulthood—in which temporality as such is to be transcended. This should strike us today as untenable. Even modern science, from evolutionary theory to the big bang theory, sees the world and life as thoroughly relative to time. There is simply no such thing in the universe as timelessness, including in human striving. Kant was wrong on both counts when he proclaimed the eternity of "the starry heavens above me and the moral law within me."[8] The view from childhood can help us overcome these temporal slumbers by reimagining moral life as fully and fundamentally narrative.

THE EXPERIENCE OF TIME

Understanding moral life's temporality can be aided by advances in the field of phenomenology. Phenomenology is the study, broadly understood, of what it means to experience being in the world. This experience has long been thought to involve existing in time. Two of the field's foundational texts have the titles *The Phenomenology of Internal Time-Consciousness* (Edmund Husserl) and *Being and Time* (Martin Heidegger). These strange and complex texts are the objects of much criticism and dispute. We cannot dwell on them in depth here. But we can use their general ideas to learn about human time from the time of childhood.

What is most important from this field for our purposes is the argument that time is more than just an observable fact "out there" in objective reality. It is not something physical like the movement of the stars, the earth's revolution around the sun, the dating of years from the event of Jesus's birth, hands on a watch, Greenwich Mean Time, or the orbit of electrons. These are merely external markers of an inner experience of time as such.

Time is inner in the sense that it is relative to its interpreter. As Heidegger rather cryptically remarks, "the Present arises in the unity of the temporalizing of temporality out of the future and [the past]."[9] What he means is that the times of the past and the future can be interpreted only in relation to an also timeful present. The experience of time is redoubled, so to speak, in time itself being experienced over time. Temporality is temporalized. Indeed, Albert Einstein's physics of relativity (invented around the same time) makes a similar point: that the measurement of time is always relative to the time of its observer. This relativity of time applies to humanity's experience not only of the larger universe but also of ourselves and our relations to one another. Being-in-the-world not only passes through time but interprets this passage through time itself through time.

This experienced or "human" time, as it may be called, is not, however, purely subjective either, as if one's past, future, and present could be interpreted or narrated entirely at will. Time can be constructed only because its meaning is already preconstructed by a larger time of history. Time has meaning insofar as it participates in already continuing experiences such as duration (that time continues at all), memory, expectation, culture, language, anxiety, care, and being-toward-death. In each case, time is experienced as not only changeable in its meaning but also invested with meaning already. Indeed, time is the very basis on which experience is possible at all. As Winnie Foster sees, rocks and trees exist in time but do not experience their own temporality. Human beings, in contrast, both are temporal (like everything else) and interpret this temporality for themselves in time.

GROWING TIME

What, then, of childhood? Childhood is perhaps the most obvious time in which humanity exists in time. But does the experience of being a child—or of having been a child—require a more complex phenomenological picture? For example, does it make a difference that the experience of temporality begins at a certain point of time? Or that there may be changes over time in the very capacity for interpreting time's meaning? Or that children may be less anxious than adults (if one may generalize) about the coming time of death? Is what Heidegger calls being-toward-death truly the most authentic experience of time?

What childhood suggests is that the human experience of time is not only interpreted within time, but also aimed toward an increasing temporal growth or expansion. The more inclusive and therefore profound experience of time is not being-toward-death but being-from-birth. No one, not even a newborn, escapes the fundamental temporal experience of once having been born. From this point of view, time itself has an ethical aim of expanding rather than contracting over time. The difference between the first breaths of an infant and the last breaths before death is not just that one anticipates the other. It is more fundamentally that an infant has a relatively narrower experience of time—relatively fewer past experiences and senses of future possibilities—while as one ages it becomes increasingly possible with more experience to interpret time across broader temporal horizons.

The experience of time as an interpreted phenomenon, in other words, has neither one size nor one direction. It can be stretched increasingly outwards in a range of interconnected ways; or by the same token it can be variously narrowed. The past can stretch more deeply, the future can extend more widely, and the present can become more complex and distended. Indeed, the anticipation of death alone, without considering time more broadly, is one way for time to be constricted. Human time has a certain teleological direction of growth from its relatively immediate experience at birth toward the increasing breadth, complexity, and inclusiveness of life's possible experiences of time over time.

Let us consider a newborn. She already has a deep past of experiences in the womb, a set of accumulated feelings, a particular body and gender, a larger implicit experience of a family history, ancestry, culture, and traditions, and an even larger-scale genetic context of biological evolution and constitution by the physical universe. All of these pasts constitute her present story in some way, however much or little understood.

At the same time, she also has an enormously wide and open future—more open, in a way, than the futures of those who are older. A newborn's life story could take her in any number of directions, some relatively preordained and others relatively not. No one, not least the newborn herself, can anticipate where this future will lead. Yet straightaway, she also experiences the fact that future possibilities are open, that there are different options to strive for in the world—that, in other words, the present is inseparable from the future.

The relative smallness or shortness of a newborn's experience of time does not lie, then, in any disconnection from time as such. It lies, rather, in how little temporal experience has been able to be temporally experienced. A newborn's self-interpretation includes a relatively immediate sense of her pasts and possible futures. This immediacy is only partly related to cognition. More profoundly, it is a matter of the degree to which a newborn has experience in interpreting her being over time. The less time one has experienced, the less one is likely to be able to experience the larger reaches of time itself. Even cognitive capabilities for interpreting time, while in part biological and psychological, grow through the experience itself of inhabiting time. It takes time to experience time more expansively. Time makes possible ever more complex experiences of time.

Take the story of Valentino Achak Deng, a boy who had to flee the civil war that came to his village in Sudan when he was seven. One of the so-called "lost boys of Sudan," his story of violence, loss of family, long marches, years in refugee camps, and eventual emigration to the United States, told by Dave Eggers in *What Is the What?*, is a story of hope because it shows Deng piecing together a time, over time, that has repeatedly been disrupted and almost ended.[10]

How does Deng make sense of his experiences and come to some larger sense of narrative meaning? He does so by weaving together the complex threads of which his temporal experience is composed. These threads include his ancestry, his early life with family and community, the horrific events he witnessed, his present life, and his future hopes and dreams. He faces temptations of nostalgia or anger for a lost past, or of repressing his long childhood trauma. He faces despair about his limited options for the future. But his aim, both as a child and then as an adult, involves drawing these dispersed threads into an imaginatively created new story, one that does not simply retell the facts but interprets their evolving significance for his own evolving present.

Childhood shows with particular clarity that human time, for children and adults both, is capable of tremendous creative plasticity. One's diverse pasts and possible futures can be interwoven over time into either broader or narrower narratives. Human beings can compartmentalize time into separated pasts whose meanings are suppressed, or rigid futures whose new meanings are closed off. One's present story can become trapped in past obsessions or traumas, lost in future utopias or anxieties, or stuck in present concerns and preoccupations. Or human beings can stretch out time, over time, from relatively small and immediate experiences of the world into widening temporal richness and significance. They can create their time into increasingly expansive narratives. Deng can invest even a deeply traumatized past, however slowly and painfully, with a new and unfolding sense of his life's growing direction.

A child-inclusive account insists that human time can grow and expand over time because this growth is precisely what is possible from life's very beginnings. Being-from-birth means being called upon to expand one's own story over time. The narrative of one's own narrative—the temporalization of one's temporality— can contract, splinter, and divide, or it can expand, fill out, and grow more whole. No one is dealt a complete or full story. Everyone must strive to create it.

DISTENDED TIME

This simple experience of time has been obscured for us today by the legacy of notions of time that are inherited from modernity. For in the Enlightenment, human time took on an especially fixed and objectified meaning.[11] Paradoxically, time came to be viewed as immutable. The universe, and humanity within it, became like a clock, moving through time with mechanical predictability. According to this view, our only job is to explain time's laws, as if we could stand apart from them. This perspective may have its benefits, such as scientific predictability. But it also has the effect of dehumanizing time itself, characterizing it as a merely empirical object divorced from the subjectivity of its observer.

As a result, insofar as children appear especially obviously to exist in time, insofar as they must change and grow in order to become adults, childhood tends to become for the Enlightenment also chiefly an object. Children exist in some strange realm where they are neither pure nature nor yet its rational observers. Because they are not yet fully self-critical, on this view, children remain chiefly in the realm of things to be observed, somehow "out there" in the mutable world of passing time instead of "in here" where time is interpreted.

The phenomenology of time, as we have seen, disputes this Cartesian view and interprets time as integral to humanity's being-in-the-world. It has unfortunately, however, followed modernity in one respect: the obscuring of the particular time of childhood. Since Heidegger, the focus has been on the other end of human life: on being-toward-death. Or, when looking backwards, human time skips over childhood to extend itself into humanity's larger past historicity, its constitution by traditions and cultures. The experience of time somehow springs fully formed into human life as a completely inherited world of meaning. But childhood does not fit neatly into either of these temporalities. It falls somewhere in between historicity and death. In fact, it is how they are connected to one another. Between the historical past and one's personal future is the personal past, which in its most basic expression is the experience of oneself as having been born.

This experience of being-from-birth is arguably humanity's most powerful experience of time. It means experiencing time as having begun to be experienced at one's own distinct coming into the world. Every human being's present experience—whether as an adult or a child, and however directed toward the past and the future—is fundamentally constituted by the experience of having at a certain point in time come into being. Obvious though it may sound, everyone will always experience their time as already having entered into time. As life develops, everyone on some level must struggle to come to terms also with their own death. But this struggle is part of a larger struggle, experienced just as profoundly by children and adults alike, to come to terms with having been born into time as a new and particular interpreter of time.

Strangely enough, one of the heroes of the phenomenological interpretation of time is deeply misunderstood without such a childist lens. I am thinking of Augustine and his frequently cited discussion of time in his autobiography, *Confessions*. This is a text, as we have already seen, that is about childhood centrally. When read apart from its larger autobiographical context, its discussion of time remains incomplete and abstract. For a range of figures, from Heidegger to Ricoeur and Derrida, Augustine suggests in one way or another how time is itself experienced within time. In fact, though, Augustine's inquiry involves a more complex experience of time stretching not only forwards toward his hoped-for future but also backwards toward his childhood past. It is this fuller experience of time that will enable us to understand the aim of narrative growth.

What prompts Augustine to write autobiographically is not principally, in fact, his movement toward death or his larger embeddedness in a particular history, important though both are. What prompts him to tell his own story is his desire to understand how his present life and future hopes arise out of his own personal past. What he aims for is not just meaning in the face of death but a larger story of his struggle for meaning over the course of his own life. The central autobiographical question is how the trajectory of his own birth, childhood, early adulthood, and maturity can be deepened into a more fully meaningful sense of direction. His God is not merely out there in the universe but the unfolding narrative meaning under-lying his own life. Why did he balk at his studies or steal pears as a youth? Looking back from later in life, he can now see a deeper story of moral struggle and growth. He can now see that it was not joyful abandon but rebellion against his own larger potential, a rebellion that he now sees as defining him still.

It is in this autobiographical light that we should read Augustine's puzzlement over time in his famous eleventh chapter. How can his search for meaning in the present, he asks, be related to his no longer experienced past and his as yet un-known future? "What, then, is time? I know well enough what it is, provided that nobody asks me; but if I am asked what it is and try to explain, I am baffled. . . . [H]ow can two [divisions of time], the past and the future, *be*, when the past no longer is and the future is not yet? As for the present, if it were always present and never moved on to become the past, it would not be time but eternity."[12] How, in other words, can the meaning and rest he seeks in life be discovered in the unfold-ing time of his particular pasts and unknown futures? How is eternity realized in one's personal movement through the world?

Augustine's answer is that time must be understood as the self's experience of its own *distentio animi*, its own "distention of the soul." The soul or mind can distend or literally "stretch apart" into its own pasts, presents, and futures. It is composed of "a present of past things, a present of present things, and a present of future things"—in the experiences, respectively, of "memory" [*meminit*], "attention" [*at-tendit*], and "expectation" [*expectat*].[13] This capacity of the mind for its own tem-poral stretching apart is so remarkable and mysterious to Augustine that he argues it could only be a gift from God. It makes the individual in some small way a par-ticipant in God's temporal fullness. From within one's own narrow and fragmented experiences of time, one's longing is to stretch or distend oneself toward a hoped-for temporal wholeness. One's deepest desire is not the negation of time in some transcending timelessness, but on the contrary the fulfillment of time, as an image of time's very Creator, in a fully whole narrative of one's life in this world.

From this angle, human temporal experiences have an implicit aim or purpose: the self's stretching toward an ever fuller temporal wholeness. Each human being longs for a complex narrative unity of its life that includes all at once its past-orient-ed memories, its future-oriented expectations, and its ongoing present-oriented experiences. It is in this temporal unity that Augustine hopes to find some measure of peace and rest, some return to the image of a Creator on the seventh day of cre-ation. And for Augustine this includes the soul's participation, however brokenly, in creation's entirety, its meaning within the full time of the cosmos. Here we find a proto-phenomenology of human time that is infused with ethical purpose: to distend oneself as fully as possible toward time's potential wholeness. Whether we know it or not, we desire to live in the broadest experience of time as possible.

One need not accept Augustine's rather harsh view of infants, seen above, or his theology, to acknowledge his point that at birth such a narrative wholeness is far from accomplished. For implicit in Augustine's view of time is that the human experience of time is something that should expand rather than stand still or contract. It is not born fully complete. Prior to the kind of empiricism that makes time a static object in modernity, Augustine is able to see time as essentially fluid and dynamic. It is an experience that can be inhabited always still more fully. Being-toward-death and being-from-birth are components of a larger task of autobiography, of the lifelong struggle to interpret one's own small experiences of time in relation to a more fully whole timefulness.

It is through childhood that this temporal struggle is most powerfully revealed. A child's shorter experience of time is in a certain sense closer to temporal wholeness than an adult's. Having fewer opportunities to experience the world makes it possible to experience that world with what could be called greater completeness or even joy. By the same token, a child is less likely to have experienced life's wider narrative possibilities. It is not that a child's past is not as deep and historically complex as an adult's, its future not as precarious and open-ended, or its present not as diverse and multifaceted. Each human being is equally self-creative and equally related to the whole time of the universe. Rather, the time of childhood cannot generally be interpreted by the child him- or herself with the same degree of distentionality, the same extent of expansiveness. Compared to adults, children begin with a temporal being-in-the-world that will tend to be more unified but less distended. The aim for adults and children both is to interpret one's life story with growing temporal wholeness. It is to create one's time into an increasingly expansive story.

The human aim, then, is not exactly to hold on to childhood innocence. It is certainly not to overcome childhood through socialization. It consists, rather, in growing narrative wholeness. Time ought to be experienced with increasing expansiveness over time. Life begins close to the hub of its slowly turning wheel and should gradually distend itself outward over time toward its own wider narrative possibilities. To this task of time's expansion there is no end. It is easily fragmented along the way and inevitably stagnated and narrowed. But, on the whole, human being in time aims toward narrative growth. As childhood shows, the meaning of time is always still to be created in time: into an ever more whole unfolding story.

TOWARD NARRATION

If the experience of time can grow in this way, it develops concretely in the manner of narrative. Narrative, for our purposes, refers to the creative interpretation of time over time. As Paul Ricoeur has said, "time becomes human time to the extent that it is organized after the manner of a narrative; narrative, in turn, is meaningful to the extent that it portrays the features of a temporal experience."[14] Augustine does not explicitly employ this ancient poetic category of narrative in his own description of time, but he implies it by wrapping his own time in the specific narrative of an autobiography. Narration is how time grows over time into meaning. Everything in time has a narrative: the universe, the earth, a flower, an ant. But it is perhaps only human beings who perform the act of narrating: of retelling the experience of time ever anew. Humanity is not just part of narratives but also a being who narrates. To be human is both to live in a world of time with others (as do all things) and to construct this world of time with others over time.

Henry Newman is a normally confident four-year-old boy who has just moved into a new house and started school. He climbs onto his father's lap in a Chinese restaurant and declares, "I want to go back to being a baby and suck my dummy [pacifier] and sleep in my cot."[15] He is struggling to reshape his own short (but to him long) life story in a way that responds to the great upheavals he is now experiencing. He is not just passively inhabiting this changing time in his life. He is also actively interpreting it over time into what he hopes will be a more meaningful narrative. This narrative is one of changes being met with comforts, anxieties being articulated to his father, and a greater sense of future security. Newman does not really want to be a baby again. In a more complex way, he wants to find his former imagined sense of stability amid new changes. He is trying to expand his narrative of himself and his world to include the possibility that what currently feels painful and destructive can be rendered meaningful and more whole.

The concept of ethical narrative today has three broad senses. These correspond roughly with the three historical forms of childism explored in chapter 1. Most influentially, the term "narrative" tends to retain today the bottom-up sense given it by the Romantics, the sense, namely, that stories express their makers' distinct authenticity or genius, something they assert in the face of habit and custom from deep within themselves. This inwardness of narrativity reflects in part the Cartesian idea of the inwardness of the human mind, but it takes that idea to perhaps its farthest conclusion. One contemporary writer insists, for example, that "every newborn is a new creation, and the unique personality of each infant child is beyond human reckoning."[16] True enough. Each self from birth is the chief author and proprietor of their own unique life.

However, such a view can be taken too far. As argued above, no one creates their own life's meaning merely for themselves. No one's story exists apart from the multiple historical, social, and relational conditions by which its direction and meaning have already been constructed. Newman cannot simply remake his life story at will, as he himself fully realizes. The purpose of narrating oneself is not just to express one's inner being, but also to construct a sense of meaning that is responsive to others and larger contexts. The narrative gift is realized only in vulnerability to larger historical time. Furthermore, insofar as each person does have a narrative gift from birth, this gift is not purely good but can also narrow and distort itself. As the ancient tragic poets understood, people are caught up in narrative forces, arising from the past and pressing toward particular futures, that it is part of their life task to struggle to make sense of.

However, recent "anti-modern" notions of narrativity go too far the other way. They insist in a top-down fashion that moral narratives should be constructed, not as expressions of individuality, but by larger historical cultures and traditions.

According to such notions, Newman's father should use the opportunity of Newman's crisis to inculcate wider social values. In this view, the self creates his or her own story of life, to be sure, but only in the limited sense of appropriating a traditional story whose horizons have already been defined. As we have seen, for example, in Hauerwas, this rather passive notion of the narrative aim is frequently defended on the basis of childhood. Childhood is when human beings are initiated into moral communities. Such a view, however, strives to create rich narratives while denying children's (as well as adults') narrative capabilities.

The truth is, as Augustine recognizes, that a narrative of life is never merely created but always also creative. Each self lives from birth in a multitemporal narrative world that she has some ability—indeed responsibility—actively to narrate into meaning for herself. No one could be initiated into narratives from historical traditions without possessing their own narrative giftedness. A narrative is never simply something to which one belongs; it is always also something one does. Having a narrative requires the capability to narrate. It requires, in other words, the ability to be creative over time, to play amid the tensions of time and weave them into a larger sense of temporal meaning. Narration rests on a gift for being fruitful and multiplying in the world, a gift not simply received but also enacted.

But neither, finally, is it the case that the human narrative aim can be adequately described by a story of passing over time through prestructured stages of human development. This lifecycle view of human time, first suggested by Aristotle, has the virtue of endowing moral life with a certain temporal concreteness. It also allows for children's growth to be understood in terms of what Erik Erikson calls "cogwheeling," that is, the growth also of parents and adults as they seek to realize their own generativity over time in the process. But it does not capture the full dynamics of either children or adults having to create their time in the world into their own growing constructed narrative. (I will return to Erikson on generativity in chapter 6.)

It is worth pausing over this influential developmental perspective for just a moment. For in one sense it takes the time of childhood very seriously; but in another sense it separates childhood time as an empirical object of study from what I am calling human time. In the process, it misses what it means for all human time to aim at child-like growth.

On the whole, the developmental narrative, at least in moral terms, suggests that narrative growth proceeds linearly in a single ethical direction. Developmentalists frequently disagree on what this direction might be. But the logic of developmentalism, as I have argued in chapter 1, requires a particular end point, usually in adulthood, toward which development should aim. Newman, for example, must be struggling in some sense to grow up, and so he is dealing with a typical four-year-old's concern (say, Eriksonian learning to take initiative). Success means moving the story along the right path toward healthy adulthood.

The fact is, though, that human narratives never merely follow a straight developmental schema. For one thing, the direction of growth is in part culturally constructed. More fundamentally, growth over time always belongs to a singular human being. It is the nature of human beings to create meaning in time specifically for themselves. Narrative growth may follow all kinds of normative or predictable patterns common in a society. But it also necessarily involves, especially when including the point of view of childhood, a self telling its own particular story in order to create its own meaningful life.

Take, for example, Sigmund Freud's theory of childhood phases of oral, anal, phallic, latent, and genital development. Whatever else one may think of these phases, they do at least move beyond views of children as either already filled with inner goodness or simply needing society's moral civilization. Indeed, the mature goal is a complex creative tension of passively experienced unconscious forces (of both the id and the superego) and their active conscious interpretation into personal meaning (by the ego and in response to others).

Freud and his followers improve on earlier developmentalists like Aristotle, Thomas, and Locke by disentangling growth in time from mere growth in reason. With other so-called "masters of suspicion," such as Karl Marx and Friedrich Nietzsche, Freud sees that rational consciousness is not the master it thinks it is in its own house, but that it remains to a large extent, and largely hidden from itself, a false consciousness able to deceive and mislead itself. Unlike Marx and Nietzsche, though, Freud makes his argument, in a certain sense, from the point of view of childhood. One of his signal accomplishments is to have shown how children's worlds are significantly more complex, dynamic, distorted, repressed, and in general filled with passive-active tension than they may appear from the outside.

For Freud, then, the developmental aim is not simply the ego's autonomy, but rather the ego's inclusive sublimation over time of the libidinal and aggressive powers of the id and the internalized cultural prohibitions of the super-ego to which its growing sense of self is all too vulnerable. "The ego, driven by the id, confined by the super-ego, repulsed by reality, struggles to master its economic task of bringing about harmony among the forces and influences working in and upon it; and we can understand how it is that so often we cannot suppress a cry: 'Life is not easy!'"[17] As for Augustine, in a way, the life aim according to Freud is a kind of autobiographical peace and rest. Though Freud does not put it this way, it is a narrative wholeness painstakingly forged over the course of time.

But Freud's narrative—as well as the developmental narratives of successors like Carl Jung, Melanie Klein, and D. W. Winnicott—ultimately falls into a Cartesian trap of scientific objectivity. Childhood may be viewed as temporally complex, but it is not agential in the sense of fundamentally self-constructing. Rather, childhood is patterned, in a way, on Enlightenment science itself: the march of progress in understanding nature now being applied to the march of progress in selves.

As a result, Freud does not escape the historical problem of defining childhood time chiefly through the lens of its developed adult goal. Few adults would be glad to interpret their own present life stories mainly as expressions of some determined stage of maturation toward something else. One's age in life might have a certain influence on one's capacities for self-narration. But everyone, young and old, experiences time fundamentally as something to be shaped and retold. Children do not primarily experience their own lives as passages through life's stages. Rather, however much they may have in common with their peers, children experience themselves as in part creators of their own unique development in time. Every single human being is narratively self-creative.

This is why developmental psychology can take us only so far in understanding what is learned from childhood about moral growth. As the childhood studies theorist Alan Prout has rightly said, "because it focuses on the outcome of adulthood, [developmental psychology] marginalizes the process of growing up and sidelines children's own actions, meanings, and cultures."[18] It may be true that human life develops in certain predictable ways over time within particular cultures. But this is an outside view of the situation that does not capture how moral life develops over time as a creative human endeavor.

Self-narration is ultimately something more than the expression of inner genius, the learning of traditional stories, or the passage through phases of a lifecycle. Each of these perspectives describes part of the elephant. But none fully accounts for the complexity of the actual experiences of narrative time in childhood. Each relies in some way on childhood time being relativized to adult time. None fully articulates what it means for narrative time to be capable of growing and expanding over time.

NARRATIVE EXPANSION

To learn in a more complex way from childhood, the narrative aim needs to be understood as fully circular. It needs to involve the whole dynamics of human time. This can be done through the concept of *narrative expansion*. What does it mean not only to live in time but also to give meaning to time over time from birth to death? It means to be born into already narrated worlds that must also be narrated in the direction of an increasingly expansive whole. One's life narrative is neither simply predetermined nor merely made up. Rather, it is fragmented and diverse across life's many pasts, futures, and presents. It is in need of constantly creative new narration. The ethical aim is the self's narrative expansion rather than its narrative stagnation or contraction. It is the creation of one's disparate experiences of time into a wider story over time.

Consider, for example, the diary of Anne Frank, written by a Jewish girl in hiding from the Nazis from the ages of thirteen to fifteen. Frank's is in a sense another autobiography, like Augustine's, but now from the point of view of a child herself. Among the many reasons it is so moving is that she gradually places her forcibly constricted life in a tiny annex in Holland into her own increasingly wide perspective. Concerns about family annoyances and self-image grow over time to include also concerns about the broader meaning of her situation. Late in the diary she declares, for instance: "Quite honestly, I can't understand that the Dutch, who are such a good, honest, upright people, should judge us [the Jews] like this, we, the most oppressed, the unhappiest, perhaps the most pitiful of all peoples of the whole world."[19]

It would have been possible for Frank's view of the world to grow more narrow and embittered, as had the views of Dutch Nazis themselves. But instead she demonstrates tremendous humanity in her struggle to understand her life more broadly, as bound up with complex histories of anti-Semitism, oppression, and resilience. Hers is an example of the effort of narrative expansion, under the most difficult of circumstances, where personal and historical time have been radically dislocated.[20]

There is in fact never a time in human life when telling one's story becomes unproblematic. Each of us from birth to death is always already narrated by a vast, complex, and in many ways unfathomable history of evolution, historical era, culture, community, family, and much more. A child in a large city in China or in a remote village in Brazil is each the inheritor of diverse strands of culture, long and complex power struggles, particular and disputed family mores, changing economic realities, and diverse global dynamics. Such a history is always fragmented and distorted. It presents no one with a coherent story that is simply given to them. Rather, life's narratives are always too narrow for living fully meaningful lives.

At the same time, every human being is capable in some way of actively narrating their larger complex narrative worlds in new and more meaningful directions. Each of us lives a particular and distinctive life from birth to death that is composed of unique experiences, feelings, and relations. My own story could not possibly be identical to the story of anyone else, least of all in my own experience of it. The narration of each individual's life is utterly singular at every moment, belonging on some level entirely to oneself. Such is humanity's being-from-birth. Children must struggle to interpret their complex surrounding worlds of meaning into their own particular narratives just as much as must adults. In a certain sense, they must do so more, being newer to their worlds. Even a newborn, as yet lacking the use of verbal language, must construct a sense of its own life's unfolding flow and growth.

The moral beauty or innocence of children consists, from this point of view, not in somehow standing apart from a corrupt world, but in being on the whole more open to narrative creativity than are their more narratively settled and structured elders. This openness, or vulnerable agency, is due to the fact that the younger the child, the smaller is likely to be her or his experience of time to be narrated. There will generally be more free play in one's life story the less one has encountered life's vast and conflicting enormity. This is different from saying that children are narratively undeveloped or blank slates. Children possess exactly the same narrative creativity as anyone else. It is different also from saying that children's stories are less profound or meaningful. For everyone is equally connected to the larger historical narratives that construct their lives and equally experiences them anew. It is to say, rather, that children are likely to embrace their unfolding narrative task more dynamically and spontaneously. The difference between children and adults is not whether they narrate time into meaning but how much experience of narrating they bring to doing so.

Narrativity is the self's passive-active capability for expanding the meaning of time over time. As noted in chapter 2, the Latin *creare* is etymologically related to childhood by the Latin *crescere*, "to arise or grow." To create is to arise and grow. We can now see that this arising and growth is not just a basic aspect of all human being but also, and at the same time, invested with temporal direction. As one's life story is created over time through new experiences, one is faced with the task of interpreting these experiences with increasing narrative complexity.

If an infant has less expansive temporal experience than an adult, she is not thereby less capable of her own temporal expansion. Likewise, throughout life, all selves, however wise or practiced, are faced with the task of their own still further narrative distention. As our narrative worlds grow, they are called upon to grow still more. Unlike in a novel, the narration of the time of a self has no final page. Even dying is a temporal experience which must at the time be narrated into meaning.

Because human narratives can expand over time, they can also shrink and contract. Indeed, they inevitably to some degree do. Selves embrace over time only parts of the histories by which they are constituted, cut out aspects of their present experiences and relations, and narrow their possibilities for the future. This pruning or shrinking of narrative time is part of what it means to narrate oneself in the first place. But it also inevitably goes too far. No one forms their own life story with fully meaningful wholeness. No one achieves a totally time-inclusive narrative identity. Each human being is born into a far-flung plethora of stories already begun and departs with a life story only partially told.

The ethical aim is therefore not narrative completeness but rather narrative expansion. Increasing narrative growth over time is the internal desire of our creative ethical being. It is the journey that childhood shows we must embark upon from our first breath to our last. The human aim is the endless end of making a meaningful story of one's time in this world.

BODYING FORTH

In the remainder of this chapter, I flesh out this description of the ethical aim in light of childhood in three particular ways. These relate to the body, relationships, and the divine. Each should help us more fully imagine the interconnectedness of the self's pasts, presents, and futures and how these diverse times may be either narrowed or expanded through the activity of narration.

The body is an appropriate starting point because it is as bodies that selves experience and interpret time most immediately. It is as flesh that one is born into time. It is in one's body that one most directly participates in time's passage over time. And it is as a biological being that one encounters the end of the experience of time in death. From a purely objective point of view, of course, time escapes any particular body. Bodies are part of the stardust and nature. But from a phenomenological point of view—that of time as lived experience—it is in the first place as an embodied being that each of us turns time into narrative. It is not the body itself that necessarily expands, but its temporal meaning to me in the world. My body is my autobiography's first, last, and closest protagonist.

The body is particularly important from the point of view of childhood. For it is in childhood that, to adapt a felicitous phrase from feminism, the self first "bodies forth" in the world.[21]

Childhood is the most obvious time in life when humanity is not only embodied but also embodied in time: as beginning, continuing, changing, and growing. It is in childhood that each self begins the lifelong journey of constructing its body's meaning in time. In other words, the body shares the same dual temporality as described above: It moves in time, and this movement is itself interpreted over time. The body is not (as Descartes thought) an object in the world separate from the mind. Rather, as Gabriel Marcel says, it is never just *a* body but always also, and more fundamentally, *my* body, *your* body, *somebody's* body.[22] Objectifying bodies is a second-order experience that presupposes a primary experience of one's own embodiment. For both children and adults, the body is the most immediate experience of being-in-the-world, of living in time as an ingesting, feeling, acting, sharing, and becoming human being.

This is why the body is a necessary element of the self's expanding narrativity. Before being an object, it is an experience of oneself in the time of the world. It is as a body that Anne Frank finds herself born into a horrifying time of history, moves from Germany to Holland, grows from thirteen to fifteen years old, uses the pen that writes her diary, is trapped in an annex and eventually discovered, is taken to Bergen-Belsen, and there dies. Likewise, no one escapes the fact that their time in the world is time as a body.

Embodiment is more primordial even than language. For the latter depends on the body's growing brain, ears, mouth, and so on. Children remind us that selves inhabit bodies before they reflect upon themselves linguistically and culturally. Embodiment is not one part of narration but narration's necessary condition. If there are such things as disembodied beings, they do not narrate: without bodies they could not experience time. It is because of the material aspect of one's being that one is capable of narration at all.

Let us take, for example, the brain. Unless I need a CAT scan or MRI, I do not generally experience my own brain as an object (and not really even then). My first and most fundamental experience of my own brain is my experience of being able to experience at all. I experience as a creature having a brain. It is this part of my body that first marries passive conditions and active choice in my own synaptic creation of new meaning. The brain is, in a sense, the record of my ongoing history of narrating. Starting as a late fetus and ending at brain death, it embodies my experiences of time itself. All human experience is at once already constructed by a surrounding world and newly constructed by a self. And this tension finds its most immediate expression in the narrative growth of connections in the brain.

From the brain we know that "growing time," as defined above, has a particular temporal starting point. As far as is currently known, the human experience of time begins (in time) in the formation late in fetal development of neurons capable of interacting with their surroundings. The earlier embryo develops a neural groove, then the beginnings of a brain and spinal chord, and eventually a nervous system able to control bodily functions. But none of these developments constitute an experience of the world. It is not until about a month into the third trimester that the cerebral hemispheres and thalamus are thought, normally, to be sufficiently formed that one could speak of the fetus interpreting sensory input with any kind of meaning. It is only at this point in time that one might be able to begin to speak of a person's own experience of time. The body is no longer just a possible object for others but also a possible subject for itself. Only here or later could one argue that time is experienced doubly, so to speak, as created into meaning over time—or, in other words, that time might start to become narrative.

This neurological experience of time continues throughout life. The self's narration of itself—its synaptic autobiography, if you will—creates new connections between neurons, grows short-term and then longer-term memories and expectations, and organizes itself through selective pruning. Adult brains tend to expand their capacities by greater synaptic specialization, and as adults age, the brain may create fewer new synaptic connections but with potentially farther-reaching narrative focus. At death (though not dying) this simultaneously brain-constructed and brain-constructing capability comes to an end.

When looked at from the point of view of childhood, the brain does not simply advance toward some adult rational state, but embodies the remarkable human capacity for expanding the experience of time over time. It receives experiences of personal time, relations over time with others, and the more abstract times of belonging to particular histories and worlds. But it also interprets these experiences into plastic meanings over the course of one's time in the world. It may be that children can "learn more" than adults in terms of more rapidly inculcating experiences and information, whereas adults might "learn more" in terms of investing experiences with wider significance. Augustine as a boy learned to speak and as an adult to construct an autobiography. But the same basic aim is being pursued throughout: the more rather than less expansive narration of one's being-in-the-world. The brain is neither a mere lump of cells nor a tool of the will but the first arena in which the self strives to create experience into wider meaning.

Another example of this bodying forth in the world, from a childist point of view, is the human expansion of the use of language. The "linguistic turn" of phenomenological and analytic philosophy in the last century is often spoken of as an entirely disembodied experience, as if human beings spring into language fully formed. In fact, as childhood teaches, language is bodily through and through. It begins in simple gestures like kicking, crying, touching, and smiling. Only later do these forms of communication develop also into speech and then writing. Speech in the sense of oral expression is an extension of the brain, mouth, ears, and so on into creating meaning in the world. Writing takes this extension still further, through neurons, eyes, and hands, into forms of language that are more formally structured. However, speech and writing are definitive of humanity only insofar as "humanity" does not include babies. The sheer physicality of human language is easily forgotten as one grows into adulthood and takes all this bodily generativity for granted. Nevertheless, at its most fundamental level, language is humanity's embodiment of meaning in time.

This means that language is implicitly narrative, and not the other way around. Language is predicated on the primal human capability for interpreting time. It can grow and have significance only as brains and bodies increase in linguistic capability. Language is only the basis for narration in the limited sense of providing it with time-tested historical, cultural, and interpersonal materials. But language, like the body, is always in the first instance experienced as *my* language, *my* speech, *my* writing. It belongs to concrete bodily experience before it then turns around and helps to invest such experience with new meaning. Language, in other words, is implicitly temporal. It exists only in the meeting of selves and societies as these change and recreate themselves over time. Language, most broadly understood, is the expansion of time into meaning.

And what of being-toward-death? Between being-from-birth and being-toward-death is suspended the possibility of the creation of an embodied narrative whole. One's story in the world not only begins in birth (or slightly before) and ends in death—the bodily bookends of life—but in between expands the bodily experience of time into a story of one's own life's meaning. Death is not merely an objective fact or an existential conundrum. It is part of the narrative each self must tell of its larger time in the world. Death from the point of view of birth is a hoped-for narrative completeness. It is the time when we hope we will be able to say that we have lived our time fully, or at least as fully as possible. The anxiety of death is for narrative beings not the anxiety so much of no longer being as that of potentially not having been, not having experienced one's short time meaningfully and to the fullest. The death of the body is not merely its reabsorption back into the universe, but, from the point of view of it being *my* body, its ultimate embrace of time. As a being who comes from dust and ends in dust, I belong finally to whatever larger narrative I imagine of all creation.

The body is therefore not just an object that passes through time but humanity's closest experience of time itself as a struggle for narrative meaning. The body and brain do not aim simply to survive, either personally or as a species. They aim more fundamentally, in light of childhood, to grow toward narrative wholeness. Even an infant like Ying Ying Fry, who has only just come into the world, faces the task of creating a vast diversity of bodily experiences into a growing narrative meaning. Likewise, for each self, the body is part of its ethical quest for larger narrativity in the world. The human story can ultimately involve giving up one's bodily life, perhaps in war or by physician-assisted suicide, for the sake of a greater narrative unity. But as my body—somebody's body—the human body overall seeks growth in meaning over time.

SHARING TIME

Another illustration of this child-inclusive narrative aim can be found in the self's re-lations to others. Other persons have to have bodies (or have had bodies or be going to have bodies) if I am to relate to them as others in the world. But they also (and in part because they have bodies) possess their own more fundamental narrative cre-ativity. It is through this relation of narrativities that we may approach each other's fuller humanity. The next chapter explores human relations in terms of moral obli-gations: the sense in which others should be treated as irreducible others in and of themselves. But in this chapter, our interest is in the pre-obligational or teleological sense in which self and others are integrated through shared narrative aims.

Consider again the stories of Winnie Foster, Valentino Achak Deng, and Anne Frank. Each is struggling to retell, in a more widely meaningful way, their own life narratives. But each is also, at the same time, bound up with the life narratives of oth-ers. Foster grows irritated with her parents, but she eventually realizes how important they are to her, having raised her so far and promised to be there no matter what in the future. Deng loses his family to war but finds a new family among the "lost boys" who share his homeland and experiences. Frank is reduced to a small circle of imme-diate others in her annex, but also impacted by larger social forces, and her autobiog-raphy includes how she defines herself in relation to them and how they define her.

For children in particular, but also for us all, selves are related to others neces-sarily. Even the body begins in relation: to a mother and a father, at the very least. My own being-in-the-world or narrative is never just about myself. No newborn lacks a genetic and cultural family ancestry. No child thrives without caretakers. No adult can take part in cultures and societies without others in cultures and so-cieties around them. In general, the human being is a social animal—as Aristotle long ago said—its meaning and story bound up with the meanings and stories of an unfathomable diversity of others.

The aim of narrative expansion in time includes these kinds of wider relations to others, because they are inherently part of the self's story. This relation amounts to more than just one another's instrumental use for their own narrative purposes. Rather, happiness itself consists in part in relating to others as distinctive storytell-ers in their own right. The different wants and desires of others are to some degree bound up with my own. My narrative includes my story with others. Whether I like it or not, my time in the world is shaped by others in the near and distant past, anticipates relations to others in the future, and belongs to complex networks of relations to others close and far in the present. Even if, with Sartre, I think hell is other people, I could not interpret my life this way without them.

This narrative relation of self to others can be called *sharing time*. From child-hood in particular we see that the self's own narration of time involves also the nar-ration of time by others. "To share" has the etymological meaning of both actively *to take part in* and passively *to be part of*. The self's narrative expansion over time requires active-passive narrativity that is fundamentally shared with others, a story created by selves and others at once. From birth, each self responds to others in their distinctive narrative particularity, and others respond to the self in the same way. This is not only *a* mother but *my* mother, not only *a* friend but *my* friend— with all the storied concreteness involved. Sharing time means narrating oneself as dynamically related to the distinctive narrating of others.

Shared stories can either expand or contract over time. On the one hand, they can increasingly include the experiences and stories of others. It is possible to use one's time in the world to involve the story of others, however painfully or joyfully, in the creation of one's own story in an increasingly complex way. It is also possible, on the other hand, out of fear or lack of imagination, to keep telling the same story over and over again or to fall into narrow clichés. Overall, however, shared time with others aims toward investing human connections with wider narrative meaning. Childhood should show us all that one's stories with others are able to grow over time.

A newborn is not accountable for her relation to the poor and starving of the world. She does indeed relate to them (for example through the cheap labor that went into making her toys), but she cannot yet form her own story in a way that is also shaped meaningfully by theirs. Her narrative experience is not yet sufficiently broad to do so. But, as a child grows, she is rightly expected to enter into increasingly wide relations with the world of others tied to her life. Others should impact how she creates her worlds of meaning in ever more extensive ways.

The vast field of others with whom a child's story is wrapped up should become an increasing part of how she unfolds her own life's meaning. Time should be narrated as fully as possible in relation to others. Ultimately, the human story from birth to death is always too narrow. Even though all human stories are connected in some way, they are never connected in ways that include all experiences of them. Such is simply impossible. Narrative expansion remains at all times a task to be accomplished in the unfolding thickness of time.

The human aim involves narrating oneself in wider rather than narrower relation to the narrative strivings of others. It includes stretching one's own story of oneself in the world to include the ways in which this story is related to and told by other such storytelling selves. To expand narratively in relation to other narrating others is to open oneself to an ever wider story of what it means to be human. It is to set oneself on the surprising and unpredictable journey of sharing time with others. As beings who start out life as parts of the stories of others, we can be fulfilled only by telling our stories with others with increasing interconnectedness. The human aim in light of children includes narrating ourselves in relation to others who themselves also narrate us.

BEYOND DEVELOPMENTALISM

If so, then we may return one last time to moral developmentalism to see why moral growth, now in relation to others, is more than a matter of lifecycle phases. I have already argued that developmentalism, past and present, helps concretize human time, but in the process also obscures children's own creative moral agency. We can now see why this is the case when it comes to sharing time with others.

Take, for example, the foundational text in moral psychology, Jean Piaget's *The Moral Judgment of the Child*. Piaget observes children's (or rather French middle class boys') games and charts a progression of three stages in their growth of moral judgment. Younger children on the whole view morality as "obedience" to adult rules and authority; older children view it as following a strict "equality"; and still older children understand it as achieving an "equity" or "justice" that accounts for "the particular situation of each."[23] Putting aside for the moment Piaget's of-ten criticized narrowly European and bourgeois lens, his achievement is to have recognized clearly that moral life expands in time. For what Piaget describes is a kind of temporal growth, not unrelated to what I have described here, in children's relations to one another.

What is problematic about Piaget's view, however, among other things, is that growth in time is understood as something that more or less passively happens to the child. Unless something interferes, there is a natural, almost biological, narra-tive that should in due course unfold. This means ultimately, however, that Piaget's story is ethically self-defeating. The purported goal of moral development is to re-spond to others in their particularity. Yet children themselves are to be viewed, not as particular selves, but as following a generalized moral path. If children, however, are full human beings, each child's moral growth over time should be viewed as in part constructed by their society and in part something of their own making. Both self and other actively create a wholly new moral relation. As a result, there is no fixed "adult" developmental aim, either for children or for adults themselves, but only increasing narrative growth in relation to others.

This difficulty of unilinear time persists in the more complex moral developmen-tal schema of Lawrence Kohlberg. Here, moral growth passes through three levels of moral capability: from "preconventional" egocentrism (typical, it is claimed, in younger children), to "conventional" satisfaction of societal expectations (typical in adolescents), to "postconventional" universalizing moral reason (usually reached, if at all, in adulthood).[24] Kohlberg admits that these three levels (each of which has two stages) do not strictly correspond to particular ages; an adult, for example, could be stuck in conventionality or even egocentrism. But Kohlberg does insist that this path is the only one along which ethical advancement may proceed. The aim of moral development in time is already determined, however little a child can understand it, toward a fully autonomous adult rationality.

Some have argued—and rightly so—that Kohlberg may be telling the wrong story, marginalizing the moral experiences of women or infantilizing cultures that value the well-being of the group. But, in addition, there is a profoundly paradoxical sense in which Kohlberg's study of children is inherently biased precisely against children. For at each stage, children are chiefly defined in terms of what they lack: first a sense of wider community, then a capacity for impartial reasoning. Growth in time is understood from the point of view of (a particular notion of) adulthood. As also in Kant, childhood is unformed adulthood. In other words, despite being empirical, the assumptions at play here mean that little is learned about the grounds of moral life from childhood itself.

Here it is notable that even the stage theory of Carol Gilligan, which is explicitly critical of Kohlberg for sidelining women's experiences and human relationality, still retains a developmental adult-centrism. In this case, based on observations of the experiences of middle class North American young women, the three stages are somewhat shifted: egocentric concern for oneself, self-sacrificing concern for others, and finally mutual or reciprocal care prioritizing the self-other relation.[25] This trajectory does in fact lead toward a more complex view of self-other dynamics. It even touches on a kind of creative moral tension between self and other. However, children are still interpreted as essentially pre-moral creatures lacking in relational capacities. Somehow the ability to care for others in a responsive and self-transforming way becomes possible only the more one approaches adulthood.

In the end, stageism excludes the full experiences of children, not because it fails to study them, but because it brings to the study of children's moral lives flatly unilinear assumptions about moral time. It sees human time from a Cartesian perspective as simply passing by, rather than as part of a narrative world that human beings also actively construct. The fact that children are earlier in the human lifecycle does not make them an incomplete species of moral being. Rather, they inhabit moral time in the same way as do adults, by both constructing and being constructed by it.

When it comes to relations with others, children's differences are at most a matter of degree rather than of kind. Any narrowness of narrative relations is not a separate egocentrism, but a relative smallness of narrative experience stemming from a relative shortness of time in the world. The more time one lives in relation to others, the greater the possibility—though not necessarily the actuality—for narrating that world more inclusively with others. Both children and adults are full human beings capable of relating to others with either increasing or decreasing expansiveness. The question is not *whether* children create narratives with others, but *how much* both children and adults are able to grow in doing so.

A more fully childist view of moral relations views each self's moral story as something that, from birth onwards, both the self and others contribute to forming. All children and adults bring to ethical relations distinct narrative capabilities of their own. Growth in time is always in part—whether one is male or female, rich or poor, young or old—constructed by oneself. Every child and adult re-narrates the larger narratives of their cultures and societies.

THE NARRATIVE BEYOND

As before, we can press our account one step further to consider its ultimate boundaries, its stretching toward its own beyond. Childhood origins can point toward ultimate hopes. In light of childhood, what would the human story expand toward at time's farthest possible fullness? What narrative can finally be imagined of narrativity as such? If there is no timeless point toward which human life aims, what, if anything, could be imagined about the nature of time's timefulness, time's unending eternity?

In Toni Morrison's novel *Beloved*, an escaped American slave in the nineteenth century slits the throat of her baby rather than surrender her back into a life of slavery, so horrifying her pursuers that they let her and her other children go. But the baby, Beloved, haunts the mother's household for many years thereafter. The hoped-for time of a new beginning enters into a kind of liminality where the dead baby still lives on. The infant's all-too-short time on earth is overtaken by the tragedy of its irreversible death. Its narrative of life contracts, one might say, toward a zero point—a life almost totally robbed of time—which, paradoxically, turns into a life whose time seems infinite, unending.

The deep sadness of a child's death has to do not only with the shortness of her time in the world but also with the smallness of her opportunity to create a story in the world for herself. Everyone, even Beloved, has a story. But not everyone gets to tell that story as fully as do others. Stories include broken attachments and losses of love and relations. Beloved's story may be the closest one could get to a god's-eye view of the shortness of human time for us all.

To imagine and give shape to narration's boundaries, its totality of beginning and eventually ending, one may find some guidance from religious symbols and myths. To expand the stories of human lives is to press them ultimately toward a time beyond time, a time continually vanishing over the visible horizon, a time at time's own edges. The full aim of narrative growth cannot finally be known, for time itself is not something one can experience as coming to an end. As with human origins, it lies finally beyond the human imagination. If one's story is always still to be created, it is always also something never fully known. It is an autobiography never finished. This does not mean, however, that this unknown itself cannot be spoken of, however hesitantly and imperfectly.

Myths are peculiar kinds of narratives. They narrate within a temporal framework what appears to be temporally transcendent. The Genesis story of the creation of the world, for example, takes place over seven "days," but is about the very creation of the earth, sun, and therefore "days" themselves—and in a sense time itself. Myths are able to mark out the ultimate horizons of narrativity. They can try to imagine human time at its farthest possible excesses: whether, for instance, as creation, new creation, the oneness of humanity, the return of the gods, the world of ancestors, a final age, life after death, nirvana, or total present mindfulness.

Such imaginations represent what I have been calling "impossible possibilities" that stretch experiences—in this case of time—beyond their knowable limits. When properly understood as mythic rather than literal, they beckon human narratives to face their own farthest boundaries. They are stories that stand in tension with the actual stories of our lives and therefore help to recreate them in light of vanishing hopes. This is why myths can be morally dangerous, but also potentially liberating. Mythic time never fully arrives but nevertheless can expand one's sense of time into greater meaning.

Each new child brings a fresh and unanticipated story into the world. At the same time, with each new child, the human story further escapes description. The theologian Jürgen Moltmann calls children "embodiments of God's hopes for us."[26] Children make as concrete as possible the sense in which humanity is capable of continuously outgrowing itself. The narratives that selves are able to make of their lives are never the final story—not even in the heights of ecstasy or the depths of despair. Rather, however impossible it may seem, human stories are always capable of narration once again. Every human being is in this sense a newborn child throughout life. Human beings are "children" of a universe whose story remains full of promise and hope.

Childhood functions in this way as an antidote to the tendencies of all manner of religious and secular fundamentalisms. For fundamentalism sees in children only new means to further a given story that a select few (usually adults) already know. In a strongly top-down way, children's own stories are to be bent into a prestructured narrative that has already been told and predetermined by nature or God.

A more fully circular view sees in children an opening for creating the world anew, beyond what even the wisest of people might imagine. Religion, from a childist point of view, is about constantly telling stories anew. Humanity in the fullness of time is part of a story always still to be unfolded. From this perspective, the claim of actual or literal knowledge of the ultimate human aim is a form of idolatry: a reduction of the whole to a mere part, a reduction of the fullness of time to narrow temporality. What lies at the limits of the human story cannot be captured in any particular story as such. A narrative theology like that of Hauerwas, starting from a particular scriptural story, is in this sense, while not fundamentalist, also idolatrous. Children and adults are not just to be initiated into existing narratives, but welcomed as images of the divine who bring to the world new capacities for narration.

TIME'S TIMEFULNESS

Human time could be perfected only in a kind of mythical eternity that is not time's overcoming but rather its fulfillment. We are temporal creatures through and through, not temporarily temporal creatures who are waiting for temporality to end. The aim of narrative growth is not nonnarrativity, the end of time, but narrativity's temporal wholeness. If God is a symbol for the world's ultimate hope, He or She does not lie outside of time but constitutes time's own perfect realization. Such a God is not *no* time but *all* time. The furthest horizon of human time is not timelessness but timefulness.

This narrative aim of the fullness of time becomes especially clear in light of children. As Karl Rahner rightly says, if a little too romantically, "childhood does not constitute past time, time that has eroded away, but rather that which remains, that which is coming to meet us as an intrinsic element in the single and enduring completeness of the time of our existence considered as a unity, that which we call the eternity of human beings as saved and redeemed."[27] For adults, childhood is not past time but a call toward (though not, as Rahner suggests, the perfection of) greater temporal completeness. It is a call toward narrative wholeness. Each human being's pasts, presents, and futures move toward, however unfathomably, a fully unified narrativity. In expanding the story of my life into time, I approach ever nearer to a kind of timeful eternity.

The divine symbolizes in many religions the possibility for time and eternity to exist in creative tension. Creator and creation (human and otherwise) are neither separate nor identical but in a living relation to one another. It is this tension that makes it possible not only to live in time but also to expand time over time infinitely. Time can always redouble itself. The eternity of human time could not be bound up with any one particular narrative but is the ultimate condition for the possibility of narrativity itself. Time is both what is narrated and the condition for narrating. It is both finite and infinite. However incompletely, each self is a child of time who creates their time into meaning through time's own expansion.

In this case, we may return to the symbolism in the previous chapter of humanity as an image of a Creator, but now in terms not just of ethical life's origin but also of its ethical aim. This aim, as mythologized in the story of Genesis 1–2, is the eternal time of a Sabbath. As images of a Creator, it is possible for human beings to transform worldly time toward its own peace and rest. In the Genesis myth, God is said to have created the world in six days and on the seventh, or Sabbath, to have rested. This day of rest should be understood, not as withdrawal from the world, but as the world's temporal fulfillment. The Sabbath is not the end of time but a day completing the other days. It is the day toward which all other days lead. It is the culmination, not the annihilation, of God's creation of the world in the time and speech of a narrative. It is an imagination, however incomplete, of time's complete narrative fullness. It is the conclusion, in fact, of the myth itself: the end of the myth in the sense of its moral and ontological fulfillment. It does not end historical time but eternally begins it. It imagines historical time as infused with infinity. The Sabbath is a narrative of the possibility of narrative possibility.

The Jewish theologian Martin Buber argues that keeping the Sabbath represents an *imitatio Dei*, an imitation of God in the form of God's imagined rest and peace. In this case, both real and mythical Sabbaths continually remind one of life's ultimate purpose and direction. "The imitation of God . . . is what becoming a blessing for the other peoples means: setting a living example of a true people, a community."[28] In imitating God, humanity embraces the possibility for transforming itself toward a fully temporal whole. Imitation does not presume an already fully narrated community, but affirms that such a community might be hoped for. It tries to regrasp a spirit of creativity that can move over the depths and darkness of chaos and give them new meaning over time. It asserts the ultimate meaningfulness of time itself.

Likewise, God's narration of the world over seven days is one possible symbol of humanity's own narrative potential. It is projection, a creation—perhaps imaginable only by human beings—of the human possibility for imitating time's fullness. It is a narrative of the unnarratable possibility of narration. It may help one stretch toward one's own more whole narrative possibilities. It is not a myth of before time or even of just the origin of time, but of time's unimaginable fullness. There would be no "rest" on the seventh day had God not gone through the six days leading up to it. Likewise, for us, the narrative aim of our lives in history finds no rest apart from that unfolding history itself. Rest and peace are not separate from time but time's inner fulfillment.

It is no accident, then, that the Creator in whose image one might imagine oneself to create is finally a Narrator. Such is the case in many kinds of mythology. In the case of Genesis 1–2, each day of mythic creation does not simply happen but is undertaken through an act of speech: "God said, 'Let there be light'; and there was light," and so on. Even God's final creation of humankind is imagined through narration: "God said, 'Let us make humankind in our image, according to our likeness.'" Narration is God's mode of creation. God as Creator is Narrator. Why? Because creation itself is infused from its very "in the beginning" with the growing of time. Like in the mythology of the Greeks, time, or Kronos, is among the first gods, part of what makes the world's creation possible. As with the Hindu god Krishna, when he appears as the charioteer in the *Bhagavad-Gita*, divine time and human time are ultimately one, however little humanity may glimpse it.

If the myth of a divine Narrator means anything in light of childhood, it means that each self is born a narrative being capable of narrating its diverse times of life toward an always greater wholeness. The Creator is not a top-down imposer of moral order, a bottom-up infuser of moral purity, nor a clockmaker setting humanity on a moral developmental path. Rather, She or He is an image of the possibility for narrative moral fullness. Humanity in the image of such a Creator or Narrator is called upon to shape its own time in the world toward an ever more complete narrative whole, a Sabbath peace and rest of time's ultimate timefulness. Narrativity expands the circle of human relations toward their own ever more diverse temporality. Human time is to be multiplied fruitfully in the direction of its own truly inclusive oneness. No one actually inhabits or can truly imagine this total unity of narration, but it beckons from the core of human being as a time-creative creature.

What is strangest of all is that life is not fixed in time but capable of temporal expansion. Yet it would be stranger still if, as originating in childhood, we could not stretch out our stories of time in the world at all.

CONCLUSION

What is admirable about children like Foster, Deng, Frank, and Beah is not that their stories have achieved some kind of unexpected maturity, but that they embrace so fully the human creative struggle for greater narrative wholeness. Disjuncture and chaos do not give way to narrowness or destruction, but stimulate new openness and growth. Their particular stories as selves with bodies and in relations with others expand rather than contract their hopes for fuller narrative meaning.

The narrative aim is never completed. It is not possible to tell every side of one's life story. The time of self-narration never ends. But in every moment along the way, from birth to death, every human being is capable of weaving the unfathomable threads of their time in the world into a more rather than less expansive narrative whole. Human fulfillment in light of children does not lie in reaching some timeless ideal, known only to the fixed laws of reason or tradition, but in creating one's own passive-active story with increasing narrative fullness. This possible wholeness changes as one's life experiences change and grow over time. But any life story can be stretched into time more fully over time. The human end never ends. It is an unfolding narrative growth.

Chapter 4

What Is Owed Each Other?

THE QUESTION OF ETHICAL aims finally gives way to a third question of ethical obligations. At a certain point, others are not just parts of my own or anyone else's story, but also irreducible human beings in and of themselves. What might be desired or hoped for runs up against what is owed to others—including oneself as an other to oneself—regardless of narrative outcomes. A child can always have better health, but some basic level of health care is morally required. Persons and societies owe others a certain dignity and respect as others in their own right.

But how should the nature of moral obligation be understood in light of children? Both historically and today, obligations have tended even more than aims to be based on the lives and experiences of adults. Especially since modernity, ethical respect has been based largely on the notion of human beings' independent autonomy. The basis for responding to others is thought to lie in the fact that others possess their own social rationality or freedom.

As feminists and others have recently pointed out, such a basis for moral life is open to various kinds of criticism. Above all, it leaves open the question of how moral "rationality" itself is to be defined and who has the power to construct it. When it comes to children, the problem becomes even more acute. For so long as human dignity is grounded in rational autonomy, children will tend to be marginalized more than any other group. This is not because children do not also possess reason and independence. It is because, in a social context defined chiefly by individual freedoms, children will generally have less experience in the world with which to exercise them in relation to others. It will be easier to think of children as taken responsibility for than as practicing responsibility themselves.

This modernistic approach has resulted in a profound paradox for contemporary moral thinking regarding childhood. On the one hand, adults are anxious about their individual and societal responsibilities toward the children around them. It is obvious that children suffer great systemic and relational harms and need to be treated with greater respect and liberated from marginalization. But on the other hand, the very grounds on which moral obligation is understood implicitly denies children their full humanity. The languages of autonomy, agency, and individuality—as well as of virtue, character, and community—can certainly be applied to children, but they are first rooted, or so I will argue, in the experiences and perspectives of adults. Merely extending them from adults to children will not make children equal.

The only way past this paradox is to reimagine the nature of moral obligation itself from a child-inclusive point of view—for children and adults both. This can be done, I argue in this chapter, by rethinking the very concept of moral responsibility in terms of responsiveness to the other. "The other" is a term developed in phenomenological ethics, most famously by Emmanuel Levinas, to describe each human being's demand for irreducibility. Here I revise this notion in a more fully childist way. I argue that each "other" demands that selves and societies respond creatively to them by decentering as far as possible their own horizons of meaning and activity. Both children and adults should expand their circles of moral relation toward others as their own new and changing "second centers." Otherness, in other words, should be creative of selfhood.

If the moral aim from the previous chapter is to expand the self's moral circle outwards into a wider narrative, the moral obligation is to expand it asymmetrically in response to each other. The first grows the self around itself, the second around not-self or otherness. Moral responsibility means shifting one's center of gravity to include others insofar as they are *not* reducible to one's narrative alone. The world I create for myself should be disrupted and stretched out as far as possible by genuine human difference. A child in poverty does not ask only for my fuller life story, but also for my radical transformation. She calls upon not only my creative powers but also my openness to her creating me. Each new child, and every human other, brings a new center of creativity into the world which demands an ever more fully decentered humanity.

HUMAN BEING AS OTHER

Thirteen-year-old Tony Anderson has been living in foster care in the United States for nine years. His mentally ill biological mother has not been able to look after him.[1] The law requires a termination at this point of his biological mother's parental rights and his legal adoption by someone judged competent to raise him. Anderson himself, however, even though recognizing the unfitness of his mother, wants her to retain her legal parenthood. He fears losing touch with her in the future and hopes one day to be able to look after her himself. In outrage he tells his lawyer, "She's my mother, ain't she? Ain't I got rights?" But, in fact, the court can decide whatever it sees fit according to established legal and ethical norms. Children do not have to be heard in such cases—seen, yes, but not heard. Anderson is lucky, thanks to dedicated adult activists, to have his particular voice represented in his case at all.

The great Enlightenment ethicists—John Locke, Jean-Jacques Rousseau, Immanuel Kant, and others—realized that they were excluding children in fundamental ways from their theories of moral obligation. The freedom, rationality, and autonomy by which they define moral humanity is explicitly understood as something children do not yet fully possess. The reason Anderson is not considered a full ethical subject before the law is that he is not thought to be independently rational. Depending on your point of view, he is either irrational, not yet strong enough to exercise reason publicly, or still in the process of developing rational capacities. Such assumptions powerfully shape moral thought today. In a world structured around agency, individuality, and autonomy, those who are relatively less independent in life will tend to be assumed, however benignly, to be second-class moral citizens.

The problem is no less acute, however, for those who challenge moral individualism from the point of view of older, premodern kinds of ethical understanding. As we have seen, such values as community, tradition, and virtue still tend to define moral life from the point of view of adults—that is, of those who hold the power to determine what values in society are most important. The select few, usually wealthy adult males, will have the greatest say in interpreting things like God's laws, historical conventions, or the requirements of nature. As long as ethical responsibility is relative to some larger communal whole, it will be defined first and foremost, again however benignly, by those with greater communal resources.

A more promising avenue is suggested by certain advances in phenomenological ethics that could be grouped together under the heading of "postmodernity." By postmodernity I broadly mean the effort to overcome the problems of modernity without returning to the problems of premodernity. Such ethics come in many shapes and sizes and have been criticized from various angles. However, the great moral challenges of the past century have given rise to some creative new thought. Genocides, wars, colonialism, and environmental disasters seem to suggest the need for ethical self-critique beyond the advances of the Enlightenment.

The most helpful among these new approaches, for our purposes, is the ethics of "the other." This is because, on the face of it at least, children are just as fully other as anyone else. If you were to say, for example, "love one another," the other here could include anyone of any age (or gender, race, or class, and so on). As understood in postmodern ethics, "otherness" refers to the moral fact that each and every human being is ultimately irreducible to anything that may be thought or said about them.[2] The human being as other transcends or disrupts all thinking, language, and narration. Humanity's experience of its world always ultimately overruns what anyone could explain about it. Moral life should include not just humanity's sameness—whether by rationality, nature, or tradition—but also its difference, diversity, nonsubstitutability, or otherness.

My argument is that this kind of ethics of otherness can include children better than the other options—but only if it too is rethought. So far, postmodern ethicists have hardly considered children at all. If they did, they would be forced to place "the other" in a more concrete circular relation to selves and societies. The other would be both an object and a subject of responsibility. It would not so much overturn shared worlds as open-endedly create new ones.

THE OTHER'S DISRUPTION

Let us start to think about ethical otherness in light of childhood by considering what is sometimes referred to as the other's ethical disruption. It would seem that disruption is something children may be particularly good at. They disrupt not only in the sense of being disruptive. They disrupt in the moral sense of demanding changes in the world. They disrupt by their very presence, their very coming into existence at birth. For example, Tony Anderson may not actually disrupt the thinking of the court, but ethically he demands it.

The fact of a child's existence, whether upon birth or otherwise, obliges persons and communities to undergo constant and unanticipated self-transformation. It asks for disruption in the sense of new feelings, narratives, actions, and relationships. Routines should change, sleep patterns be thrown off, priorities shifted, and relationships and institutions restructured. Such, indeed, is generally why adults take care of children, parents have them, and teachers go into teaching. Being with children draws one into fresh and surprising horizons of meaning, as does being with adults.

Whether in fact adults and societies respond to children's moral disruptiveness is a matter of degree, and to some degree they inevitably fail. But each new child nevertheless contains within her- or himself the unique moral power to oblige fundamental changes in the lives of those around them. Each new child creates in others and in society at large a distinctive new moral responsibility to respond to *this* particular child.

At the same time, children are also constantly disrupted. Rightly or wrongly, disruption is a necessary part of every child's (and adult's) life. Often against her own immediate wishes, a child's experiences are reshaped by those around her. The baby who cries for milk will not always get it. The toddler who hits another child is told to stop. The older child who does not like to do her homework nonetheless has to buckle down. Not only must children disrupt adults, but adults must also disrupt children. A child's (or adult's) life should not necessarily take its own free course. Moreover, as children grow and mature, they ought to learn increasingly to disrupt themselves: that is, to change themselves in response to experiences and others around them, however uncomfortably or even painfully. Being able to be disrupted by others is part of what it means ethically to be human.

Let us consider again Annabelle Jones, the eleven-year-old girl growing up in deep poverty in New York's South Bronx. Does her unspoken cry for help in any way disrupt us? The answer has to be yes and no. Anyone who is not completely numb to her humanity must feel the sting of moral failure, both society's and one's own, as she faces tremendous social marginalization when it comes to health, life expectancy, education, and future potential. The only way not to feel morally disrupted by her is through self-comforting narratives ("history is full of inequalities," "she deserves her situation because . . . ," "at least she's better off than some," and so on). Such narratives are normal responses to difference. But they are also finally insufficient. What they do not account for is the possibility of my own disruption by another. Jones is not just part of society; she is *this* particular human being. Whether or not one allows oneself to be disrupted by her, from an ethical point of view she is still disruptive.

The ethical problem here is not just that human relations do not make themselves hospitable to otherness. In a more complex way, it is that human relations fail to make a response to otherness by in turn recreating themselves. There is much that, in Jones's case, could be done: take a train to her neighborhood (like Jonathan Kozol does) and get to know her; help other children in similar situations; lobby politicians; teach in deprived schools; donate to children's organizations—the list is endless. The problem is not just a lack of appreciation for her distinctiveness, but also a lack of a self-creative relationship to it. It is a disconnection between her otherness and my selfhood.

I am called upon not only to be disrupted by the other but also to disrupt and recreate myself in the process. I already inhabit a family, a set of relations, a culture, a society—in other words, a vast and complex set of ethical narratives. But others demand that I also somehow refashion them in unanticipated new ways. As children particularly show, what is ethically obliged from me is not *no* self but a *new* self. My existing stories of what it means to live and act in the world are not to be abandoned but transformed. Moral disruption calls for a kind of vulnerability to the other, a willingness to open myself up to them. It calls for play: thinking and acting beyond my own existing habits. It calls for a particular person or group's simultaneously passive welcoming and active change.

This kind of moral disruption is different from saying that the other is to be recognized as another social agent. The language of agency is one of the central moral languages of much talk about childhood today. However, as we saw in chapter 2, humanity is not reducible to agency even as a simple ontological fact. Human beings are also, and at the very same time, passively shaped by societies and one another. Agency is always tied up with vulnerability, in childhood and adulthood both.

The ethics of agency arises, in fact, chiefly from modernity. Because of this, it can understand ethical otherness only in the sense of "othering": as having agency taken away. Children can of course act in their worlds for themselves just as much as can adults. But children are excluded from societies, not simply because they are not afforded sufficient agency, but more profoundly because they are not welcomed as society's passive-active others. The more fundamental ethical fact is not agency but disruption.

Neither can excluding the other, ethically speaking, be overcome by negating the self. A radically deconstructive ethics of the other tends to make this self-ab-negating claim. Overcoming modernity is sometimes thought to necessitate over-coming selfhood as such. One influential ethicist argues, for example, that the oth-er requires selfhood to be "taken hold of from without, seized by something else . . . [in a way that] that knocks me out of orbit."[3] Otherness becomes all-powerful.

If, however, responsibility to others demanded a purely passive self, this would be a disaster above all for children. No child merely asks for my ethical vertigo or deconstruction. She asks instead for my new response. A child obliges me in a more complex way to enter into other-responsive self-creativity. Rather than knocking me out of orbit, my orbit should be further expanded. The other in their otherness should form, not my only but my *second* center of meaning. A pure ethics of decon-struction assumes that others do not rely on the initiatives of selves and societies. It makes otherness selfhood's opposite. As children demonstrate, however, other-ness does not call for breaking moral relations so much as for their endlessly more radical stretching out.

Ethical disruption in light of childhood should be understood, in other words, as not linear but circular. It does not move unilaterally either from or against the self. Rather, disruption by the other calls, in the same moment, for self-disruption in response. As Richard Kearney has described it, "the challenge . . . is to envisage the existence of a narrative self prepared to work through the pain of the past in dialogue with its Others."[4] The other calls for the self's both passive responsive-ness and active responsibility. It calls for a dynamic ethical circle of shared world-creativity. My own world of meaning must be recreated ever anew in response to the singular world-creativity of others. The other's disruption of me should lead to my own widening horizons. My narrative of myself must stretch out in openness to the irreducibility of others to it.

THE OTHER AS DECENTERING THE SELF

The difference between aims and obligations in ethics is that the former expand the self's circle of meaning over time around the self at the center, while the latter disrupt or distort the self around the second center of another. The other never becomes the self, not even another self just like me. Indeed, in a certain sense, the self is also other to itself and should treat itself accordingly. But neither can the self ever fully extend itself toward the other. Rather, otherness introduces a new kind of creative tension into moral life, one that expands the self in the new sense of asym-metrically distorting it. It calls the self to new self-creation beyond what it could ever have imagined or anticipated alone.

This kind of obligational moral creativity can be described as moral life's de-centering into an ellipse: a circle with not just one center but two. The self's moral world should become like the orbit of the Earth around the Sun, a distended circle with a second invisible focus, as in the following figure.

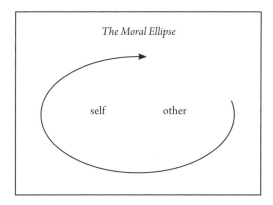

The self is responsible for its own asymmetrical decentering by orbiting its life around not just itself but also others in their irreducible otherness. Morally speaking, otherness is the self's irreducible second center. The Greek *ellipsis* means "absent" or "left out." The root is the same as that for the grammatical ellipsis: The other should be a moral . . . to me. It should interrupt me by its moral absence or irreducibility. It is not merely present to my understanding but also utterly escapes it. From the point of view of ethical obligations rather than aims, circular relations to others should distort and disrupt the self around double or multiple centers of creativity.

Decentering is not exactly the same as discourse. An ethics of discourse, such as that of Jürgen Habermas, assumes the largely adult perspective of a subject fully experienced in social argumentation. It obliges the free and equal participation of all in social dialogue. The other is included in Habermasian discourse theory only insofar as the other can take advantage of intersubjective procedures of social rationality. Habermas describes the basic ethical obligation as follows: "Only those norms can claim to be valid that meet (or could meet) with the approval of all affected in their capacity *as participants in a practical discourse*."[5] This capacity for discourse makes a number of adult-biased assumptions: ability to explicate one's own and others' social claims, experience in approving or disapproving of them, practice in practical discourse itself, and means to carry it out through language proficiency, use of media, and political education.

Children can in fact participate in social discourse. The problem is that, as a group, they have less experience than adults in doing so. Perhaps adults can stand in for children; but in this case children are objects of discourse and no longer actual participants. Perhaps children can participate on their own behalf. However, on the whole children's relatively fewer experiences in the world means that their participation is relatively less likely to change the debate. No matter how open or plural a society may be, children will generally rely more than adults on social discourse being conducted for them. Under a schema of discursive procedures, no matter how fair or inclusive, children will always be systematically marginalized.

A newborn can hardly discourse publicly at all (in Habermas's sense). A six-year-old may stand in less strong a position to consider the legitimacy of something like going to war (even though children are as affected by war as anyone else). But adults too have varying discursive experience and power in social argumentation. The fact that at least a third of humanity requires discourse to be carried out significantly on its behalf undermines the claim of discourse ethics to include the participation of all. Habermas argues that discourse ethics is for "restoring a consensus that has been disrupted."[6] But for children—and, indeed, for anyone insofar as they are other—it should be just as much the other way around: restoring disruption to what has become consensus.

Much less can moral decentering be reduced to John Rawls's widely influential procedures of social fairness. Rawls imagines that a just society can be founded on each self following rules of impartiality. In his view, individuals should place a metaphorical "veil of ignorance" over their own particular situations in society in order to imagine what it would mean to treat other persons equally and fairly.[7]

No self could entirely set apart their own interpretations in this way. But even to the extent that it may be possible, it is in principle *more* possible the more experience one has had of relations with others and society. One does not generally expect children to exhibit the same impartiality as their elders. What is more, the less one has the resources to represent one's own voice, the less others exercising fairness are likely to recognize one's voice and interests in the first place. Children like Anderson are systematically excluded from Rawlsian justice in two interconnected ways: They are less likely to have their social interests understood by others; and they are less experienced in the processes of social fairness that might correct this kind of marginalization. Impartiality understood as a rationalizing procedure is in fact unavoidably partial.

Discourse, fairness, and justice all depend on a more profound moral fact: that it is possible to respond to one another's irreducible otherness. The other does not decenter selves and societies merely through participation, but in a more dynamically elliptical way through the disruption of selves' and societies' basic assumptions. Moral life requires not just agency but a passive-active relation of self and other that allows for the creation of unanticipated new relations. The other must disrupt the hermeneutical or narrative circle of moral life by demanding that it shift toward as yet undiscovered moral terrain.

Moral life's decentering responsibility is of necessity endless and uncharted. It sets the self on previously unimagined trajectories of meaning. It does not eviscerate self-narration, but demands new self-narration that has been stretched toward being narrated also in response to the other. The Tony Andersons, Annabelle Joneses, and Anne Franks of the world do not narrate me in the same way that I narrate myself. Rather, they narrate me in the redoubled or elliptical sense of demanding my own self-narration from a second disrupting center. Responsiveness to the other is simultaneously deconstructive and reconstructive, undoing selfhood and reinventing it anew. The self is not called by the other to less self-creativity but rather to more: to greater self-innovation and self-transformation in light of others' differences.

Indeed, the self should gain as many centers of meaning as there are others in the world. It is obliged to decenter itself, not only endlessly by *each* other, but also endlessly by *every* other. The self's narrative orbit is to be reshaped by the gravitational pull of all others near and far. Some others may have larger legitimate claims on myself, such as my own child in contrast with a neighbor's, or a starving child in contrast with a well-fed one. But overall, the call from others is infinite and never able fully to be met. It can only shape me to one degree or another. A totally disrupted or deferred self would make no difference to anyone at all. It would especially not respond to the otherness of a child, who asks for my deeper rather than dislocated selfhood, my self-broadening rather than self-abnegating response. I should create my own narratives and worlds of meaning with growing responsiveness to the multiple othernesses around me.

"HERE I AM"

Emmanuel Levinas calls this kind of ethical responsibility to otherness a demand that I stand before the other in the attitude of "here I am" (*me voici*). The "I" is placed in the "accusative," as he calls it, both grammatically as the object of the other and morally as being required to respond. It is in this naked "face to face" that the other as other commands me. "My exposure to another in my responsibility for him takes place without a decision on my part. . . . It is exposure to the openness of a face . . . a passivity more passive still than the passivity of matter."[8]

The face of the other, for Levinas, is not first of all the recipient of my response, but rather its ethical origin. The other confronts me unexpectedly, disrupting what I think my response should have been. The other commands my "hospitality" to its otherness and even my "expiation."[9] And ultimately, for Levinas, my response of "here I am" before the other exposes me to the other as a trace of the Wholly Other, issuing the ethical command from infinity.[10]

This "here I am" in Levinas does not, however, go quite far enough: It does not reach the responsiveness required either toward or of children. It is true that, beyond reason and discourse, I must expose myself to each child's unspoken otherness. What could be a more powerful response to children's social marginalization than opening oneself to their moral "faces"? The problem, however, as the quotation above indicates, is that Levinas understands this "here I am" as reducing the self to an absolute "passivity." The other person becomes my all-powerful God. Can a totally passive conception of responsibility call me to feed this child, rescue that one from war, teach this other one about the world, encourage yet another to find her own voice? No, because it does not require me actively to transform myself, to recreate my own life in a more fully responsive way.

We can see the problem here by examining Levinas's biblical illustrations of this "here I am." For in many of its most crucial instances, the ethical response "here I am" in the Bible is not only to God or to others generally but to or from children. Levinas touches on children in his symbolism of the other as "the stranger, the widow, and the orphan."[11] But, this symbolism of "orphans" tends to remain abstract. There are no actual orphans in Levinas's writings.

The very first and most important "here I am" in the Bible takes place in the story of Abraham and his son Isaac. Abraham says "here I am" three times, structuring his own shifting narrative path at Mount Moriah: once to God, when God commands Isaac's sacrifice; once to Isaac, when Isaac asks where the sacrificial offering is; and once to the angel who at the last moment stays Abraham's hand as he is about to kill his son. Without the central "here I am" to his son, Abraham's story would lack moral integrity or pathos. It would simply tell of Abraham's complete obedience to God's orders. The second "here I am" to Isaac is Abraham's only (if inadequate) ethical moment amid an otherwise ethically horrifying tale. It is the "here I am" to his son that makes Abraham an ethical person, one accountable not only to God but also to humanity.

Of course, we do not find any meaningful agency in Isaac himself, and his voice is limited only to the question he asks his father. He is merely led and bound. Nevertheless, Abraham's "here I am" to Isaac, insofar as it is ethical, is far from being merely passive. Rather, it shows a complex inner struggle to give his son some kind of meaningful response. Because Isaac is his child, Abraham cannot simply receive his moral demand but must also give some response to it of his own. If there is moral failure on Abraham's part, it is that he does not remake himself enough. Furthermore, Abraham is not even passive before God, for God's command requires that he act.

Another important use of the phrase "here I am" in the Hebrew Bible is when it is spoken by a child himself, Samuel, first in answer to the call of God, and second in answer to his master Eli. It involves his own taking on social responsibility, a little like in the childhood prophesy of Jeremiah.[12]

The only time "Here I am" appears in the New Testament gospels is in the response of Mary to the angel Gabriel upon hearing that she will give birth to Jesus, her first child. "Here I am" may be the only possible response to what Gabriel himself recognizes must seem to her "impossible": her virginal and, as it turns out, divine motherhood. Here again the other in question is paradigmatically a child— indeed, the story claims, God *as* child. As for just about any parent, the news of a coming child is one of the greatest of ethical calls to respond "here I am." Again, in contrast to Levinas, the response is not simply passive or "accusative." It is also a call for new activity and new selfhood. In Mary's case, the "here I am" marks the origin simultaneously of her motherhood and her discipleship, her activity of welcoming a child into the world and her recreating herself in ways she cannot anticipate.

As these illustrations suggest, children may be the ethical other par excellence. It is before children that humanity is most profoundly called upon to respond "here I am." This is not because children are somehow more pure and innocent than adults, or that they are truer embodiments of God. Nor, on the contrary, is it because they are in special need of discipline and care. It is because children most fully embody the demand to give others one's own new response. Children are at once the most easily ignored and the most morally disruptive other. They make the sharpest command for selves and societies to open and remake themselves.

In light of childhood, the ethical "here I am" is therefore an obligation to create a more expanded other-self relation. The responsible self is not so much uncentered as decentered. The kind of openness called for by another, whether child or adult, is not self-denial but self-expansion. Likewise, both children and adults are obliged by others not merely to negate themselves but to grow.

THE OTHER'S CREATIVITY

The moral command of the other is therefore that my own narrative in the world be created not only by myself but also, and at the same time, by the other. One could say, continuing the biblical symbolism discussed above, that children as others are the fullest images of a Creator, now appearing to command humanity's ever-renewed fruitfulness and multiplication. To respond "here I am" to the other is to open myself to self- and social recreation in light of the other's particular other-creativity of the world. The self's ethical decentering is a response to the other as a singular child and image of God, a gift of irreducible newness in the world. The face of the other endlessly and unfathomably stretches out my own orbit of moral imagination. As Lisa Guenther has put it, "the emergence of this child demands a responsibility that it also makes possible, simply by showing its face."[13] The face of a child is paradigmatic of the demand that I recreate myself anew in response to each new other.

Children too are obliged by this self-creative responsibility. For each child is a world-creative self capable of greater self-decentering in response to others. Children least of all should be required to make themselves merely passive before others. If children's orbits of meaning cannot always be morally disrupted to the same degree as those of adults, this is not because children bear no responsibility at all. It is because the worlds that children are as yet able to create are relatively smaller in scope, being constructed around relatively fewer experiences of relations to others in the first place.

But children can and should recreate themselves in response to their creation by others. Just like adults, they too are called upon to increase rather than decrease the expansiveness of their world of relations. A newborn has already begun to create social worlds decentered by others as he or she responds to parents and siblings, takes in new meanings and cultures, and begins an ever changing lifelong journey of moral growth. The more experience one has of others in the world, the more one should be expected in principle to disrupt oneself and respond to them. Responsibility is a matter of degree rather than kind. For everyone, it should grow rather than shrink over time.

The other does not create me solely, for I am also created by myself—as well as by my society, history, biological nature, and many other factors. Human beings share a buzzing narrative world shaped in many directions. What otherness adds to this moral circulation is the obligation for me to recenter the world I inhabit in response to the irreducibly other centers of world creativity around me. I should say to the other: "Here I am, ready also to be created by you." In a way, each other is my Creator, another origin of my moral being. But I can embrace the other as making demands on me only by remaking myself. I can treat others as other only by expanding my own always limited moral horizons.

ONE ANOTHER'S DESTRUCTION

If humanity is capable of this kind of other-responsiveness, then why from the day it enters the world does it inevitably everywhere fall short? What can be learned from childhood about the origins of humanity's equally unfathomable other-dehumanization? The answers from history explored in chapter 1 are each incomplete, for the reasons we have examined. Can an elliptical perspective based on other-responsiveness learn from childhood more fully?

I spoke in chapter 2 of a basic or ontological "evil" of humanity as world creativity's opposite: world destruction. This evil, I argued, involves a simultaneously active depravity and passive deprivation that conspire in moral life's constant fixation and narrowing. From birth each self begins not only to create meaning but also to starve itself and be starved by others of wider meaningful potential. Active and passive evil are intrinsically related because human being itself is active and passive. It is not separate from the world but a socially embodied being-in-the-world. Humanity already finds itself at birth in an ethical spiral that destroys humanity.

Evil becomes even more complicated when we consider what it could mean for moral obligations. For now the kind of destruction at play is not just of the self but of the creative connection between self and otherness. The opposite of self-decentering is not self-centeredness. The point of responding to others is not to destroy the self but to expand it. But neither does evil consist in losing the self to the other. For the other demands that it make a difference precisely to the self. The moral problem consists, rather, in the self's creating a response to the other that is not expansive but narrowing. In this case, humanity's creative imperative undermines itself. Moral destructiveness is tragic. It uses the self's creative potential to destroy not just the self or the other but the possibility for a growing relation between them.

For example, as I have already suggested, one of the profoundest problems facing children today, in rich and poor countries alike, is the unprecedented means of mass media to manipulate children's lives and imaginations. Enola Aird has argued that not only does the media create endless desires in children, just as in adults, but it also specifically targets children in order to create within them a "lifetime brand loyalty."[14] Why is this practice ethically problematic? It is not exactly because children are not treated as agents; on the contrary, it is their agency in which advertisers are most interested. Nor is it because the adults in charge of advertising and its regulation, including government and parents, are not unaware of the fact that harm is being done. The moral problem is that the relation of advertisers to children is unresponsive to what makes children other and distinctive. Rather than acting differently in light of children's particular vulnerabilities, mass media seeks to take advantage of them for its own narrow purposes. In the process, whatever other benefits it creates, it also becomes a destructive force for children and society.

Let us turn to Levinas again for a starting point in clarifying the underlying moral problem. For in the Levinasian schema, the face of the other calls me specifically *not* to do its otherness violence. It is essentially a prohibition. The other is what Levinas calls "otherwise than being." The other is of a different moral order than the ordinary give and take of the world. Without responsibility, "*esse* [or being] is *interesse*; essence is interest. . . . War is the deed or the drama of the essence's interest."[15] The world as it actually *is*, in other words, is on some level violent through and through. Ordinary states of affairs reduce otherness to sameness.

This account works for children up to a point. It is, again, an advance on traditional premodern and modern perspectives. Children, after all, are perhaps the most susceptible group to being done violence by the ordinary course of human relations. A world structured purely around the competition of interests—as in the current state of mass media advertising—would favor those with the most experience and power to advance them.

But, we must ask, does the opposite of responsibility to children lie in the self's and society's being as such? And, is it fair to imply that children therefore start out life fundamentally violent before they grow in other-responsiveness? Does not Levinas enjoin a rather Kantian top-down view of humanity as by nature initially corrupt? Broadly speaking, does moral evil, in the sense of the failure of moral obligation, require selves to transcend their own very being?

Reducing evil to violence ultimately makes it impossible to understand either how adults should respond to children or how children can be moral themselves. A strict dualism of selfhood and otherness, being and responsibility, agency and passivity, does not permit their self-creative relation. Violence is not answered by negating the world as such. It is answered by expanding worldly creativity.

The opposite of ethical responsibility is not violence but destruction. From the day each of us is born, we both create and destroy our worlds. In most circumstances, a newborn both fills her parents' hearts with joy and makes their lives more difficult. Likewise, a parent does their best to respond to their child by making as good a life for her as they can, but in the process inevitably also constricts and harms her. The problem again is tragic. Human evil does not lie in human being as such, but in human being's self-defeating capacity for its own dehumanization. The capacity to create worlds—in this case in response to otherness—also inevitably, to one degree or another, devolves into destroying them. Destruction is creativity fallen short.

The failure to respond to otherness is neither a simple assertion of selfhood nor a simple loss of selfhood. It is a failure of the self to create the other a sufficiently self-decentered response. It is not moral creativity's nonuse but rather its misuse, not its negation but rather its privation. Responsibility to some extent always fails. Few know this more poignantly than adults responsible for children. Good and evil are not two forces at war, locked in a Manichean dualism of responsibility and being. The more profound human experience, starting in childhood, is that evil is part and parcel of humanity's very efforts to do good in the world. It is a perversion or disease of the fundamentally positive human possibility for creating meaningful relations. Those who do the greatest evil—the Hitlers and Maos of the world—do so thinking they are doing the greatest good. Those who do the greatest good, the Gandhis and Mother Theresas, do so admitting how acutely they have fallen short.

The other commands that I recreate my own relations to them ever more expansively. While I always extend myself toward them too narrowly, I am also always capable of greater responsiveness. The problem is not that everything I do is mired in violence, however much this is certainly the case. The problem, in a deeper sense, is that I never sufficiently exercise my ability to create a fuller response. I never do what I could for Annabelle Jones, even if I do something. Evil is the incapability for imagining such things as how to provide children with better protections and resources. It is wrapped, as Hannah Arendt says, in its own unending banality, the banality of not going further than one does.

SOCIAL REPRODUCTION

In the remainder of this chapter I expand on this concept of decentering responsibility in three areas: interpersonal relations, social justice, and universal love. Each of these areas of moral obligation is used to point toward some of the possible meanings of responding creatively to otherness.

In the most immediate area of interpersonal relations, consider again the eight-year-old girl Ying Ying Fry, who was adopted from China as an infant. Her story involves many different intersecting relationships: to her unknown biological mother and family; as an infant to her new American parents; as an eight-year-old to herself as an infant; to her parents when she is eight; to the readers of her book; and so on. Relations to others are multiple, complex, and overlapping, and they pull selves toward others in many directions at once.

Fry's relations with her parents are particularly instructive for us here. Fry is able to open herself as an infant and growing child to the particular lives of her parents. And her parents are able to open their own worlds up to new and unanticipated decentering by the unique experiences introduced into it by Fry. They are able to journey together to explore her unknown past, to enter into her unanticipated questions and feelings, to imagine what her first months might have been like, to inhabit the blank space of her absent family of origin, and to create a new family among themselves. Each of these are aspects of Fry's and her parents' irreducible otherness, to which Fry and her parents are able to create new responses. Fry's parents in particular neither merely impose their own meanings on the evolving relationship nor step back as if afraid that they could only do her harm. Instead, they respond to each other as singular others.

Morally speaking, immediate relations to others demand what could be called social reproduction. While from an adult point of view this metaphor might suggest the mere replication of the self, here I use it along lines implied by the biological reproduction of children to evoke the creation of a new relation to an entirely other human being. One self is made into two; two are made into three; and so on. To quote Alfred North Whitehead, in a different context, "the many become one, and are increased by one."[16] Immediate relations of self and other are not based on selfhood or otherness alone, but on the capacity to give birth to shared new meaning. As in biological reproduction, moral reproduction is both actively done and passively undergone. The other recreates me through the relation's invisible umbilical uncoiling.

To live a life unresponsive to the others with whom one interacts is to narrow not only others but also oneself. It is to constrict the scope of one's own possible humanity. Just as Fry's parents embrace their own changing lives, selves can reproduce themselves in fuller ways by being changed by others in their otherness. Responsibility is not just a laudable altruism but a widening of one's being-in-the-world.

Social reproduction is elliptical. It does not treat others merely as objects on which to impose my own ideals; nor as wholly separate subjects; nor, finally, as dialogue partners in development. In a more complex way, the other—and paradigmatically the child—stands in a moral tension with the self by demanding wider moral relations. What can change and grow over time is how far the other decenters the self. As H. R. Niebuhr has said, a responsible self "comes to knowledge of itself in the presence of other selves and . . . its very nature is that of a being which lives in response to other selves."[17] Or, in more elliptical terms, a responsible self approaches the other as its own second center of meaning. The other is morally present as an irreducibly second focal point for myself—a presence that is also an absence—that calls for an always more expanded response than has yet been formed.

A responsible response to the other is to this particular other: an other also constituted by a concretely evolving narrative life of its own. A child does not ask me simply to be bowled over by her absolute alterity. She is not just *the* orphan but *this particular* orphan. She asks that, in responding to her, I do so in relation to her own distinctive history, ancestry, birth, infancy, personality, hopes, and anxieties. It is only in relation to the other's unique and changing narrativity—and not just otherness in general—that it is possible for the self truly to expand itself. When singularity is considered from the point of view of childhood, it becomes impossible to brush aside its particular being-in-the-world. The task is to account for this concreteness as fully as possible.

Others populate everyday life and oblige one endlessly to retell one's own complex life story. Self-narration should embrace its own asymmetrical narration by others, its moral reproduction through other's newness. As Bonnie Miller-McLemore has said of caring for children as a parent, there "is a wisdom that somehow emerges in the chaos, stops us dead in our tracks, and heightens our awareness."[18] This wisdom is not that everything I knew and felt before is wrong. It is that, in light of childhood, relations can expand previously settled horizons. They can be shaped by each other's gravitational pull. Others too are centers of meaning that should stretch me out further—without destroying me as another other—toward ever wider relations. Moral responsibility transforms us into Silas Marners who take in orphans only to find our little worlds reborn.

SOCIAL JUSTICE

Sofia Monim, ten years old and the eldest of five children in a poor family in Sudan, has the job of collecting water several times a day for her family. As Cindi Katz tells her story in *Growing Up Global*, Monim is small and timid and must jostle with the other children who crowd around the local well fetching water.[19] Monim's job helps her family survive but also keeps her from attending school. The village's gradual development over the years has had both positive and negative results for its children. Those who collect water, like Monim, save time because of the construction of a more accessible pipeline. Those who fetch wood for their families now have to spend more time doing so because environmental degradation means the wood is farther away. But in either case, work takes the place of education and makes it more difficult for children to lift themselves out of poverty.

In the realm of broader ethical relations, responding to others comes face to face with the power of social systems. It almost goes without saying that historical injustice has systematically marginalized a great many others, especially children. Feminists have rightly argued that narrow definitions of social justice have prevented women and girls from having a say in defining what is just and fair in the first place. As long as men hold central social, political, economic, and cultural power, women's otherness will only receive its due from the point of view of men; that is, it won't receive its full due at all. Similar claims can be made along the lines of race, ethnicity, and class. How much more so, then, must social justice work to make itself responsive to childhood.

Considering children like Monim makes understanding justice especially problematic. A newborn has less power to make her voice heard in society, no matter how equal that society may be. A four-year-old is unlikely to have broad enough experience to assert her own social claims as much as an adult. A ten-year-old like Monim should not be expected to form political arguments or organizations purely on her own behalf. Recognizing these limitations of social and political capability is not to marginalize children or to say that they lack social agency. Clearly Monim's social agency is great. It is to say that children will not gain social justice if to do so they have to act as if they were adults. The problem for children is that historical understandings of social justice itself, even current ones, are primarily centered on the experiences and perspectives of adults, thus requiring childist reimagining.

It is in the area of larger social systems that considerations of childhood have arguably led to children's greatest historical dehumanization. Plato believes, as already mentioned, that children's utter unruliness requires that society tell them the "noble lie" that, by nature, they are born into a fixed social class.[20] Any sense of inventiveness allowed to take root in childhood, Plato believes, would lead society into chaos or tyranny. Aristotle places children at the bottom of his ideal social hierarchy, aristocracy, because, as "part of" their parents, "the product belongs to the producer."[21] The order of moral reason dictates that wise aristocrats should rule over adult male heads of households, husbands over wives, and parents over children. Even Jesus's welcoming of children as the first in the kingdom of heaven does not actually challenge children's status as "the least among us" in this world. Quite often in history, children's social marginalization has been justified by a supposedly elevated place in the beyond.

Modernity, too, defines social justice on chiefly adult grounds. Locke insists, as we have seen, that because children only gradually develop reason, their greatest social virtue is not liberty but obedience: "He that is not used to submit his will to the reason of others, when he is young, will scarce hearken or submit to his own reason, when he is of an age to make use of it."[22] Rousseau emphasizes the bottom-up necessity of cultivating children's natural inner self-love so that it has the strength to withstand social corruption. But this means, he argues, that children must be barred from the larger social world until they grow up, in order that they can remain for as long as possible in a state of private nature.[23] Kant claims that children's lack of higher moral autonomy makes them slaves to lower animal desires and thus bereft of any capability for "generosity" or "duties toward others." On the contrary, for the sake of social justice, "everything in education depends upon establishing correct principles, and leading children to understand and accept them."[24]

None of these founding modern theorists of social justice resolves the kinds of injustices found in the lives of children like Sophia Monim, Ying Ying Fry, or Ishmael Beah. These children are not simply parts of larger social hierarchies, nor are they merely free or autonomous individuals. More importantly, they are bound up with systems of social power that are unresponsive to their particular otherness. It is through wider exercises of power, for example, that Beah's family life is destroyed and that he comes to be drafted to fight in war. It is also through larger organizations like UNICEF that he is rescued and given the opportunity to express his own voice. Children are not mere playthings of power, but they reveal the great depths to which power shapes all human lives, even as those lives remain particular and creative. Selves are neither wholly dependent on nor independent of social systems, but rather thoroughly interdependent.

A response to power that included children would not rest content with extending to all equal social agency. In such a system, children would still be marginalized, as diverse agents with differing amounts of experience in the world competed for social influence. Rather, a child-inclusive society would be one able to decenter itself around even its most vulnerable others. It may be adults who are primarily responsible for bringing about widescale social justice—though far from entirely—because they generally have more experience and resources to do so. But the underlying moral obligation is to expand rather than contract the sphere of social inclusiveness in light of those most easily left out of it.

SOCIAL EXPANSION

A good and just society is therefore a matter of its expansiveness, its ability to respond to difference. It is one that contains practices and mechanisms of disruption and decentering that enable it to expand itself to include its own greatest possible creativity by otherness. It is something like this kind of expansiveness that Martin Luther King Jr. argues from his jail cell in Birmingham, Alabama is the ultimate goal of social justice: "to create the kind of tension in society that will help men rise from the dark depths of prejudice and racism to the majestic heights of understanding and brotherhood."[25] The goal of justice is not simply to oppose power, but to turn destructive social tensions into creative social tensions that are more radically inclusive of difference. As societies reproduce themselves in response to their actual lived diversities, they are able to transcend narrow abuses of power and stretch themselves toward their own more fully shared humanity.

Children can stand up to social oppression for themselves. For example, seven-year-old Linda Brown was instrumental in instigating the *Brown v. Board of Education* decision in 1954 that desegregated American schools. Of course, Brown was surrounded by others in her cause: her father (for whom the case is named), family, lawyers, activists, a liberating culture, democratic institutions, and a moment in history without which she could not have done what she did. The decentering of the American school system was not just the result of individuals exercising their liberties. More fundamentally, it was the result of individuals and groups expanding their own and their society's moral imaginations to include previously marginalized others in shared new horizons. Taking responsibility for children like Brown and Monim involves remaking social structures in ways that are more rather than less responsive to others' obscured voices and experiences. It requires social systems to open up to greater disruption by otherness.

The purpose of networks of social relations is not to overcome natural violence with social constraint, nor to welcome natural innocence into overcoming social corruption. Thomas Hobbes is only half right when he says that life in a state of nature would be "solitary, poor, nasty, brutish, and short." It would be more accurate to say that it would be oppressive, narrow, and exclusionary.

The reason for social structures, from an ethical point of view, is to expand systems of interdependent relations as diversely as possible. The worth or value of social systems should be judged by the degree of their other-responsiveness. Social justice is measured by the extent to which social systems multiply the centers of meaning through which they are created. A noncentered society (anarchy) would be just as oppressive as a single-centered society (totalitarianism). Both extremes deny what children above all teach: that otherness demands that societies' centers of power be as responsive to difference as possible.

The next chapter will develop this conception of social justice in light of a new interpretation of human rights. But a broader illustration can be provided by noting some of the ways in which social justice has been extended or contracted in the moral history of the United States. Creative decentering is evident, for example, in the country's founding constitutional expansion of political power from the aristocracy to white male landowners; the subsequent widening of voting rights after the Civil War to include African American men and, in the twentieth century, women; the provision toward the end of the nineteenth century of education not only to well-off children, but to children universally; more recent processes of racial desegregation and of women's increasing economic and cultural opportunities; and, more recently still, legal protections for children against violence in the home and for a social voice. In each of these cases, moral progress consists in having found a way to expand cultures and policies beyond what had previously been imagined. In each case, social justice means responding to a wider diversity of otherness within a group. Others become newly creative centers of the whole social dynamics.

In contrast, social narrowing or destruction has included the disenfranchisement of Native Americans; centuries of slavery in which economic gain for some came at the price of the disempowerment of others; women's and children's economic marginalization as they were separated into a private sphere during industrialization; declining opportunities for the working classes in late-nineteenth-century laissez-faire capitalism; the failure in the twentieth century to extend needed health insurance and social security beyond the elderly (who can fight for it for themselves) to children (who often cannot); a recent growing de facto school segregation; and children's increasing rates of incarceration for crime, instead of rehabilitation. In such instances, the social imagination becomes narrowed. The particular experiences and capabilities of others become more profoundly excluded. What could have been created among diverse ways of life is destroyed by habit, complacency, obtuseness, bigotry, divisiveness, or fear. Social power is consolidated instead of diversified.

The more demanding and rewarding path has always been for social systems to decenter themselves by wider and more dynamic social creativity. It has been to fashion together a more perfect union, a fuller *e pluribus unum*, a richer and more other-responsive sharing of power.

A perfectly just society cannot be known in advance because no one person or group can anticipate the results of inclusive social creativity. But it is possible to articulate justice's direction, which is to increase other-responsiveness. From a childist point of view, the moral ideal is not maximum autonomous freedom but maximum social decentering. As related to one another, others are owed society's most creatively distended response possible. I alone cannot achieve this response to the others in my society by myself. I will never as an individual be able to feed all the poor, give care to all the sick, attend to all the homeless, protect all the vulnerable, hear all the ignored, tell all the stories. For this effort, others need social structures. Insofar as these structures remain unresponsive to difference, they remain narrow and unjust. Insofar as they are other-decentered, they achieve some measure of the fullness of their own possible humanity. Social justice is the obligation to reproduce the structures and narratives of societies in ways creative of wider social creativity.

TRANSFORMING LOVE

No one can know exactly where moral decentering should ultimately lead. To use a term from the anthropologist Victor Turner, moral responsibility is "liminal": It presses selves and societies into a constant ritual of the deconstructing and restructuring of human relations. Like bringing a child into the world, social responsibility sets me and you on new journeys toward the unknown. Like a Renoir brushstroke, each other in society refigures the whole canvas. The decentering of selves and societies in response to otherness is inherently open-ended. It is an endless coming of age.

This suggests that, as in previous chapters, moral life also presses the human imagination constantly toward its own beyond. Present horizons of understanding are both coordinates for shared life and boundaries needing to be transcended. In the previous two chapters, childhood pointed us toward human being's primordial origins and narrative timefulness. Now it brings us to the equally unfathomable borderland of others as other absolutely.

Such liminal horizons cannot be described literally, for they lie of necessity beyond any particular understanding. But they can be described symbolically or mythically, not as an alternative or hidden ethical basis, but as a stretching of the sense of obligation toward what I have been calling its impossible possibilities.

The hard work of attending to the particularity of childhood is not to be brushed aside by a human or divine rulebook. Rather, considerations of the beyond or the divine are useful for our purposes only insofar as they press moral life toward otherness in its inherent inscrutability. Otherness is never—and could never be—responded to fully. Self-decentering in response to others ultimately places into question all that the self actually knows and does. Yet, strangely, at the heart of being human, a wider response to others is nonetheless always also possible.

The ethical term that perhaps comes closest in Western religions to naming the self's unlimited obligation to the other is *love*. Love can of course mean many things, moral and otherwise. It can be reduced to either self-sacrifice, the other's suffocation in my own desires, the sentimental elevation of another's purity, or even the "tough love" of imposing on others my own values. But it can also involve a self-transforming response to others—and to oneself as another other. In this case, love is unending and excessive, constantly revealing new horizons of meaning, drawing selves and societies into journeys of self-transcendence. In response to children in particular, but also in response to any other, humanity is finally called upon to love by reimagining its own sense of humanity.

Such excess is encouraged in some of the symbolism of love in the Bible. The poetry of the Psalms and the Song of Songs is sometimes wild with divine intoxication, as the beloved other draws the poet toward the sublime. The prophets sometimes announce that, despite Israel's waywardness, God's love still persists. Paul's letters come back to the constant "how much more" of loving and hoping through grace. And the love command of Jesus involves extending love for one another even to one's enemies: "Love your enemies, do good to those who hate you, bless those who curse you, pray for those who abuse you."[26] In these and other instances, moral obligation is pressed toward its own scandalous superabundance. Human limits are stretched beyond what seems reasonable or possible.

But these excessive forms of love are always set within larger historical communities: a nation of Israel, a marriage, a social covenant, a community of disciples, a new humanity. They do not destroy ordinary human relations but demand their more radical transformation. "Love your enemies" immediately precedes Jesus's restatement of the ancient golden rule: "Do to others as you would have them do to you."[27] The golden rule is possibly the most ubiquitous moral norm in human history. But here one is reminded of its most extreme possible implications. Treating others as you would like to be treated yourself ultimately includes even the way you treat your enemies, those precisely trying to destroy you. They may be love's greatest test. Such excesses come not to destroy but to distend relations.

Moral love is not reducible, in this case, to the merely reciprocal give-and-take in which I should return what I receive. It requires the self to decenter itself whether the other responds in kind or not. I am obliged to respond to others with the radical degree of responsiveness that I myself would hope to receive from them. Doing to others "as you would have them do to you" ultimately turns the tables and puts me in the place of "the other," so that I may better experience what the other is truly owed by me.

The command is also not simply for self-sacrifice. The self remains in the equation, both as responsible self and owed other. Love means other-responsive self-decentering. It asks for two, not just one, centers of moral relations. It disrupts the orbit of moral self-understanding to the point of unfathomable excess in which other and self are truly related.

What if this other to be loved is a child? A child soldier taking me hostage, my own child, or a child in poverty? Love for a child in this moral sense is not love for otherness abstractly, but for this other in particular. And because of this, love is not just created by myself, but arises first of all from the other in its own particular otherness. The other creates my responsibility to love him. He commands me to love his concrete and timeful appearance in the world. It is not me but this particular child who initiates my endless decentering. This child is my own other moral center. And so, in a way, this child is a face of God, a trace of the beyond, issuing the love command to me from beyond my own world of meaning. If I must transform myself and my actions, it is because here stands before me a new and unanticipated creator of moral worlds.

LOVE'S HYPERBOLE

Our circular imagery ultimately suggests that love decenters selves hyperbolically. In geometry, a hyperbola is a form of ellipse, but one in which its second center "exceeds" (from the Greek *huperbole*) the orbit of its first, so that it never closes back in on itself. It opens or curves outward infinitely, disappearing into the beyond. The image of a hyperbole is a more child-inclusive way to revise the traditional concept of altruism or self-sacrifice. Love is hyperbolic, from a childist point of view, in that it includes a moment of self-opening excess. This excess is not the whole of love but its self-opening movement. It is not self-negating but self-stretching. What is hyperbolic is that self-other relations should on some level decenter the self beyond its own present limits. Relations demand always still more than can actually be imagined.

Love in this ethical sense does not break apart the self-other relation but invests it with infinite creative tension. Selves and societies are ultimately responsible for embarking on journeys of self-decentering that transcend what can possibly be anticipated. My responsibility toward the other should involve an experience of vertigo or liminality, in which certainty and meaning are placed into question. This infinite opening cannot, from a child-centered point of view, evict the self altogether, for then the child/other would receive no response from this particular self. The kind of love a child commands, morally, is not *any* response but *my* response—whether as parent, fellow member of society, or even stranger. The other decenters the self hyperbolically by asking the self to take the risk of extending its orbit of meaning beyond its own present course.

What is more, children too are called upon in exactly the same way to hyperbolically decenter themselves. The love command is also for children. Even the youngest child is obliged to exceed herself in response to others, to create new relations beyond her present horizons, to expand her own moral worlds. This possibility does not suddenly materialize at some "age of reason," but grows throughout life's increasing social experiences.

Likewise, for children, love is not merely self-sacrificial. Just as a child does not demand my self-destruction, nor should a child be required to destroy him- or herself for me. Rather, love is self-decentering. It is not destructive but creative. The other asks the self to enter into radically new relations. Love requires always still more precisely of a self.

Love is from this angle more complicated than sometimes imagined in postmodernity. Jean-Luc Marion has described ethical love as "two gazes, invisible forever, expos[ing] themselves each to the other in the crossing of their reciprocal aims."[28] This kind of "exposure" or "crossing" remains rather static. It falls short of the dynamics of genuine human interdependency. Moral responsibility toward a child is not only self-exposing but also self-transformative. I am to be deconstructed by the other by reconstructing myself. The relation is not just a crossing of two gazes but a widening of the moral circle. It stretches the self's gaze toward new and unknown horizons. Love expands a concretely existing relation in the world to include its creation not only by the self but also by the other.

The endlessness of love has been classically symbolized in Western traditions by myths of God. God appears in a glass darkly as my own greatest inner possibility. This God is the very epitome of love. God is a word or symbol that can be used to describe (among other things) what humanity ultimately aspires to when it aspires to love. From this angle, even though God cannot finally be known, human beings can be affirmed ultimately as images of God as love. Or, rather, they are broken images in need of their own transformation *toward* love. The image of God is a mirror in which to view the infinite depths of love that I might imagine are hidden within myself.

This moral symbolism for love's beyond can, by definition, take on an infinite variety of forms: father, mother, king, whirlwind, angel, son, and so on. The forms are infinite because something infinite is being described.It can also receive infinite possible interpretations. Phenomenologically speaking, God as love is a human experience: the experience of the possibility of loving still more. Selves should love one another, not just as they already do, but in a hyperbolic way that imitates the infinite kind of love that a Creator may be imagined to have for its creations. Human beings might then be affirmed as able to love one another in their ever fuller particular and concrete earthly otherness.

Love is an act of self-creativity. It is not only fruitful but multiplying. It not only enlarges the self's narrative circle but distends it around diverse creative centers and ultimately the otherness of all. Such love can be imagined, as John Chrysostom puts it, as a Creator's call for moral artistry: "To each of you fathers and mothers, I say, just as we see artists fashioning their paintings and statues with great precision, so we must care for these wondrous statues of ours."[29] Or again, as it has been pictured recently by Sallie McFague, God can mean loving parenthood: "We should become mothers and fathers to our world, extending those natural instincts we all have, whether or not we have children of our bodies (or adopted children), to . . . universal parenthood."[30] Such myths and symbols of love as divine artistry or parenthood allow selves to imagine themselves as able to exceed their own all too narrow horizons in response to difference.

Love in light of children is not self-serving or self-sacrificing but self-transforming. It does not change the world by imposing an already created narrative upon it from above, as if one or another tradition already contained the answer to all human relations. Nor does it transform the self solely through the other, as if the self did not also have to recreate itself in response. Nor can love finally rely on the gradual development of human relations over time. For at some point, especially in light of children, love must be disturbed by excess, by what disrupts understanding and stretches it outwards toward the unknown otherness of each and every world-creative other.

This means, at the end of our ethical trilogy, that other-responsiveness brings us full circle back to the beginning. For the ability to respond decenteredly to one another is finally an expression, though now in terms of moral obligation, of humanity's original world creativity. Human beings can extend themselves to one another in responsiveness and love only because they are born able to recreate their existing worlds of meaning anew. At bottom, selves can open themselves to being transformed by others because they are capable of self-transformation in the first place. Likewise, others continue to exceed selves because others are just as world-creative too. Moral relations can always stretch themselves beyond themselves. It is this possibility that, as in love both for and of a child, allows responsibility toward others always to expand and grow.

CONCLUSION

Obligational ethics can account for childhood only by moving beyond traditional hierarchies and modern individualism in all their various forms. Moral obligation is not about collectiveness or autonomy but responsiveness to the other. Childism calls for a moral poetics of otherness. Selves and societies are obliged by others to recreate their moral worlds ever more decenteredly. What unites children and adults as fellow moral beings is the requirement of expanding other-responsiveness, of the creation of a more differently inclusive humanity.

Children may on the whole have less experience of self-decentering, and adults in principle may therefore have wider obligations. But all human beings are obliged to open themselves up to the irreducibility of others in increasingly broad ways. This decentering responsibility—this making others second creators of one's own worlds—begins at birth and should grow throughout life without end. It does not reach some age of rational maturity but continues to be able to expand until death. It transcends present horizons and challenges the limits of moral imagination without end.

Our moral poetics thus takes on a third and still more ethically complex dimension. Chapter 2 argued that human being in light of childhood is circular in the simplest sense that each human being is born and lives in an already constructed moral world that he or she must also reconstruct into his or her own world of meaning. Chapter 3 showed that the ethical aim is to expand rather than contract the self's circle of relations with others over time toward an ever broader and more inclusive narrative whole. In this chapter we have seen that this circle also requires distortion or decentering. Another kind of expansion is called for in which selves and societies continually disrupt themselves in response to the second centers of meaning of others in their otherness. Moral life, in sum, is at once self-creative, self-narrative, and other-responsive. It demands, as childhood teaches, a growing imagination of humanity.

PART III

PRACTICE

Chapter 5

Human Rights in Light of Childhood

THE IDEAS OF THE previous three chapters have implications for any area of moral life. In the following three chapters I offer but three examples. The application of theory to practice is not a one-way street: theory sheds light on action just as understanding action changes theory—in a hermeneutical circle, as it were. However, if the ethics of childhood calls for anything, it calls for addressing moral relations not only abstractly but also in their practical concreteness.

I start in this chapter with the practice of human rights. I do so because despite being intended to unite humanity, "human" rights were in fact originally developed *not* to apply to the third of humanity who happen to be children. Indeed, the Enlightenment architects of human rights formulated them explicitly *over against* childhood, as a specific realm for adulthood. As a result, their application to children today has proven deeply problematic. Children have certainly held various human rights throughout history, and they increasingly do so in the contemporary world. Through documents like the 1989 United Nations Convention on the Rights of the Child, rights today are one of the most important ways to think about and improve children's lives. But the very concept of human rights is burdened by a profound antichild ethical basis. It has traditionally viewed human beings through the lenses of independence, autonomy, and individualism, which, it turns out, are not even true to adulthood.

If human rights are truly to be "human," and if they are to be less frustrated in their actual implementation, then they need to be fundamentally rethought in light of childhood. Only through a new childist ethical grounding can human rights hope to expand the actual humanity of societies. This will require thinking of them, not as freedoms, entitlements, or even expressions of agency, but as responses to social otherness. Rights are not protections of individual autonomy but expanders of interdependent creativity. Childhood must save human rights from itself.

HUMAN RIGHTS WITHOUT CHILDREN

Consider, for example, the legal right for persons to be heard in court. Legal rights are one instance of broader ethical rights. To be heard would seem to be one of the most basic human rights one could have, part of the right to due process and to having a social voice. It is protected for children specifically in Article 12 of the Convention on the Rights of the Child. Yet, as we saw in the case of Tony Anderson in the previous chapter, it is not particularly well applied to children. Anderson is denied the right to make his own views heard in court even in the face of the possibility of the court's termination of the parenting rights of his mother. As Lewis Pitts has pointed out, a child's right to be heard in court is not, as for adults, the same as their right to decide: the latter belongs only to the judge. Yet, even being heard is systematically denied children (and not adults) in most courts around the world because children are thought not to be capable of expressing what might be in their own best interests.[1]

The debate about whether this and other kinds of rights are owed to children is greatly hampered by a lack of understanding of what "rights" actually are. The evolution of human rights theory is a great deal more complex and disputed than often thought. On the one hand, those who challenge the idea that human rights (or some of them) might be applicable to children tend to reduce rights to simple expressions of freedom or individuality. On the other hand, those who defend children's rights have not seriously confronted the original historical arguments that children should not have them.

One could argue that human rights are not even products of modernity. Most accounts trace them to the earliest surviving rights document, the sixth-century BCE clay cuneiform Cyrus Cylinder, which not only guaranteed religious liberty (including, it is thought, for the biblical Jews then in Babylonian exile), but effectively abolished the institution of slavery across ancient Persia. The third-century BCE Buddhist nonviolent charter in India known as the Edicts of Ashoka established many social rights such as to uniform sentencing for prisoners. And European human rights law dates to at least medieval England, when King John was forced in 1215 CE to sign the Magna Carta, enshrining most famously the right to habeas corpus (i.e., to not be unlawfully imprisoned) as well as children's (though possibly only *adult* children's) rights not to be dispossessed of their inheritance.

Nevertheless, it is in Enlightenment modernity, starting in the seventeenth century, that human rights theory began to be developed in ethically systematic ways. But here we find, not a single view, but a significant diversity of human rights bases. And this diversity turns out to be connected with the three different attitudes toward children explored in chapter 1. For human rights' three most influential architects—John Locke, Jean-Jacques Rousseau, and Immanuel Kant—each happen to embrace, as we have seen, a different tradition of thought about childhood. What each believes about the nature of human rights is fundamentally and explicitly bound up with what each believes about childhood. It is these connections that need to be deconstructed if human rights today are to become fully human.

The first systematic human rights theorist is generally thought to be John Locke. His argument in *Two Treatises on Government* is that humanity's "natural rights," as he calls them, stem from the duty that each individual owes to its Maker to advance its own "self-preservation."[2] What persons must be allowed to preserve in society is what Locke calls their "property": in the broad sense of their life, liberty, and estate (belongings). The rights to "life, liberty, and the pursuit of happiness" in the United States' *Declaration of Independence* are directly Lockean in this sense. Rights provide individuals with the means to preserve their most basic natural being.

This view of human rights is entirely consonant with what we have already seen is Locke's equally influential view of childhood. Locke views children developmentally: as starting out life as white pages that need to be gradually molded over time toward enlightened social reason. By natural law, children have the same interest in self-preservation as anyone else—indeed, given their relative social weakness, an even greater interest. But, because they have not yet reached the age of reason, children lack the fully developed capacities to exercise social freedom without doing themselves and others harm.[3]

It is precisely because they too deserve preservation, then, that children cannot yet be granted societies' freedoms and rights. Children's rights would contradict the very purpose of rights in the first place. In fact, children should not only have no right to their own "property," Locke argues, but they should be the "temporary property" of their parents, who are the ones most likely able to ensure their self-preservation for them.[4] The paradox here can be explained by the fact that, for Locke, human rights are grounded in a *developed* capability for social reasoning, which, as available only to adults (indeed, he thought, only to landowning men), excludes children by necessity. Children demonstrate humanity's *potential* for social rights, but they are not yet ready to hold social rights themselves. This view remains widely prevalent today.

A century later, the eighteenth-century French philosopher Jean-Jacques Rousseau provides a different account of human rights, which one might expect, from what we have seen, to be more child-friendly. His more bottom-up way of thinking would seem to open up wider rights-inclusiveness. However, he too excludes children explicitly. Rights, in Rousseau's view, exist to enable persons to form societies according to their "general will," that is, their freely chosen collective agreement.[5] Against the tyranny of the powerful few, rights allow all to participate in a general social contract. This view informs the distinctively egalitarian and fraternal ideals of the French Revolution, as in the first article of its Declaration of the Rights of Man and of the Citizen: "Men are born and remain free and equal in rights. Social distinctions may be founded only upon the general good."

But the consequence is again paradoxical when it comes to children. As we have seen, Rousseau claims to have a high regard for childhood as the very origin of goodness in society, the source of all resistance to social corruption. But it is precisely because of this natural innocence, he argues, that children must be carefully sheltered from public life. Children do not possess the moral strength, hardened by worldly experience, to hold rights without becoming quickly corrupted. Children need to be nurtured for as long as possible in the private sanctity of the home, preferably by a sanctified mother and then a wise tutor, until such a time as their God-given goodness may be able to stand up for itself against vice and influence.[6] What is more, in an argument that has also been applied to women and minorities, society itself depends on children remaining in a separate private sphere, so that public life may continuously be infused with natural goodness over time. This privatization of pure childhood is another widely accepted view today.

Finally, a third grounding for human rights is provided by the late-eighteenth-century German philosopher Immanuel Kant, and along with it a third reason for systematically excluding children that continues to influence current assumptions. According to Kant, rights exist less to preserve natural liberties or to further the general will than to institute humanity's rational "autonomy," its capacity for moral self-legislation. Human beings are on one level just like animals: driven by irrational and heteronomous wants, instincts, needs, and desires. But on another level, they surpass animals in being capable of regulating their wants and desires by self-given rationality. They can transcend nature by imposing on it the duties of universal moral law. Each human being is owed rights because each ultimately possesses the dignity of being an autonomous moral lawgiver and therefore end in themselves. "He who violates the rights of men intends to make use of the person of others merely as means, without considering that, as rational beings, they must always be esteemed at the same time as ends."[7]

The one great exception again, however, turns out to be children. As we have seen, Kant views children as starting out life like animals: wholly captive to irrational wants and desires. Their morally autonomous higher reason has to be cultivated in a top-down fashion through education and discipline. The result in terms of rights is actually a little more complex than in Locke or Rousseau. On the one hand, children do in fact belong to the universal human rights community in the limited sense that they deserve to be treated as *objects* of dignity and respect. They have a certain inborn moral reason, however weak. "Hence parents cannot regard their child as, in a manner, a thing of their own making; for a being endowed with freedom cannot be so regarded."[8] On the other hand, only adults can be said to be *subjects* of human rights, since only they are in principle capable of using reason autonomously to legislate over their own desires. Only adults can be expected to be able to subordinate their animal instincts to higher moral law.

Thus, Kant too sees children as the exception (that proves the rule) to universal "human" rights. Indeed, he insists on "the right of the parents to the management and training of the child, so long as it is itself incapable of making proper use of its body as an organism, and of its mind as an understanding."[9] Children are not property, as in Locke; nor are they sequestered into the private sphere, as in Rousseau. Perhaps surprisingly, it is Kant's more authoritarian thinking that at least allows for a small measure of children's public dignity. But, all the same, children are to be confined to the rule of the home because they are not yet autonomous individuals capable of bearing the rights and duties that constitute citizenship.

To return to our example, history therefore provides at least three basic reasons why a thirteen-year-old like Anderson should not be heard in court. First, under Lockean assumptions, he lacks the maturity to be able to comprehend what is in his own best interests. These interests must be determined by adults, given their greater rationality. Second, under Rousseauian thinking, Anderson may know what is best for himself, but he is ignorant of the larger ways of the world. Someone older and more experienced, who has been tested and strengthened by participation in public life, must protect him from the dangers he cannot understand. Finally, from a Kantian perspective, Anderson does deserve to be treated with a modicum of human dignity. However, he is still largely beholden to immediate wants and desires and therefore lacks the moral discipline to make rationally autonomous choices for himself.

The very foundations of modern human rights theory are, as a result, utterly adult-centered. The chairs and tables are too high, the faucets out of reach, for children to be members of the human rights regime. In all three major justifications in modernity for why human beings should have rights, children end up lacking what Hannah Arendt has called (though in connection with other groups) "the right to have rights" in the first place. Because it is based on an imagined rational individuality, modern human rights theory is grounded precisely in *opposition* to childhood.

Of course, these kinds of grounds have been used to exclude other groups from human rights too, such as women, racial and ethnic minorities, and colonized non-Europeans. Public moral "rationality" can and generally will be defined narrowly by those with the power to impose their own images on society. However, while women and minorities have gradually been able to fight for social rights for themselves, by asserting their own moral rationality too, the modernistic foundations on which they can do so are inherently less available to children. So long as human rights are understood as expressions of social independence, then children will remain second-class citizens.

SPECTERS OF RIGHTS TODAY

One would expect that the past century, in which children's rights have made significant gains in actual practice, would see a correspondingly more child-inclusive progress in human rights theory. Few today would dispute that Anne Frank, for example, had a right to nondiscrimination and life, Ishmael Beah not to be recruited into war, altar boys not to be sexually abused by priests, Annabelle Jones to a decent education, and Ying Ying Fry to express her own voice through writing her book.

Strangely, however, contemporary human rights theory almost seems to have forgotten that children exist. With rare exceptions, human rights theorists today hardly even mention such a thing as childhood. If Locke, Rousseau, and Kant at least considered whether or not children are human rights subjects, their conclusion—that children are not—is now part of the white noise of human rights ethics. Rights are routinely ascribed to "men and women" as if that covered everyone. Thus, for example, one of the most widely read texts on human rights theory in recent years, Jack Donnelly's *Universal Human Rights in Theory and Practice*, based on a largely Kantian ethics of "individual autonomy," devotes exactly half a page, out of close to three hundred on "universal" human rights, to rights in relation to children, and then only to register surprise at how quickly the Convention on the Rights of the Child came into force.[10]

In contrast, during the same period of the twentieth century, many of the most important international human rights agreements and advances in national laws have been driven by concerns for children centrally. Lawyers and advocates "on the ground" have increasingly responded to children's poverty, needs for health care and education, discrimination, abuse, and lack of legal and social voice with explicitly human rights language. This disjuncture between theory and practice has been driven from both sides. Human rights theorists do not apply their work to children. And children's rights practitioners do not recognize human rights' deeply adult-centered premises.

There are currently three major ethical theories about the nature of human rights. (I leave aside the not unrelated question of how rights may be extended to animals and ecosystems.) Perhaps the most widely held of these comes out of Anglo-American analytic philosophy and is known as "will theory." Will theorists such as Donnelly, H. L. A. Hart, Alan Gewirth, and John Rawls argue—chiefly relying on Kant, but also on Locke—that human rights exist to protect individuals' social freedoms, liberties, or autonomy. Hart revived human rights ethics in the 1950s by arguing that all particular legal and social rights are based on one fundamental moral right: "the equal right of all men to be free."[11] The word "men" is understood here to apply also to "women" but not to "children." For, as Hart fully acknowledges without finding it controversial, rights belong only to "any adult human being capable of choice."[12] In accordance with the same reasoning as one finds in Kant, only adults have the rational capacities to express their wills or choices in society for themselves.

John Rawls is perhaps the most influential ethicist in this tradition. For him, the first and most important principle of social justice is that "each person is to have an equal right to the most extensive scheme of equal basic liberties compatible with a similar scheme of liberties for others."[13] A rights-holder, for Rawls, is anyone who has the capacity to place their own personal interests behind a "veil of ignorance" that ensures their objective impartially toward others. But impartiality requires experience of others in the world that allows one to put oneself in their different shoes. This capacity may in fact not belong to anyone at all (as Rawls's critics argue), since others are not reducible to what selves may be able to imagine about them. But it may belong least of all to those with the least worldly experience, namely, children.

As for Kant, will theorists such as these can certainly include children as human rights *objects*. Children too can be granted, according to this perspective, a basic set of rights to be treated without violence and with dignity and respect. However, children are not as likely to be understood as full human rights *subjects*. A Rawlsian schema of "equal basic liberties" requires extensive capacities for understanding larger societal contexts and consequences. A two-year-old with little worldly experience is likely to be less full a participant in such a system. Even an eleven-year-old like Jones should not have to have her rights to health support and education based on whether she can justify them through procedures of public discourse (or on whether an adult can justify them for her). In a sense, they should be provided to her whether she can give public reasons for them or not.

A second way of justifying human rights is known as "interest theory." Interest theorists see human rights as grounded, not in autonomy, but in furthering basic human interests, needs, or goods. One of its most influential proponents, John Finnis, uses Thomas Aquinas's natural law ethics to argue that human rights exist to advance "basic forms of human good."[14] The seven most fundamental such goods or interests, to which individuals therefore have rights, are to life, the acquisition of knowledge, play, aesthetic expression, sociability, practical reasonableness, and religion. These are "rights" because human nature is such that everyone has a fundamental interest in them. A similar rights logic underlies Martha Nussbaum's Aristotelian grounding of rights in what she calls human life's "functional capabilities."[15] Her list of these basic capabilities is similar to Finnis's goods. Each person is owed rights to the basic building blocks that make human life possible and worthwhile. Interest theory is arguably more open to children's rights than is will theory. It is easier to picture children as possessing basic human interests or needs. Even a newborn claims as a public interest its own life, play, and family.

But interest theory retains the essential ambiguity of the Aristotelian and Thomistic history of thought about children, also shared by Locke, on which it is based. That is, it views rights as means for basic human development. For children in particular, this means that rights will generally be interpreted from an adult rather than child point of view. The rights to the acquisition of knowledge and practical reasonableness, for example, or to Nussbaum's functional capabilities, are rights to things that are usually possessed by adults to higher degrees. This is because it is precisely adults who get to define social aims in the first place. The one possible exception is the right to play; but even play, as we have seen, can be interpreted as a means for development into adulthood rather than an interest in and of itself.

The difficulty here lies in *who* defines what interests and goods are truly basic or fundamental. Such a problem has long bedeviled those without power. But it works against children inherently. Goods-oriented thinking has tended historically to interpret childhood through the lens of what children *are not yet*, namely, developed adults. While women, for example, can at least in principle acquire the power to influence how societies define and prioritize their interests, on the whole children are more likely to have their interests defined by others—and the more so the younger the child. Children, then, will tend to be included in interest rights chiefly from the point of view of adults rather than as different others.

There is, however, a third view of human rights that holds still more promise for children, though still not enough. This is a "civil rights" approach that grew out of social liberation movements and figures such as Dorothy Day, Mohandas Gandhi, Simone de Beauvoir, Martin Luther King Jr., and Gustavo Gutiérrez. Here, human rights are understood in the more Marxist sense of the means to free entire social groups from economic, racial, gender, and other large-scale systematic oppressions. The basic human right, in this case, is less to individual freedom or the meeting of interests as it is to inclusion in social power. All rights are based on the fundamental civil right to a public voice, agency, and participation. This tradition grows in part out of Rousseau's view that social corruptions are to be overcome through increasing inclusion in the general will. More radically, this view also recognizes how even the general will of a society can be subject to systematic distortion, so that social power must always be broadened through grassroots movements.

Such a view has proven more useful for children's rights advocates than the other two possibilities above. It recognizes children as a distinctively marginalized social group. Children, just as much as other oppressed "minorities," have a right to social participation on their own behalf. Children's rights are a question not just of freedoms or of interests but also of inclusions in power.

However, this kind of bottom-up approach still suffers from some of the ambiguities of its history. Although children are capable of significantly greater social participation than is generally assumed, they should not be expected to bring about their own systemic liberation for themselves. The younger the child, the more, on the whole, will she or he rely for gaining civil rights on others who are precisely not children but adults. Civil rights movements have always recognized the interdependency of human groups on each other. But, unlike groups such as women and adult minorities, children will remain forever less socially empowered than adults so long as they have to gain power for themselves. Age genuinely affects one's ability to take political action, express public views, organize grassroots movements, hold positions of influence, and press for new political agendas. Even in an ideal society, few children will occupy university professorships. The analogy of children's rights to other historically oppressed groups' rights does not quite do justice to the distinctive worlds and experiences of children themselves.

While advances have been made in human rights theory in recent decades, therefore, these still do not include the perspective of childhood centrally. This is because in no case has childhood served to transform the basic meaning of human rights as such. Top-down, developmental, and bottom-up assumptions about children continue to define the parameters of the discussion. It is true that there are some glimmers of hope. However, rights will always only be extended to children in a piecemeal way until the ethical foundations of rights are reshaped in light of them.

GLOBAL CHILDREN'S RIGHTS

A first step toward more child-responsive rights can be taken by examining the major international children's rights agreements of the twentieth century. These rights agreements do not develop particularly novel human rights groundings, but they do show why human rights can be extended to include children's actual experiences. Here we find a creative and expansive struggle, albeit with varying degrees of success, to apply human rights to the one group in history that has been most systematically denied them. Through these concrete struggles, rights have in effect approached nearer to children's moral otherness. It has been on the global stage that children's rights have most clearly embraced what Paul Gordon Lauren, referring to human rights in general, calls "visions seen of a world of possibilities."[16] As Barbara Bennett Woodhouse has observed, attention to actual children's rights has meant that "illusions of autonomy, so dear to adult-centric schemes of rights, would dissolve, making room for the reality of dependency and interdependency."[17] Listening to children's rights agreements is a way of listening more attentively to the true complexity, circularity, and dynamism of human rights as such.

The first truly global rights agreement enacted in all of history is the League of Nations' 1924 Geneva Declaration of the Rights of the Child. It contains only five rights, and they are all what have since been termed "provision" rights, that is, rights to receive national and international aid. They are premised on what the 1924 *Declaration* calls the "duty" that "mankind owes to the Child." They include children's rights to normal development, nutrition and health, priority of aid in distress, the means to an eventual livelihood, and being brought up in the consciousness of owing service to others. There is also a subtheme of what are known as "protection" rights, that is, rights against harm or violence. For two of the above rights also call, secondarily, for children's shelter and nonexploitation. But the overall thrust is to provide children, mindful of their special vulnerability, with the basic necessities for living and thriving in the world.

Provision rights are sometimes referred to by legal scholars as "positive" rights, or rights to states' and societies' active aid and support. They are what is thought to be in children's "best interests," just as in interest theory above. But we can now see that, in deeper historical terms, they arise out of a kind of ethical developmentalism. That is, from Aristotle to al-Ghazali and from Thomas to Locke, ethicists have long felt that what society fundamentally owes to children are the positive means for developing their social potential. Likewise, as we have seen, this view has already shaped human rights theory directly, through Locke's idea of rights as means for natural self-preservation. Why, though, are such rights now thought to be applicable to children themselves? It seems that the nations of the world came to see children as not necessarily able to receive all basic needs solely from their families. Along with similar women's, labor, and antipoverty movements of the time—as well as the beginnings of children's universal education—a movement arose to recognize children's legitimate claim to basic public investments.

The horrors of World War II, however, made it clear to many that such rights for children are not sufficient. The next great evolution in international children's rights is the United Nations' 1959 Declaration of the Rights of the Child. On the one hand, this new declaration shares all the same provision rights as the one in 1924, even adding more wide-ranging ones such as to "a name and a nationality," "wherever possible, grow[ing] up in the care and under the responsibility of parents," and "the benefits of social security." On the other hand, its now ten children's rights include also a number of separate rights to social protection. These have been called "negative" rights, since they are rights *against* being done violence or harm. They reflect the tone of the then recently created United Nations' founding charter—the 1948 Universal Declaration of Human Rights—which is of an almost entirely protection rights nature.

Thus, the first right in the 1959 Declaration is to protection against racial, sexual, religious, political, national, birth, and other kinds of discrimination. Other protection rights are against "all forms of neglect, cruelty, and exploitation," separation from parents, trafficking, and employment. After the terrible violence, genocides, and discriminations of the war, which clearly affected children as much as they did adults, children's and human rights documents have to account for children's deep vulnerability to harm from others and groups.

Protection rights have long been afforded to adults, but only recently have they been extended to children. This is because children's protection has historically been considered the responsibility of families. But we can see from history that protection rights for children also reflect profound ethical traditions. They are in essence top-down rights to live with social dignity and order against people's tendencies for violence, manipulation, and abuse. Why, then, are such rights suddenly thought applicable to children? It appears that world war and the Holocaust may have shattered the myth of families' ability to protect children fully. Indeed, many would soon realize that children also need public protection against abuse *within* families. Children are as much, if not more, in need of rights against social harm as anyone else.

The 1959 Declaration also shows that children require both positive and negative rights at once. Provision rights are still more numerous in this declaration than protection rights. But a link between the two is established. Developmental resources are less likely to be effective if they are not framed by state-imposed protections. And protections need to be backed up by states stepping in with meaningful support for children's interests. The two kinds of rights, from a child's point of view, are thoroughly interdependent.

THE CONVENTION ON THE RIGHTS OF THE CHILD

Thirty years later, the United Nations' 1989 Convention on the Rights of the Child (hereafter CRC) reshaped children's international rights in an even more complex way still, and in two major respects.

First, it contains all the rights of the above previous international agreements, but extends them now into forty distinct children's rights, each spelled out in much greater detail.[18] Approximately sixteen of these forty rights could be said to reiterate rights from the previous declarations.[19] Even here, though, the rights are further elaborated upon: the right to nondiscrimination, for example, now refers also to disability and birth status. An additional eighteen or so rights are entirely new rights of the same provision and protection kinds. New provision rights include, for example, the right to an official government "identity" (article 8) and to an "adequate standard of living" when it cannot be provided by parents (article 27). New protection rights include those against sexual abuse (article 34), "torture or other cruel, inhuman, or degrading treatment or punishment" (article 37), and drafting into armed conflict (article 38).

These additions in the CRC continue the trend from the 1959 *Declaration* toward greater rights to protection. Indeed, provision and protection rights are now roughly equal in number: depending on exactly how they are counted, eighteen and sixteen rights, respectively. This shift arguably reflects a deepening recognition of the extent of children's social vulnerability, especially in the face of adult and systemic power. Not only is it natural to extend the right not to be harmed to children, but children arguably need this right most especially.

But second, and even more significantly, the 1989 CRC adds an entirely new category of children's rights, namely what are known as "participation" rights. These are rights to act and be heard in society for oneself. Participation rights are much like the civil rights described above. They have their roots in Rousseau's right to participation in society's general will. They do not provide aid or protect from harm, but rather enable public agency. The six participation rights in the CRC consist, briefly, in the following: to be heard (article 12); to freedom of expression (13); to freedom of thought, conscience, and religion (14); to freedom of association and assembly (15); to privacy (16); and to access to appropriate information and mass media (17). These in essence grant children the right to shape their public worlds actively for themselves.

Participation rights reflect a long historical view of humanity that I have described as bottom-up. Human beings, according to this view, are born essentially just and good. They should be given the freedom to influence society on their own behalf so that the corruptions of collective life may be resisted and overcome. Participation rights aim to create societies based on genuine inclusiveness instead of the will of a powerful few. In civil rights terms, they allow power to be exercised from the ground up instead of oppressively. What is most revolutionary about the 1989 CRC is that it extends this insight about humanity, based on what is after all the essentially childist notion that humanity is free and good from birth, to actual children themselves. No previous international agreement—and very few national laws—had previously promoted rights of this kind specifically for children.

It is the CRC's inclusion of participation rights that has produced the document's greatest opposition. It is the chief reason the CRC has not been ratified by the United States (the only country not to do so besides Somalia, which has no functioning government). These opponents take the traditional Lockean and Kantian view that children cannot hold public liberties without doing themselves and others harm. Perhaps children need a level of public provisions and protections (though even this is disputable to some), but they should not be given the same liberties as adults to speak and act in the public realm for themselves. Connected with this criticism is the essentially Lockean argument that children's freedoms will conflict with the freedoms of parents to raise their children as they see fit. Children are not their own rights-holders but rather in the temporary care of their parents until such a time as they can act in the world for themselves. Indeed, even Rousseau makes the claim, as we have seen, that children should be confined to the private sphere until they are strong enough to confront the world.

But these criticisms are misguided, and in at least four important respects.[20] First, when it comes to actual children, the freedom to participate in society is just as important as it is for adults. Empirically speaking, children are actors not simply in private families but also in larger public systems. As we saw in our discussion of the childhood studies movement in chapter 2, children consume mass media, respond to poverty, take views on politics, negotiate health systems, contribute to culture, and in general participate in one way or another across the entire public spectrum. If children have limited social experience—and the more so the younger the child—this does not mean that they are not social participants. Adults too have varying degrees of social capability, from the most violent criminal to the wisest head of state. But the purpose of social participation is not simply to include the voices of those deemed most experienced or rational. It is to include the fullest possible diversity of humanity.

Second, children's public freedoms do not conflict with the child-rearing rights of parents. As the CRC shows, children's public freedoms can coexist with the rights of parents to provide, protect, and advocate for them. At least seven of the CRC's rights are centrally concerned with children's rights to families, and many others touch on family life in other ways. For example, article 9 calls for children's right, except in exceptional circumstances, not to be separated from their parents. When it comes to the realm of public discourse, children's rights *should* sometimes conflict with those of their parents (and others), such as in cases of domestic violence. When it comes to the private realm of the home, as we will see in the next chapter, the language of rights is necessary but not alone sufficient. However, without public rights, children have less recourse when parents cause them significant harm, others in the community do them violence, or societies fail to provide adequately for them.

Third, although children's rights to social participation are relatively new, they are based on an ancient historical tradition of children bringing to society something uniquely worthy and good. Children have been valued as public agents long before the advent of modern rights language. They have worked alongside parents, contributed to religious and cultural meaning, been able to assemble and express their views, and made their own educational, economic, and vocational choices. If there is a sense in which children need special protections and aid, there is also an equally important sense in which they bring to society special and unique capabilities. From this angle, the CRC's extension of participation rights to children is a way of rectifying modernist human rights theory's rigid adult-centrism. It also overcomes an industrial-era radical separation of the public and private spheres of life. If children are in some sense origins of good in society, they should be able to contribute to society's active shaping.

Finally, critics of children's participation rights presume an overly adult-centered idea of "participation" itself. The CRC offers the opportunity to reimagine public social participation in a way that centrally also includes children. Social participation may not entirely consist, as Enlightenment theorists believed, in the capability for independent rational autonomy. It may consist more fully, in light of childhood, in what I have been calling interdependent social creativity. That is, the right to participation might more fundamentally be understood as a right to the creative formation of societies in conjunction with others. In this case, as we will see, children's participation in the public realm is not just a limited version of adult participation, but a model for social participation as such. Openness to children's participation rights will help us reimagine social life in a more creative, dynamic, and circular way.

However, the larger conclusion to be drawn from these evolving children's rights agreements, culminating in the CRC, is more complex than just asserting children's rights to social participation, important though these are. The larger conclusion is that children's rights cannot finally be reduced to any one of the above kinds of rights discourse alone. Nor, more fundamentally, can they be fully explained by any one of the major traditional kinds of human rights theory or historical childist ethics. Rather, children show that human rights must include provision, protection, and participation rights all at once in a more fully interdependent way. We will have to press more decisively beyond existing rights groundings if we are to discover from children what makes human rights truly human.

RIGHTS AS RESPONSIBILITIES

So far in this book, I have argued that to be moral is to create shared worlds over time and in response to each other. This poetic moral capability belongs to adults and children alike from birth to death. Its aim is to remake selves' narratives of life together more rather than less expansively over time. And it obliges selves and societies to form increasingly decentered responses to others in their otherness. The remainder of this chapter uses these ideas to argue that human rights are not social expressions of individuality but social responsibilities to difference.

It is no accident that, like the children's rights agreements discussed above, this kind of postmodern approach has its immediate roots in the horrors of the twentieth century. When history is written, the past century will be seen as a time of great technological, humanitarian, and gender advances, but also one of massive violence, brutal war, nuclear weapons, genocide, racism, culture clashes, and climate change. All of these disproportionately affect children.

The great founding ethicist of otherness, Emmanuel Levinas, was a Jewish survivor of the Holocaust. His response to the problem of mass human disorder is not merely to reapply more vigorously the human rights discourse of modernity. This discourse had ultimately proven all too tragically inadequate. Nazism, Stalinism, Maoism, and the many other totalitarianisms of the twentieth century and today are not wrong because they are irrational. On the contrary, they are wrong because they are *too* rational. They advance visions of highly rationalized societies based on all too strongly held convictions.

Against the hopes of modernity, rationalism has proven itself as capable of moral self-righteousness and violence as in previous centuries (and still today) as religion. As Levinas and others have rightly seen, the clearest response to social tyranny—which is exactly the problem Enlightenment ethicists wished to solve—is the disruption and questioning of social rationality itself. This means questioning historical assumptions from the point of view of the other. Only in the face of each other's irreducible differences can we hope to create societies that transcend their own profoundest marginalizations. The poetic humanism of this book similarly hopes to rethink moral life postrationalistically—which does not mean irrationally, but rather inclusively. Rights language is often rejected by postmodernists for precisely these reasons. It is time, however, for the sake of children, to reclaim and revise it.

Human rights, in a more fundamentally human sense, are markers of social responsibility to otherness. Their purpose is not to universalize social relations but to create more diversely expansive ones. The aim of human rights should be to decenter the powers and laws that define society in order to multiply as far as possible the diversity of its centers of social creativity. Childhood shows that human beings are not so much rationally autonomous individuals as responsively interdependent others. Each particular human right should instill a specific historical construction of the meaning of being human in relation to each other. Each is justified, ethically and socially, by its capacity to help reconstruct historical constructions with greater rather than lesser inclusivity of others.

The remainder of this chapter defends and clarifies this new vision of human rights in light of childhood. This vision applies equally to children and adults, but it cannot be understood on the usual adult-centered grounds. There are an infinite possible number of "other" centers of society that societies ought to respond to. Cultures and subcultures are also irreducibly diverse. However, what others and other cultures share is an intersubjective capability for world creativity. Rights should function to distend and decenter, as opposed to contract and consolidate, social creativity among humanity. Existing social relations should be made more rather than less fully responsive to humanity's true diversity of lived experience.

THE CIRCLE OF HUMAN RIGHTS

The 1989 CRC does not, of course, explain itself in terms of responsibility to others, nor do its defenders. However, because of its multidimensional complexity, as seen above, it does help us begin to imagine what such a vision might look like.

This is because the CRC's three sides allow us to picture human rights in light of childhood in the form of an expanding circle, as follows:

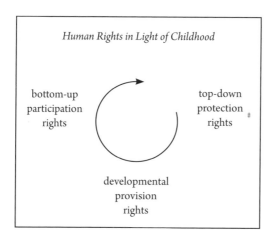

The basic ethical trajectory of each kind of right here is tied to the others. Their traditional linearity is only a partial expression of their more dynamic circular whole. Each kind of right is just one expression of the more profound social right to be a creative center of society. Each stretches the circle of society further outwards. Together they revolve around humanity's more fundamental social responsibility to expand the horizons of its own humanity. The fuller trajectory is not straight but decentering, elliptical, centrifugal.

We can understand this dynamism of human rights by looking at how, especially but not only for children, each kind of right in the CRC is a different kind of response to human otherness—and at how, as a result, each kind is related to the other two.

Let us start with protection rights. These, I have argued, construct top-down moral standards imposed against a tendency for harm and violence. In light of childhood, this violation cannot be understood simply as the individual being robbed of autonomy. Rather, in a more dynamic and relational way, what is to be protected is others' irreducibility to one another and the group. Protection rights should identify those protected as not only agential but also vulnerable. They should call for one another's greater responsiveness to difference. Not to be abused or exploited means not to be reduced to others' narratives and powers, not to be denied a particular social creativity of one's own.

Take, for example, the 2005 *Williamson* case denying the right of Christian schools in the United Kingdom to practice corporal punishment.[21] The argument for this right was that it protected parents' and schools' religious freedoms. However, as the court rightly saw, this ignores the rights of the least powerful parties in the situation, namely, the children being punished (as well as all British children whose right against cruel and unusual punishment in schools might therefore be placed in question). Freedoms of those with social power—in this case school administrators and teachers—must always be balanced against the possible exploitation of others—such as children—who are less likely to be heard or accounted for. When children are taken as centrally into account as adults, they gain the right to protection of their own distinctiveness in the situation.

If so, then protection rights must also be understood in relation to other kinds of rights to provision and participation. On the one hand, the *Williamson* children are not just being protected as others; they are also being ensured the provision right to an adequate education. Rights such as those to nondiscrimination and nonexploitation in part require that marginalized groups receive a share of social resources, such as health care, social services, knowledge of rights, and family and community support. On the other hand, being protected in one's otherness also contributes toward one's rights to social participation. Children who are not threatened with violence in schools will also be more fully able to speak up in them. Or, to take an adult example, women's gains in domestic violence rights came about in part as a result of rights to vote, work, and be heard. Social participation requires not simply the freedom to be autonomous but the active-passive opportunity to contribute toward the group. Public protections need constantly to be defined through the voices and agency of others in their concrete and singular otherness. If those with the least experience and power are to be protected against exploitation and harm, they must have the right to society's most energetic and welcoming response to their particular social creativity.

Similar considerations hold for provision rights, such as to health care, welfare, and social aid. Such rights are not merely rights to the passive reception of social goods. This would mean they were chiefly defined by those with the greatest power to distribute them. Rather, from a childist point of view, provision rights are means for including otherness more fully in the creation of society. They are not generous entitlements, but rather part of what is required for human beings to make their own distinctive contributions. Provisions are both active and passive at once, gifts from the whole of society that encourage the expression of the gifts of otherness within it. Education, for example, is a circular rather than linear process of expanding to respond to each new generation's social innovativeness. Health care is not just a public handout to the needy but a social response to what particular others require for social inclusion. The provision of social security after retirement is not a passively received reward but part of what is needed for those no longer able to work to continue to contribute to society in new ways.

This again means that provision rights, like protection rights, help to support other kinds of rights around the more fundamental right to society's response to one's difference. On the one hand, to be provided, say, an education or health resources enables (and relies upon) a robust regime of social protections. The distribution of social goods must be done without discrimination, abuse, or exploitation if those goods are truly to broaden social relations. Such is especially the case for children, who are more likely than virtually any other group to be denied provision for their interests. On the other hand, provision rights also depend on one another's inclusive social participation. How societies increase the good of their members should be determined, not just by the few, but by the voices, associations, and cultural influences of the widest possible plurality of others. The more widely otherness is heard, the more effectively will social provisions serve their function of building up the social good. Only then do social investments expand rather than contract the circle of the social whole.

Finally, rights to participation are likewise expressions of the fundamental right to other-responsiveness. They are more than just enablers of freedom or agency. They are means for the inclusion of increasingly diverse others in the dynamics of social creativity. No one makes a difference in her world merely by herself or in a social vacuum. Rather, young and old, male and female, poor and rich alike have their social voices constructed in passive-active relation to many layers of already constructed social meaning. Without history, cultures, power structures, and personal relations, it would be impossible to participate meaningfully in society at all. The purpose of participation rights is not to free selves from one another but to create more diversely inclusive societies.

And so, once again, even participation rights turn out, in light of children, to be fully reliant on other kinds of rights. On the one hand, freedoms to expression, culture, assembly, and religion all depend for their fuller realization on protections of otherness against discrimination, abuses of power, actual or threatened violence, and the like. A child growing up oppressed by racism is likely to have a more difficult time having her voice make a social difference. Participation precisely means *making a difference*. On the other hand, participation rights also rely on developmental provisions, that is, rights to receive society's positive investments and aid. The freedom to participate as a singular other depends in part on having been provided an education, health care, and support. The diversity of otherness truly constructs a whole society only insofar as that society invests itself in protecting and empowering the otherness by which it is constituted.

The reason these different kinds of rights are intimately bound up with one another is not that, as modernity supposed, all human beings are rational individuals. Rather, it is that all human beings are creatively other. Rights are really responsibilities. They are how societies and their members respond to one another in their otherness. They proclaim each and every other person a distinct and worthy creator of social worlds. Because others are never reducible to the group, and because each new birth brings another other into the world, human rights should include others in society as diversely as possible. They should constantly decenter how social relations are created over time. Societies should be on the lookout especially for those who are marginalized in order to grow toward their own larger humanity.

EXPANDING THE CIRCLE

If such is the case, then the forces aligned against human rights are more powerful and profound than generally imagined. Indeed, they are unavoidable. The wider inclusion of others in societies will always face tendencies toward social consolidation and narrowing. In chapter 4 I referred to this problem as the proclivity for social destruction. Human beings' abilities to expand moral relations are always shadowed by their historical and personal abilities to narrow them. Social tensions need to be constantly reworked in order to become more diversely responsive. Actual human history attests that both individuals and societies respond to otherness only to one or another degree. The only conclusion that could be imagined to this process is a mythic one of a wholly inclusive humanity, but even myths are always constructed too constrictedly.

How, then, can one properly judge whether a human right will widen rather than contract the circle of a society? How can the social contract, which is necessarily binding and limiting, resist its own tendency toward social contraction? How, as historically entrenched beings-in-the-world, can individuals and leaders recognize the specific ways in which their societies ought to become more other-responsive?

The perspective of those most likely to be marginalized—namely, children— shows that the only reliable criterion is how far rights respond to others as social creators. A right achieves its aim only insofar as it responds to persons and groups in their interdependent dynamism. Any one arc of the circle of rights obscuring the others will prove finally self-defeating. It will result in either impositions of power, narrowed goods, or meaningless liberties. To create more expansive societies is to increase members' abilities to create worlds together.

Let us take, as an example, the rights of poor children in the United States such as those of the 11-year-old girl Annabelle Jones whom we met in the introduction. Jones is a citizen of her country with all the rights afforded to children of her age. She is legally protected against abuse and exploitation, owed provisions of an education and at least emergency medicine, and afforded a measure of participatory free speech and assembly. These are only a few of the thousands of public rights she possesses. And yet, despite all this, Jones stands at the far periphery of social inclusion when compared with most other children and adults. She is less protected against violence and harm, receives lower overall social support, and has a more limited public voice. So she would seem to represent a clear case of an "other" human being whose human rights do not in fact make her particularly central to her own society. She is a member of a human rights community, but in a relatively constricted way.

For the Joneses of the world to receive fuller social rights, they would have to be imagined by the social whole as more fully valued centers of social creativity. Their distinctive experiences and capabilities as social others would have to be all at once welcomed, protected, and cultivated. Their moral, legal, and political communities would have to take an active responsibility for decentering themselves around what makes them distinct.

Protection, provision, and participation rights are but partial expressions of the fundamental human right to be responded to as an other creator of society. To be protected against violence fundamentally means to be protected against having one's otherness marginalized or destroyed. To be provided social resources is to be given the means for making one's own creative social contribution. And to be able to participate in society is to have the opportunity to bring one's own distinctive contribution into the creativity of the whole.

These top-down, developmental, and bottom-up vectors of social creativity combine to resist the contraction and encourage the expansion of inclusively responsive social worlds. They should spread out as widely as possible the seeds of shared life. They add up to a larger circular dynamics in which society expands its own genuine humanity. Shortening any one side of the circle stunts and narrows the whole. Each human being ought, all at once, not to have their social creativity violated, to have it positively supported by social investments, and to express it to the widest extent they can as a singular other. These dimensions check and balance one another. They never achieve perfect harmony. But they are united by the goal of including others as centrally as possible in the shaping of societies.

Human rights are social responsibilities in that they create the conditions necessary for responding through society to each other. At the center of collective life lies the basic right to be another creator of society. It is the right to be treated by one's social surroundings as another valued maker of the social world. Human rights bind others together in their social interdependency. They are how societies decenter themselves in response to their own fuller human differences, and therefore how they expand their own humanity. They are markers in the public realm of the moral demand for responsiveness to others' creativity.

Human rights require a whole social circle because human beings create meaning and relations in whole ways. All selves are born into already constructed social horizons that they must also reconstruct into meaning for themselves. The question for human rights is not whether persons are able to recreate their social worlds, but how expansively they are enabled to do so in relation to each other. Part of this expansiveness depends on selves, and part depends on social conditions. It is a matter of stretching the circle of human relations ever more elliptically outwards. The dynamics of social creativity has always already begun. The issue is how widely it is permitted to grow.

It is often thought that "rights" and "responsibilities" are opposed. This, however, is a modernistic fallacy. It assumes that rights are means for expressing one's own individual autonomy, while responsibilities are ways of reaching out to others in their vulnerability. It also often assumes that rights are public and responsibilities private. From a childist point of view, these are false dichotomies that ignore the depths to which human beings are dynamically interdependent. Selves are not subjects *or* objects but active-passive beings-in-the-world. Properly understood, rights *are* responsibilities. They are means by which societies respond to the fuller social creativity of their members.

THE RIGHTS OF CHILDREN AND ADULTS

To say that rights are responses to otherness is not to say that everyone's rights should be exactly the same. It is only to say that everyone should have the same fundamental right to share in creating society. Everyone should be treated as a full member of the human circle.

Children, for example, should on the whole have greater rights to the provision of an education, for their relatively fewer years of experience in a society means that they need education more than do most adults. They are owed it more, not because they are not yet autonomous or developed, but because an education is required in most societies for fuller social creativity. The right to an education both depends on and advances protection rights like those against gender discrimination and labor exploitation, as well as participation rights like the expression of one's own interests and voice. Adults have rights to education too, and for similarly multidimensional reasons. But the broadest possible social creativity demands giving greater educational priority to children, since on the whole children require more learning experiences in order to contribute to societies as others.

In contrast, adults on the whole should have greater rights, for example, to hold political office. Wielding power is not merely a form of social participation. It is also a protection against domination by the few and a means for determining distributions of social provisions. It therefore depends on having had broad experience in the world. Children, however, should have more expansive rights to political representation than today they generally do. Countries should seek to better hear children's political voices through such means as systematic legislative priority, children's parliaments, and possibly an automatic vote at birth that children can activate when they desire. These and other such measures are already being taken or explored in many countries. Their purpose, from an ethical point of view, is not to make children into mini-adults, but to find creative ways to represent children's differences in democracy—which, after all, is supposed to be inclusive of all and not just some. However, making laws and representing otherness does rely on having related to others in diverse and wide ways.

The same can be said for the rights to marry, smoke, join the military, buy alcohol, or own property. In each case, some age can legitimately be set, however much it may also be culturally conditioned, below which such rights would destroy rather than support a larger rights circle. Marriage prior to adulthood is exploitative and impedes education, especially for girls. Joining the military, except in the most extreme circumstances, will likely narrow children's long-term social, psychological, and economic prospects. At the same time, a right such as to government social security should be afforded the elderly and the young, among others, since those in the middle are more likely able to work. In general, rights should be held equally by all unless there is a particular reason to restrict them. The criterion should be whether a particular right is more or less responsive to otherness.

The central right in all societies is not the right to act autonomously but rather the right to be included in the creation of social relations. Particular rights are justified by the extent to which they enable social relations to expand so as to include social difference, rather than narrow so as to exclude it. The means by which humanity creates more other-inclusive social worlds are multiple and diverse. They are themselves expressions of human being as socially inventive. There is no universal yardstick for human rights except for social creativity itself. Human rights become more fully "human" to the extent that they broaden and decenter life lived in common. They become less fully human insofar as they fail to respond to the endless diversity of human experience.

The actual multiplicity of rights in most societies attests to their endless need for dynamism and growth. As history shows, not only can rights grow in number, but they can also grow in kind. Most human rights that are widely accepted today would have been barely imaginable in the past. It took long and painful struggles to create rights to such things as public education, habeas corpus, women's and minorities' votes, and nondiscrimination. And these and other struggles continue today.

Rights have to be forged within social contexts that are always too narrow. The social whole has constantly to recreate itself. New rights may be threats to the established order, but they are legitimate insofar as they stretch that order to become more diversely inclusive. Human rights in light of childhood are markers, not of individual autonomy, but of boundless shared creativity. Rights are another form of social construction. As the history of the rights of children clearly shows, the language of rights must retain an inventive plasticity if it is to further a society's broader humanity. Only in this way does humanity become more responsible to its own humanity.

RIGHTS AND NATURE

It is important, finally, to note that human rights so understood always point to something beyond what has so far been imagined. In this sense, human rights are markers not only of otherness but also of excess. Their function involves pressing societies beyond their own settled moral horizons. They not only create social worlds but also stretch them beyond their own existing limits. Human beings from birth onwards are called upon to create their own greater possible humanity. Human rights receive their meaning and legitimacy from their ability to stretch the circle of humanity further outward toward its own self-transcending humanization. If so, then childhood leads us finally to rethink existing human rights theory in at least two further respects.

First, human rights in light of childhood exceed their traditional limits by being able to extend themselves to nonhuman "others" like animals, plants, and ecosystems.

Of course, rights talk has already been applied for some time to such beings. However, contemporary human rights theory inherits from modernity the paradoxical problem of extending rights to beings in the world who do not necessarily share humanity's autonomous reason. If it is difficult to include children in such regimes, it is even more difficult to include animals and nature. It is children's supposed closeness to "nature," in fact, that excludes them in the first place.

The usual way in which such an extension is made is to treat non-human entities as nevertheless sharing in certain human characteristics. This, indeed, is how rights first came to be extended in small ways from adults to children. In this manner, animals can be said to feel pleasure and pain and so to have a certain independent rationality of their own. Even ecosystems can be said to have a rational "interest" in their own well-being. Alternatively, rights can be extended to nature in an instrumental sense, whereby nature needs protection for the sake of human beings. To protect the right of rainforests to survival, for example, is necessary for avoiding humanity's extinction.

The language of otherness allows us to turn this equation around. If human rights are expansions of responsibility toward others, they invite us ultimately to imagine humanity's connections with every living other that shares its world. If human beings are not just rational individuals but interdependent world-creators, then they are open to seeing themselves as members of a larger natural environment. All life on some level involves an element of passive-active creativity, from the simplest organism to the most complex ecosystem, from the newborn child to the whole global community, from the rainforest to the urban city.

This interdependency with nature is thinkable when rights are considered in light of childhood. One of the horizons toward which childhood presses humanity is the roots of humanity in biological life. As philosophers and theologians of childhood have often suggested, children are in a sense nature's most immediate human expression. How one understands childhood—negatively, positively, neutrally, or otherwise—deeply affects how one understands nature. If, as I have argued, childhood is world-creative, we can likewise connect human experience to the teeming creativity of all life. To create societies is in part to create a relation to the creativity of the natural world. It is to include, however well or poorly, bodies, animals, plants, and ecologies. Nature and humanity are not divided by a line of moral rationality—the one objective and the other subjective, as Descartes would have it—but bound by their interdependent creativity.

As with children, this broadening of the grounds of rights does not mean that the same rights are owed to every living creature and system. Nor is it to say that animals, plants, and the like are somehow to be treated as analogously human. Rather, it is to say that what is meant by our own "humanity" should be stretched out also to include the nonhuman others that construct it too. The circle of human relations belongs also to a wider circle of nature. Human beings are fully biological creatures whose being-in-the-world is expressed in part through their biological relations to plants, animals, and the Earth. As human societies expand rights to nature, they are expanding their own humanity.

As we saw in chapter 3, children remind us of this especially. Being a body is not experienced in the first place as participating in a separate objective reality. Bodies become empirical objects only through a secondary analytical distance—a distance that itself depends on a primary experiential connection. Phenomenologically speaking, the body and brain and biological life in general are experienced most immediately and fully as activities of world creativity. It is as embodied beings—in synapses, sensations, and movements—that selves and others form meaning. What is more, societies persist throughout time only in their continued embodiment in each new generation.

To extend "human rights" to nature is to recognize that however "other" nature may be, it is also bound up with our own human being. To exclude animals and ecosystems from social rights is to narrow social creativity. It is to forget that societies are biological. Human beings certainly have an added layer of intelligence—though this too is part of their natural evolution—but such a fact should only make human beings *more* responsible to their worlds. A flower too creates a world. It is at once constructed by and reconstructs its given natural environment. A salamander, dog, or chimpanzee does so with some degree of self-consciousness, and hence with wider world-responsive complexity. Human world creativity is ultimately even more expansive still. Our brains and bodies are such that we can create lasting cultures over time, self-transforming symbol systems, and powerful societies. In other words, we can stretch our worlds to include an especially wide diversity of otherness. Our brains and bodies are also such that we can be infinitely more destructive, not only of one another but also of nature and, potentially, of all planetary life.

This means that biological life demands some level of extension of rights in a full circle of protections, provisions, and participation. As with childhood, protection rights are perhaps the most obvious: noncruelty to animals, not exploiting livestock through "inhumane" conditions, not destroying the fragile global environment. But nature also asks of human societies a level of provision: whether in care for animals, proper investment in the land, or maintenance of forests and seas. And since nature is not only an object but also an agent in human being, it deserves a measure of societal participation. Pets and animals should be able to live in their own ways among us, plant life to change our self-understanding, and biological forces like sexuality and evolution to be respected and responded to. This does not mean that birds should have the right to vote. It means that natural creatures should help to create our worlds in their fullest possible diversity of otherness.

RIGHTS AND RELIGION

The other sense in which human rights extend "beyond humanity" in its modernistic sense concerns the kind of moral excess imaginable through religion. It is often thought that rights and religion are opposed. The one deals with public reason, the other private feeling; the one is rational and inclusive, the other nonrational and sectarian. As we have seen, it is often religious leaders who oppose rights language most strongly when it comes to children.

However, as this book has labored to show, any such distinction is finally self-defeating. You do not have to believe in some particular God or gods to believe in human rights. But you do have to believe in the power of the human imagination to expand itself toward its own unknown beyond. What is thought to be true by reason or nature must always be open to being self-transcended. Childhood shows that the capacity to create worlds of meaning with others is more primordial than the capacity to think empirically or autonomously. Were humanity not able to create new worlds, it would also not be able to discover laws of physics, invent mathematical formulas, develop languages and cultures, or live together in social systems. It would never have become humanity.

Even modernity itself points to human rights' religious dimensions. Locke, as we have seen, understands rights as duties of self-preservation that each individual owes to their Maker. To have rights is to have been endowed with primordial worth. For Rousseau, rights exist to draw into society the natural goodness that is given to each individual by its Author. The newborn's innocent gift at birth is a mystery that transcends its own inevitable historical corruption. Kant argues that human rights protect moral autonomy and dignity for beings made in the image of God's reason. What is more, according to Kant the result of being moral is to make one worthy of happiness not on earth but in eternal heaven.

Religious language is less often found in understandings of human rights today. Religion may involve specific kinds of rights—such as the right to practice or not practice a religion freely—but it is rarely considered part of having rights in the first place. Perhaps the chief exception is the kind of civil rights thinking known as "liberationism"—such as in the work of Mohandas Gandhi and Martin Luther King Jr.—in which religion helps provide moral horizons beyond the oppressions of history. There are also religious movements that make use of rights language for specific ends—for example, Christian "right to life" groups, or Muslims who support sharia laws—but such movements do not generally understand rights as the fundamental basis of societies.

The most important reason not to introduce religion into rights discourse is that, even as I have developed it here, rights discourse should apply to any "other" regardless of particular religiosity. A newborn, for example, is not yet exactly of any particular religious persuasion, but that should not prevent him or her from being treated as another creative other in the world. When religious and worldly powers are conflated, the latter is capable of exceptional narrowness and violence, since it can convince itself that it speaks for the will of God. This, I argued above, is idolatry: the reduction of the ultimate to the merely proximate, the unknowable to the known, the infinite to finitude. For such reasons, it is generally wise and more creatively inclusive to make a distinction between religious and political systems.

In the end, however, none of this means that religion cannot play a role in describing human rights ethics. In fact, there is something religious—in a broad sense—about human rights' very aim of expanding a society's otherness. Religious symbols and myths are distinctively able to point the imagination toward its own as yet unrealized beyond. When aware of its historical limitations, religion can function poetically, as it were, to help regrasp humanity's very possibility for wider possibilities.

To expand human rights means, in an ultimate sense, to open up the personal and social imagination toward its own creative excess. The purpose of human rights is to disrupt and transform existing social understanding and practice. It is easiest to see this by looking into the historical past. What was taken as unwaveringly reasonable—for example, the denial of education rights to poor children, or the exclusion of the voting rights of women—often turns out to be based on a limited understanding of human society. Although religion can be deeply destructive—and, like anything else, inevitably is—it can also press the human rights struggle toward what is not yet imagined. It can open societies up to wider approximations of a fully other-responsive world.

In chapter 4 I spoke of moral "hyperbole": pressing self-other relations to the point of self-excess. Hyperbole in human rights means embracing the possibility of society's self-transcendence. It means becoming vulnerable to renewal. It can open societies up to what exceeds existing realities, to visions of humanity as it might ultimately become. The greatest ethical excess is to try and imagine a society fully decentered by all otherness at once. No such society has ever existed, nor could it ever be imagined by any person or group. But through a kind of hyperbolic excess of imagination, a pointing to a mythic beyond, rights may be opened up toward more radically responsive new horizons.

Religious symbols are historically and culturally specific because, like all human language, they are human creations. The central such symbol I have played with in this book is that of humanity as an image of a Creator. Phenomenologically speaking, this terminology can be used to describe the human experience of its own strange world-creativity. The divine is a way of naming human being's most primal experience from the depths of childhood of being able continuously to create worlds of meaning and relations.

Such symbolisms, like all language, are inherently diverse and new ones can and should be created over time. But they can be helpful for the advance of human rights insofar as they press societies toward their own ultimate possibilities. A recent interpretation of children's rights uses the symbolism of "the image of God" to insist on the goodness of children's (and therefore adults') embodiment: "At the end of the day children have rights because they have human bodies. And that means, from a Christian point of view, that they are made in the image of the Word who took flesh and came into the world."[22] We can now interpret this kind of symbolism, more broadly, to support children's and adults' creative being-in-the-world. Children's bodies, as all human bodies, are the first sites of social creativity. Imagining one another as images of the divine can help to imagine the radical extent of social responsibility to otherness.

Human rights can thus be argued to have a certain religious dimension insofar as rights are societies' responses to their own moral beyond. Rights exist in order to press the human social imagination toward its own unmet horizons of otherness. They are not just excessive for the time being—that is, until a time when all others are fully included—but excessive by definition. The ideal human rights regime is not static but dynamic, not constant but expanding, not just here and now but always crossing new boundaries. This is another way of saying that a fully successful human rights regime cannot finally be imagined. No society should view itself as having completely responded to the others within it; for each other is an irreducible creator of worlds for itself. But saying so is also to say that what seems impossible about human rights can still be embraced as humanity's possibility, in an ultimate if never realized sense.

CONCLUSION

Children will gain full human rights only insofar as human rights themselves are fundamentally reimagined. Children are not too irrational, too weak, or too undeveloped to belong to the full human rights community. A fully human society can be constructed only insofar as rights are understood as social responsibilities to one another. From this angle, human rights include all of humanity, from the least to the most experienced and powerful.

Human rights are social responsibilities to the human diversity of otherness. The most fundamental right is to be included as another social creator. It is to make one's society a difference. This means all at once being protected against marginalization, being provided social resources, and being able to participate as an other for oneself. The underlying purpose of human rights is painfully but joyfully to expand the circumference of a society's unfathomable humanity.

Chapter 6

The Generative Family

A SECOND WAY TO consider some of the practical implications of childism is to think about the ethical dimensions of life in families. Of course, discussion of children has historically included families centrally. From the point of view of childhood, it is clearly important for human beings to take part in close kin networks. The birth of each new person in the world is, in a way, the rebirth of family: a bodily bond to a mother and father, an emotional and economic bond to a household, a genetic bond to a larger ancestry, and a cultural bond to a kin group. In all its great variety of historical forms, the family as a social institution has in part existed to protect, support, and nurture children.

However, it is precisely because of this obvious interconnection of families and children that a childist approach to families becomes problematic. For it means that today's ethical assumptions about family life—about its meanings, purposes, and obligations—are that much more profoundly mired in fixed historical assumptions. If, as we have found, these assumptions are less than fully child-centered, then the close association of families with children paradoxically makes it more difficult to think about families in a more child-inclusive way. The situation is much like that for women, for whom assumptions about historical connections to family life have also often proven marginalizing of women's actual experiences. But since children are perhaps more dependent on families than anyone else—while at the same generally less able to mount their own critiques of them—a more fully child-centered ethics of family life requires especially creative new thinking.

The need for fresh perspectives is also suggested by the highly contentious nature of family life in most contemporary societies. Many of the deep moral divisions within countries and across the globe concern issues of child-rearing, family values, gender relations, marriage, and connections between home and society. The problem is sometimes described as a "culture war" between those wishing to embrace new family forms and those seeking a return to old ones. Family ethics raises a whole hive of issues connected with gender, economics, culture, and morality.

However, as I will endeavor to show in this chapter, the problem as usually understood does not pay sufficient attention to children. This is especially the case in the United States, on which this chapter will focus. Just as with human rights, human families have not been conceptualized along sufficiently child-centered lines, either historically or today—indeed, in some ways, less so today than before. In reality, contemporary debates about families tend to revolve around the problems and experiences of adults: how to parent, balancing home and work, gender disparities between mothers and fathers, the changing meaning of marriage, the legitimacy of same-sex marriage, new methods of assisted reproduction, the passing on of traditional values, and so on. These issues are related to children, but chiefly from the point of view of adults. If family ethics has only recently been shaped from the perspectives of women, even less so has it responded to the agency and experiences of children.

From a childist point of view, the ethical purpose of families is not sharing values, personal development, or self-sacrifice. For children and adults both, it is the most immediate arena in which to create meaning with others. To describe this family ethics, I borrow a term from Erik Erikson: namely, generativity. But I use it in a somewhat different way. Generativity should refer to both adults' and children's dynamic and decentering creativity of close, interdependent worlds. Adults are generatively responsible for broadening the generative responsibility of children. Children in turn are generatively responsible for widening in generative responsibility toward family members and others in society. The well-being of children meets the obligations of adults and the interests of society in the fundamental family aim of expanding the circle of human responsiveness.

WHY THE CULTURE WARS?

Many ethicists in the United States today dismiss family issues as matters of merely private concern. Families have retreated in the popular imagination, especially but not only in developed societies, into an increasingly small world of the home.[1] From this point of view, family is an ethical subject only for traditionalists and self-righteous moralizers. Or, at most, family ethics must be left to the moral worlds of diverse cultures.

But in fact, as we have seen, philosophical and religious ethicists of all stripes have historically considered family life to be of tremendous social significance. This is all the more the case when considering children. Until the twentieth century, the most powerful philosophical and religious minds wrote about family relations extensively. Family forms and ideals differ considerably across time and place. But it is rare to find historical ethical thinking that does not consider close, personal bonds to be of social significance. When one considers children in particular, families are not only private relations but also parts of life in society.

Families are an almost universal human phenomenon: from ancient multigenerational patriarchal households, to working agricultural homesteads, to the industrial and postindustrial era's increasingly small nuclear homes. If human rights are meant to be universal but have always in fact fallen short, families are in reality universal, though in a great diversity of forms. Everyone is born into one or another kind of family, a set of immediate personal relations, whether they like it or not. If anything has persisted from prehistoric societies to the present—through all known historical cultures and despite the devastations of wars, exploitations, and injustices—it is a persistent belief among humankind in the need to create and sustain some kind of family life. The most important question is not whether to live in families, but how.

In the past, family debates also reached high pitches, especially in times of great social upheaval: the challenge to family clans during the rise of ancient city-states; increasing consent to marriage during feudalism; the critique of church family law during the Reformation; the rise of national family law in early modernity; the separation of private and public spheres through industrialization; and so on. So also today are new problems raised and divisions intensified when faced with challenges around gender, race, class, and globalization. As in the past, a changing world can give rise to deepening polarizations or to creative new thinking and practices. The way forward is once again to transform what has proven historically useful in response to those experiences that have been historically marginalized.

The culture wars over the ethics of family life today are less about whether family is important than about what exactly the family's importance consists in. As with children's rights, the most trenchant differences among contemporary family ethicists reflect profound disagreements among our three, major, historical approaches. The best way to understand today's culture wars is as a dispute, not between the past and the present, but between top-down, bottom-up, and developmental tendencies of thinking, albeit in new ways. It is because these alternatives so powerfully shape history that today's differences often appear so intractable. The first step in developing more child-responsive thinking is to unpack what these differences are.

One of the prime drivers of today's culture wars—not only in the United States but also globally—is a reinvigorated top-down desire to invest families with greater moral authority. Today's world is perceived, from this angle, to be sliding into moral relativism and disorder. Parents are urged to become stricter, marriages to be strengthened, and families in general to be more highly valued by societies. As the ethicist Jean Bethke Elshtain has put it, what is needed is "a revamped defense of family authority" and for child rearing to center on "inculcating moral limits and constraints."[2] As for (the later) Plato, Augustine, and Calvin, children need families as their first instillers of larger moral beliefs. Or, as another contemporary ethicist puts it bluntly: "Parents commit themselves to initiating their children into the human inheritance and, more particularly, into the stories that depict their way of life. In so doing, they shape, mold, and civilize their children."[3] What has been lost today, according to this view, is the authority of parents, supported by strong marriages and communities, to invest children with moral discipline.

What is primarily different in such approaches compared to the past is how to understand the moral threat. Generally this threat was historically ascribed to humanity's inborn animality (Plato) or original sin (Augustine). It is a kind of biological or spiritual disorderliness. Today, however, the threat is more likely to be understood as some kind of individualism or egoism. Humanity is capable of learning to be moral but faces an inborn natural selfishness or lack of cultural virtues. As a result, families are necessary as the most important instillers of social values.

Above all, according to this view, families should avoid raising children too permissively. As the communitarian theologian Stanley Hauerwas puts it, "we . . . raise our children permissively, because we fear 'imposing' our values on them and psychologically damaging them."[4] Children should not be left to their own devices, since today's cultures of relativism and market competition will only encourage their innate selfishness. Instead, children need to be morally stiffened by the firm hand of tradition. According to one popular psychologist, when "children are viewed as consumers of parental services," parents cannot become "assertive enough to exercise [their] parenting responsibility."[5] "Responsibility" here means parents' imposition of moral values on children.

The benefit of such approaches is that they take child rearing exceptionally seriously as a social and moral concern. In a time of intrusive mass media, impersonal marketplaces, and ideologies of endless self-fulfillment, families are indeed vital for transmitting shared histories, teaching communal values, and encouraging larger senses of responsibility. The chief drawback, however, is that children (and to a certain extent adults) are thereby treated as chiefly passive receptors of society's moral initiation. Childhood in particular is robbed of the kind of social agency by which human beings may be said to shape their worlds for themselves. Paradoxically, children must learn to take part in historically constructed moral worlds without being considered capable of historical construction themselves. The truth is, however, that even newborns can and should participate in creating moral relations.

The chief critics of such views adopt, in a way, an opposed bottom-up approach. The argument here is not that families are not important. Rather, much as we have seen in the theories of historical figures like Chrysostom, Rousseau, and Schleiermacher, it is that the primary purpose of families is to welcome and strengthen each new human being's distinctive gifts to society. Families intercede in the opposite direction: not by initiating children into adult social norms, but by encouraging children's own growing capabilities. Families serve the vital function of introducing goodness and purity into an otherwise corrupted world. They nurture, protect, and delight in each child's—and hence also each adult's—inner goodness and simplicity.

Today, such an approach tends less to emphasize childhood's moral innocence than its moral freedom, diversity, and agency. After Freud, it is difficult to see children as uncomplicated, asexual, or nonaggressive. Instead, what families liberate is each particular self's powerful inner resources and wisdom. As a United Nations World Summit document puts it, families are important because "all children must be given the chance to find their identity and realize their worth."[6] Theologically speaking, families can be said to nurture children as God's "unique gifts" to the world.[7] Or, poetically: "[Parents] are bows, God is the archer, and our children are the arrows. God is in charge, loves our children more than we ever can, and uses us as instruments of that love."[8] Against the mass public marketplace, families are private wellsprings of joy, freedom, and hope.

Such an approach to family life today also sometimes opposes not only social corruption but systemically distorted power. Sylvia Ann Hewlett and Cornel West have argued, for example, that "one of the best-kept secrets of the last thirty years is that big business, government, and the wider culture have waged a silent war against parents, undermining the work that they do."[9] What societies need, they contend, is a movement of parents' (though, interestingly, not children's) liberation. Parents face "a society that glorifies size, strength, and self-sufficiency [in which] anyone who is small, weak, or needful is treated with contempt."[10] When children are targets of the driving profits of mega-corporations like MacDonalds and Disney, families are the last bastions to stand up against gender stereotypes, consumerism, and conformity. Family life preserves what the ethicist Jürgen Habermas calls the "lifeworld" of immediate human relations against their "colonization" by the impersonal forces of the marketplace.[11]

The appeal of such a view is that it insists on parents' and sometimes children's agency. It affirms humanity's inborn goodness and giftedness. The close personal relations of the home are seen as regenerating forces in a utilitarian world, opening societies to the great diversity of human experience. The difficulty with this approach, however, is that it risks the child's and family's oversentimentalization. Children, like adults, are complex human beings who both bring goodness and joy into the world and are flawed and destructive. As the theologian Reinhold Niebuhr said in the 1940s, when a new cult of domesticity was on the rise, "there is no possibility of the family escaping the fault of regarding its own weal and woe as more important to the whole [of society] than it really is."[12] To place family life on too high a moral pedestal is to ignore its own important moral struggles, as well as its dependency on supports from the larger world. If families are the origin of society's good, then societies—beyond not interfering with them—can owe families very little. Once again, only one side of the family circle is affirmed: this time, its ability to infuse society with new agency and gifts.

Although it is not so directly involved in the culture wars, there is still a third tendency in thinking about family ethics that powerfully influences contemporary debates. Here, the chief purpose of family life is not so much social moralization or nurturing goodness as it is advancing moral development. According to this view, families should strive, alongside schools and other social and cultural institutions, to cultivate children's—as well as adults'—emotional, intellectual, and moral formation. This in turn furthers the development and progress of societies. Human nature turns out useful or not depending on the degree to which it is well socialized. While ethical development is most importantly applied to children, it also takes place in parents as they learn to care for others, and in societies as they become better at supporting them. Like for historical figures such as Aristotle, Thomas, and Locke, families are small societies charged with educating humanity toward the larger common good.

This developmental function of families tends to be understood today not only biologically but also psychologically. Its classic and still widely used statement is found in Diana Baumrind's 1966 argument for what she calls "authoritative" parenting. This is explicitly opposed to "authoritarian" (or what I would call top-down) and "permissive" (or bottom-up) parenting. "The authoritative parent [unlike the permissive parent] . . . attempts to direct the child's activities but [unlike the authoritarian parent] in a rational, issue-oriented manner. She encourages verbal give and take, and shares with the child the reasoning behind her policy."[13] Good parenting neither imposes values nor liberates agency but engages in a two-way dialogue that cultivates children's increasing moral rationality.

A contemporary theological version of this argument—based, not surprisingly, on Thomas Aquinas—is the Catholic Church's natural law conception of family ethics as involving a "principle of subsidiarity." This principle holds that more powerful social institutions like government, business, and the church should "furnish help" (*subsidium*) to smaller social institutions like families and marriages, but without taking over the unique functions that those smaller institutions can better perform for themselves.[14] As Aristotle noted long ago, families create unique natural bonds based on parents' significantly greater likelihood of investing in their children's well-being than anyone else. But parents also depend on wider social investments that they alone cannot secure, such as cultural meaning, professional support, economic stability, and government aid. As the saying goes, it takes a village to raise a child. These concentric circles of extended family, community, schools, culture, states, and religion do not replace families but support them in the task of raising children to become fully socialized.

The chief advantage of this third ethical approach, especially for today, is that it unites families' private and public functions into a larger whole. Rather than imposing a public order on private relations, or protecting private goodness from a corrupt public world, families are dialogical institutions that combine both interpersonal and societal resources to develop children's moral capabilities. The disadvantage, however, as throughout history, is that childhood is thereby interpreted primarily through the lens of what children are not yet: namely, developed adults. Insights about development turn into a morality of developmentalism. The chief purpose of family life becomes helping children to grow up into adults. While this may seem an obvious goal, it obscures the ethical sense in which children are diverse and other moral agents in and of themselves. Family responsibility should not be based, as the philosopher Hans Jonas unfortunately phrases it, on children's "demanding impotence of being-not-yet."[15] Children contribute just as fully as adults to the creation of family and societal meaning. Family life is not just a means to an end but a full expression of being human.

A NEW GENERATIVITY

Each of these approaches captures something important about family life, but each does so in a one-sided way. Families should impart values, welcome gifts, and develop capabilities all at once. They should respond to children in their fullest possible moral complexity as capable of wrong, bringing new goodness, and becoming more socialized over time. We have less trouble viewing adults today in these diverse ways simultaneously. In order to rethink family life, for children and adults both, we need to think more broadly and child-responsively. Here I propose doing so through a new ethics of family generativity.

"Generativity" is most prominently associated with the developmental psychologist Erik Erikson. He defines it as "the interest [of parents and other adults] in establishing and guiding the next generation."[16] This interest, he claims, advances a natural adult desire to pass on wisdom and knowledge to the young, including both one's own children and other young people. Generativity in turn "cogwheels" with children's natural needs and capabilities, creating a circle of generative care that promotes development in adults and children at once.

However, Erikson understands generativity as characterizing only one particular stage of the lifecycle, a stage of middle adulthood when people typically raise their children and become settled in their careers. Because each stage of life incorporates the gains of earlier stages, generativity belongs in a way to older adults too and builds on gains that have already been made in earlier developmental phases. But, as the point of view formulated in this book suggests, such a definition ultimately ends up excluding the moral complexity of children. For children become, in this view, generativity's objects and not also its subjects. Generativity, the foundation of families, is applied by adults *to* children, but not enacted by children themselves. Children are seen as developing *toward* generative capabilities but are by definition not yet generative themselves.

In contrast, I define family generativity as the kind of moral creativity that should be exercised by all family members, from the youngest to the oldest. It is not confined to one phase of the lifecycle or one particular family culture. All children take an interest and satisfaction in shaping their family and social relations and nurturing others around them. The difference between children and adults is not a matter of the kind of activity they engage in but rather of their degree of generative experience in the world and, therefore, their breadth of generative responsibility. In other words, I expand the notion of family generativity to include the world-creativity of being human.

Generativity can be understood in such a way only if it learns specifically from the ways in which generativity is practiced by children. For in children, generativity means not simply guiding others but growing in other-responsiveness over time. Both children and adults are responsible for creating increasingly dynamic relationships in the world. The generative family is an ever-expanding circle of interdependent responsibility. The central ethical responsibility of families in light of children is to cultivate, in children and adults alike, ethical responsibility itself. Family generativity grows to the extent that each and every other in the family contributes to creating the family whole.

This generative family circle can be described broadly as follows. Each newborn comes into a family world that has already been constructed beforehand. Families in part assign historical roles, pass on cultures, and create ongoing family narratives. Both children and adults are shaped by families in part passively. However, human beings also join family relations as absolutely irreducible others. Such is equally the case for newborns and newlyweds and regardless of age or experience. Indeed, families confront persons with human otherness in the starkest and most immediate terms. The circle of family relations is at once already passively constructed and always to be actively constructed anew. Finally, each family member is also called upon to respond to all the others precisely in their otherness. Not only do they demand responsiveness, but they must also increasingly respond. Selves' family obligations involve their already constructed relations' continual self-decentering over time.

In general, families fall short of their possibilities for moral generativity insofar as they exclude members from the whole family generative task. They fulfill them insofar as, on the contrary, they are responsive to their members' experiences, narratives, and differences. This they do through the retelling of family stories, the remaking of family rituals, and the evolution of family dynamics. Generativity of this interdependent kind fully includes children of all ages.

Take, for example, the case of an infant like Ying Ying Fry. Adopted from China, she is forced at a very early age to create a sense of family amid abandonment, serial parenting, new smells, tastes, and sounds, and a new and alien culture. This would be a challenge for anyone, child or adult. For a baby or child, the ability to create meaningful family relations in such a situation depends particularly on the investment and support of other family members. She requires an especially dynamic response to what makes her distinctive and other. And she must herself respond to new others in highly creative, new ways. What she faces is a microcosm of what faces all members of families throughout life.

It is true that, as Erikson would say, Fry relies to a great extent on the nurturing generativity of her adoptive parents. They face the great tasks of new parents everywhere. But this is only part of the picture. In a more profound sense, Fry relies on a kind of parental generativity that welcomes and cultivates her own generativity, too. Her deepest desire is not just to receive family care but to become a caring member of a family herself. She is not so much dependent as interdependent. As a full human being, Fry does not need just to be given support but to participate in a full circle of relations. She does not ask merely to be loved but also to have the opportunity to love others. This, one could say, is her human right.

The reason childhood is so central to family life is that it calls for interpersonal generativity of the most expansive and dynamic kind. Family life is most fully stretched as it welcomes a new person into it. At the same time, it is the beginning of a child's larger cycle of generative relations in the world. Bonnie Miller-McLemore articulates this more dynamic kind of family generativity when she argues that "society has infantilized children as fundamentally incapable of constructive thought and action . . . [when] instead, at the center [of families] should stand the gradual transfer of appropriate responsibility."[17] Families exist not just to create worlds for children but, in a more complex way, to create worlds in which children can function as world creators. Family generativity is realized only insofar as it presses family dynamics to embrace an ever more decentered family responsibility—a circle constantly expanding to include its own diversity of otherness.

GENERATIVE PARENTING

Parenting is such a profound generative responsibility because it decenters the parent around others who are only just beginning to learn to decenter themselves around others for themselves. It is, in a sense, the "beginning" of the moral circle, its first steps in expansion and growth. To put it differently, parenting stands at the beginning of the moral process whereby children begin to expand (or contract) their worlds in response to others. It requires a kind of self-excessive love that does not destroy the self in self-sacrifice but rather opens the self to new self-creation in light of others. Parenting demands not just self-expression or self-denial but the more dynamic practice of other-responsive self-decentering. It asks for the enlargement of one's own humanity for the sake of the enlargement of the humanity of one's child. The ethical purpose of parenting is to love others by enabling others to love.

Parents are obliged by children to stretch themselves in radical and unanticipated new directions. They are called upon to respond to the most basic of others' needs, to give up sleep and freedoms, to invest in schooling and activities, to worry about another's future, to be involved yet gradually to let go. Parenting is generative of not only the world of the child but a fully circular parent-child relation, of which the child is increasingly generative also. In a sense, as Christine Gudorf has put it, parental "self-sacrificing love is always aimed at the establishment of mutual love."[18] What should be mutual here is responsiveness. The parent is more responsively generative the more he or she helps the child grow in generativity. Parenting should generate generativity. It should creatively decenter the parent in response to the creative decentering capabilities of the child. It does not complete the circle but welcomes the child to take part ever more expansively in it.

In this way, families also contain the central function of contributing to the larger creativity or generativity of societies. Families are meaningful worlds in themselves, but they are also parts of larger cycles of human community and power. The intimate dynamics of family life are bound up both passively and actively with markets, mass media, and government. Cultivating children's responsibilities to others is already connected from birth onwards with responding creatively to larger social histories and forces. As Lisa Sowle Cahill has argued, "humans have a natural capacity for intimacy, empathy, compassion, and altruism that can be learned and fostered in close associations like the family and gradually extended, with the help of cultural symbol systems and the communications media, to larger and larger communities."[19] This "extension" of human relational capacities is not just the application of values learned in the family to the larger world. It is the extension of the capacity for moral extension itself: for broadening oneself in response to others in one's world.

The home is the first site of expanding responsibility because it brings others together in the most immediate and concrete ways. The purpose of parents and children creating meaningful family worlds is to create meaningful worlds as such. But for children in particular, though also to some extent for adults, the dynamics of family relations are also training grounds for the dynamics of contributing to culture and society. Family generativity produces social generativity, as well as vice versa. It is in the intimate sphere of family life that persons generally first begin to create worlds of meaning in response to others, which is the central capability of responsible life in society as human beings.

To call families "generative," therefore, is to say that the fundamental ethical purpose of family life is to create shared worlds with others. Being human involves not just living alongside others but also making new narratives with them and responding singularly to them. Family generativity arises out of a variety of biological, psychological, social, cultural, traditional, historical, and spiritual constructions. It does not spring from nothing. But its underlying ethical purpose is neither to impose nor to overcome such conditions, but rather to reconstruct them in new ways responsive to each new person. Such is the generativity of love. It is neither self-centered nor self-sacrificial but self-decentering.

THE FAMILY CIRCLE

If families are generative in this way, the key ethical question in family life is how other-responsiveness may be expanded over time rather than narrowed. The great otherness of each new human being in the world prevents us from answering this question with any kind of rigid moralism. There may be kinds of family relation that on the whole prove more morally generative than others, and there are certainly ways of destroying family generativity profoundly. But as the most immediate sphere of responsiveness to each other that most people experience in their lifetimes, families are and should be each unique. Family norms should ultimately be grounded in norms of humanity. From a child-centered point of view, families both belong to particular social histories and recreate them in their own distinctive ways.

In a similar way to previous chapters, it is possible to break family generativity down into three interdependent arcs. As these reinforce one another, a family circle may become more dynamic and expansive. As they are cut short or ignored, family life will tend to become ethically narrow or destructive. Thus a whole family dynamics can be pictured in the following way.

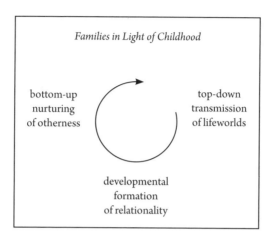

Families all at once transmit shared lifeworlds, form evolving relations over time, and nurture each other's otherness. What do these add up to? A responsibility, shared by children and adults alike, to create increasingly expansive family worlds.

NURTURING OTHERNESS

Let us take as an example the complexities of family life portrayed in Jhumpa Lahiri's novel *The Namesake*.[20] Gogol Ganguli is the eldest of two children whose parents immigrated to the United States from India just before he was born. As he grows up, he struggles to be part of a thriving Bengali community while also becoming thoroughly Americanized. The arc of the story takes him farther and farther away from family relations after he leaves home, but then back to a deeper understanding of the experiences of his parents and their own earlier efforts to raise him. He learns that he has his strange name not only because Nikolai Gogol is his father's favorite novelist, but more specifically because, by a strange fluke, one of Gogol's novels saved his father's life as a youth in a train crash. The son comes to see his father less as a cultural caricature and more as a distinctive other person in his own right. The father has all these years worked hard to act responsibly toward his son without smothering him, and his son now learns better to respond to the creativity and vulnerabilities of his father.

Part of a dynamic and healthy family circle is the bottom-up nurturing of each family member's distinctive otherness. Each new human being, I argued in chapter 2, is a gift to those around them. This gift is complex, since it involves both passively having been given certain gifts, such as natural talents and cultural inheritances, and actively giving these in one's own distinctive ways to the world. Parents and children give themselves to each other in a fully interdependent way. There is no immediate sense in which either Gogol or his father can open themselves to what is distinctive about the other. Rather, given the vast webs of relation that define family dynamics, otherness is something, especially in children but also in parents, that must be responded to creatively over the experience of time. The question is how this responsiveness to one another can grow rather than contract.

What happens to a family when a new "other" enters into it—whether through birth, adoption, marriage, or any other means—is that family dynamics are transformed as a whole. Each new other is not simply, as modernity suggests, an added autonomous individual. Rather, like a new color introduced into a painting, what was there remains but now in a wholly new light. Each other introduces into already existing family relations a disruptive and promising new field of family possibilities. And this disruption and promise changes further as others in families, both children and adults, evolve and change over time.

A newborn, to take the most powerful new other, transforms the whole world of a family in many new ways. On the one hand, she shares common histories, such as genetics, ancestry, traditions, class, culture, time, and place. On the other hand, as a singular other, she shapes these conditions in altogether new ways, both for herself and for others. Genetics are modified, traditions given new meanings, money spent differently, culture reinterpreted, and time itself invested with new range and possibility. This otherness of a new child in a family is both objective and subjective at once: her particular and visible being-in-the-world is different, but so also are the ways in which she recreates this being-in-the-world for herself and in response to others. The family should not be taken over by each new other or sacrificed to it. Nor should the family simply incorporate each new other into its existing narratives. Rather, to one degree or another, the family ought to be renarrated and decentered in creative new ways.

Such is also the case, from a childist point of view, not only in response to children but also in response to parents, stepparents, grandparents, relatives, or anyone else. Families are on the whole social institutions in which their members have to be welcomed regardless of their peculiarities and differences. This welcoming has its limits when family members are violent or profoundly destructive. Abuse and neglect attack the very foundations of family other-responsiveness. But a family is also capable of tremendous self-transformation. It has the capacity for hospitality to strangers, including the first and ultimate strangers to the world: newborns. It can generate new stories that include what is most colorful in humanity, what is rejected and despised elsewhere in society, what makes human beings parts of shared humanity no matter what.

The nurturing of otherness in families is the responsibility of all, but it falls most extensively on parents. It is parents who, in principle at least, have the widest moral experience with which to create dynamic family wholes. It is parents who expand families in the first place. As Aristotle says, parents are generally more fully invested than anyone else in their children's well-being and growth. As we can now see, this investment must be placed in each child, not merely as the parents' property, as Aristotle thought, but as a singular other who also creates the family world. The parental responsibility is to render the diversity of others in families generative of meaningful family relations. Both parents and children depend for meaning on each other. But parents have the wider obligation to create an inclusive family creativity.

Such a responsibility belongs also to children, since children are also full human beings. As children grow and mature, they do not suddenly discover a capability, at an ontologically distinct phase of moral maturity, for responding generatively to others as others. Rather, this capability is a gift from birth. As for parents, even though it may start out small, it can be either expanded or contracted over time. A newborn changes in response to the difference of parents as he or she adapts to food and sleep, smiles and plays, and opens further over time to the vaster complexities of others' lives. Older children and adolescents can grow in other-responsibility as their relations to others become more wide-ranging and diverse. However much more widely for adults, there is no one in a family who is not responsible for nurturing the others' otherness more fully.

TRANSMITTING LIFEWORLDS

But second, families are also top-down institutions that help to transmit larger historical lifeworlds. Gogol's parents' complex efforts to transmit their inherited cultures in a new cultural environment are only a particularly visible representation of the task of families everywhere. It is through family, in large part, that each human being begins and continues the lifelong journey of interpreting the meaning of their cultural, historical, and communal worlds for themselves. Families may perform this task with more or less self-consciousness or dynamism, but they cannot avoid performing it altogether. Part of the circle of family relations is the appropriation of shared historical narratives to generate new narratives for present life. As we saw in chapter 3, social narration is not simply a matter of passively adopting traditions. It is the passive-active creation of larger meaning over time.

Part of the dynamics of family relations lies, therefore, in interpreting historical inheritances into new personal and family narratives. Families have an important responsibility for situating human life in relation to larger historical horizons. Families are already parts of wider moral cultures; indeed, the very institution of family itself is culturally constructed. But the conditions that shape and make possible family life also have to be appropriated in relation to particular family worlds and family members. Sometimes larger historical heritages need to be rejected as too narrow: for example, if they exclude female interpretation through sexism. Most historical traditions, as we have seen, do not adequately include the experiences and perspectives of children. But family relations cannot avoid the ethical responsibility of reconstructing historical narratives into increasingly shared meaning over time.

It is a mistake once again to think that this interpretive task falls only on parents. One can understand why, in a time of market intrusions and radical individualism, parents need to take this responsibility especially seriously—perhaps more seriously than in the past. But from a child-centered point of view, it is clear that children do not just passively absorb the narratives that are fed to them by adults. Rather, each child is a full human being who both is narrated by her world and narrates it anew for herself. Were this not the case, children could not grow in the very capacity for narration. Viewing children as merely recipients of moral values is counterproductive and dehumanizing. It does not account for the many ways in which children themselves narrate family life. The ethical question is the degree to which families are able to generate cultural meaning with each other.

The greater responsibility for a family's narrative world falls on parents, not because parents alone understand narratives, but because they have wider narrative experience. Having children should not solidify parents' historical values but challenge them to grow and deepen. It is a transformative experience that should be met, not with anxious fixations on a supposedly unchanging past, but with more complex interpretations for the present. Parents have been tested through more years than their children by relations, challenges, and disappointments in the world. They have had to create diverse kinds of new stories culminating, perhaps, in the most socially creative act possible: reproduction in the form of another human being. Compared to their children, parents can in principle be expected to be able to generate family meaning, not in a different way, but from a broader temporal and hence narrative perspective.

DEVELOPING RELATIONALITY

Finally, families also have a third ethical task of developing relationality. By "relationality" I mean the capability to form mutually generative bonds with others. Families are composed not only of others and lifeworlds but also interdependent relations. Gogol and his parents are always related, even when he is not speaking to them; but this relation ultimately manages to grow into a more complex bond over time. Relationality does not mean, as Erikson suggests, that families meet the needs of parents and children in two fundamentally different ways. There is a developmental path from childhood to adulthood, but it is not from pregenerativity to generativity. Rather, it is from a child's relatively more immediate relationality to relationality that may include wider mutual generativity over time. This temporal continuum means that children and adults share the same ethical task of generating over time ever more expansive relational capabilities.

The difference in developmental aims for children and parents is a matter not of kind but of degree. Children's relatively shorter experience in the world means that they are able to generate social relations in generally more immediate and narrow ways. Children have to learn how to respond to others more broadly in order to create wider social narratives. Overall, they need to learn over time—as do adults—how to form more complex and meaningful relations to those with whom they share their lives.

The fundamental reason why families are developmental institutions is that human relations are temporal. From a childist point of view, relationships are not fixed in one particular point in time; rather, they constantly evolve and grow. Families are able to stretch out human time in distinctive ways. They persist over time as a set of lasting human relations. They integrate ancestors and descendents. They unite histories and futures of different families through marriage. They tie together overlapping lifecycles of youth, adulthood, and old age. They celebrate and mourn the ultimate times of each new birth and death. All human relations are temporal, but families are one of the most powerful ways in which narrative time is created into relations.

Overall, putting all three sides of this circle together, families succeed or fail ethically to the extent that they expand or contract in generativity. Generativity, in its ethical sense, means creating worlds of meaning with others. It includes all at once nurturing otherness, transmitting lifeworlds, and developing relationality. These tasks support one another. The more a family responds to its members' otherness, the more its inherited histories will find meaning and its relationships form mutually. The more these histories are creatively engaged, the more resources are found for complex relations and the more assumptions can be critiqued through difference. And the more complexly a family develops relationality over time, the more it can respond to each other's distinctive otherness and interpret family histories into meaning.

Families are close relations of others who create interdependent worlds of meaning with one another over time. Each member of a family is responsible for stretching out this circle of shared life more expansively over time in response to each other. Family is, in a way, the first generator of social generativity, the beginning of temporal and responsive social creativity. Families are not a separate sphere but part of the creation of shared humanity.

THE DYNAMICS OF LOVE

All of this suggests, furthermore, that however much families construct themselves over time, their ethical horizons are endless. There is no end to family responsibility. From the hidden depths of ancestry to unknowable descendents, from each new member to each new experience, families constantly exceed themselves. Taking responsibility for one another in families—for both adults and children—is both satisfying and difficult. Being a child in a family means starting on a lifelong journey of constructing and reconstructing ever new relations. Having a child means embarking on a timeless and unbounded love.

I argued in chapter 4 that selves must ultimately be open to decentering themselves in response to others beyond anticipation. This excessive self-transformation can be called love. It is not the same as self-sacrifice. Nor does it mean that others are there for selves' endless satisfaction. Instead, it means—and especially in light of childhood—that through love, human beings are called upon to respond to each other always more expansively than they can imagine.

This pressing toward what lies at the limits of experience has traditionally been symbolized through religion, which can play at transporting the imagination toward its own beyond. Not only have all religions had a great deal to say about families, but they also frequently symbolize the divine in family terms: Mother, Father, ancestors, great ancestor, and so on. As in earlier chapters, religion can be interpreted as a diversity of historical human creations that attempt, in part, to regrasp the ultimate meaning of human creativity itself. A Creator, Brahma, demiurge, or Great Spirit is not, phenomenologically speaking, an objective cosmic being, but rather a reflection or image of what may be said to be most primordial in human experience. Religion looks through the lens of human life, the only kind of lens we have, for what lies at its own farthest borderlands or very horizons of visibility.

When it looks through the experience of children in families, religion cannot be reduced to what is often today a simplistic moralism in which family love is thought to follow a predetermined divine plan. A merely top-down family ethics destroys the generativity that families should be all about. Instead, family love should liberate family generativity. Generativity is an expression, in a sense, of the genesis of humanity itself. In this case, family love involves an element of creative excess. It creates not only new people but also unanticipated new relations. Families can generate new responses to otherness beyond what might otherwise be possible. To "do to others as you would have them do to you" becomes only more self-transforming in the context of families, where others can appear to one another in their greatest immediacy and concreteness.

Families are ordinarily thought of as arenas of love in a more proximate and static sense. Parents are often believed to love their children by sheer natural disposition. Children in turn love their parents out of gratitude and need. Such is very much the case up to a point. It is more or less what Erikson means by generativity: a view of parent-child love that goes back to Aristotle and Locke and that captures the experientially valid point that parents and children are in some sense parts of one another.

But the creative and broken nature of human life, including in families, means that natural disposition is never enough. Natural love only takes family relations so far. What it does not account for is the larger ethical necessity of creating new relations distinctively responsive to difference. Both parents and children respond to others at once creatively and destructively. Parents should love their children not only as extensions of themselves but also as irreducible others who extend the relation beyond what they could otherwise have imagined. Children likewise should love their parents not only as their natural creators but also as generative others. Part of family relations is to embrace the joy and hope of the unimaginable, of love's superabundance.

Without this kind of creative excess, family love easily devolves into mere mutual self-satisfaction or one-sided self-sacrifice. The first destroys family members' otherness, the second their selfhood. Family relations should instead open themselves up to interdependent growth. As Don Browning and others have said, "the core of [family] love is the capacity to endure modifications of experience."[21] What this means from a child-centered point of view is that each family member adds something new and distinctive that should change the family whole. To love in families is to make yourself vulnerable to open-ended self-transformation.

Is it not, after all, this expanding possibility—this voyage into new horizons—that prompts people to form families in the first place? Human beings do not embrace family generativity solely because of the urges of genetics. Biology is for human beings, as I have argued, a part but not the whole of the experience of creating meaning. Rather, selves enter into families as whole and complex human beings who wish to love whole and complex others. Genetics is but one part of a larger human generativity. The deeper desire is for new relations that will broaden human experience. Even the acts of reproduction and birthing are embodied meetings of others in their otherness, in their differences of gender or age.

Children are at once passive recipients of an already formed family world and active contributors toward it. They too should constantly exceed themselves in greater loving response to others over time. The newborn, toddler, older child, and teenager never cease being called upon ethically to stretch themselves beyond what they can imagine. They should always challenge their own existing relational limits. No child or parent ever responds to another's concrete differences fully. This falling short is part of what makes family life a productive crucible of meaning. It is also what makes it susceptible to destruction and violence. Parents bear the wider responsibility for family love because their moral horizons should be more practiced in expansiveness. But children are just as fully capable of growing in moral love as well.

However anticipated or long sought for, the arrival of a newborn transcends all expectations. What you should expect when you're expecting is to have your expectations overturned. Love for a child is not reducible to creating the child in your own image. Nor does it come down to creating yourself in the image of your child. It should mean instead creating new family horizons. It is a hyperbolic adventure, opening toward the unknown. Only in this way can families respond to the distinctive experiences and creativity of the child. Family generativity constantly transcends itself by embracing the generativity of all.

It is this moral excessiveness, furthermore, that explains why families can be powerful training grounds—for children and adults alike—for moral life in society. If all one learned in family relations was to love others as parts of oneself, extending this to wider social relations would result in a barren and utilitarian life. A child would grow up to care about neighbors, coworkers, fellow citizens, and strangers only as extensions of her own ambitions and goals. As a parent, he would fail to stretch himself into the unanticipated depths opened up by a child of his own. The golden rule would be reduced to a merely reciprocal obligation to do for others insofar as they can do for you.

As Lisa Sowle Cahill has argued, "families [can] succeed in forming members in an ethos of mutuality, equality, and solidarity and in subsuming kin loyalty under compassion for the 'neighbor,' the 'stranger,' and the 'enemy.'"[22] Families can function as training grounds for children's and adults' capacities for wider responsibility. They are usually where selves most directly experience the need to love others beyond their own expectations. As Pamela Couture puts it, "love and generosity are the fundamental relationship of neighbor to neighbor."[23] Love in families is the most immediate arena of love of neighbor and even enemy. It requires stretching oneself beyond what is natural or comfortable toward others in their differences. This is not just a child's aim but humanity's lifelong moral task.

Family love, from the perspective of childhood, is based on the larger human responsibility to generate a more inclusive humanity. It is often in families that one's sense of shared humanity is most profoundly experienced and tested. Families are opportunities for extending oneself toward other human beings in concretely interdependent ways. They are not, of course, the only means for doing so. But in few other areas of life are most people called upon to recreate themselves over time more radically. Of course, by the same token, families have also proven among the most profound arenas for self- and other-destruction. Nevertheless, the difficult and endless task of family love is to create more expansively responsive relations to one another. Such is family generativity in its ecstatic pressing beyond.

GENERATIVITY AS GENDERED

What might this kind of family generativity imply about gender? It is to some extent through the biological and cultural differences of gender that families are generated at all. The question of gender has been part of family ethics for millennia, and it is especially important today. Moreover, it has and still does revolve significantly around responsibilities toward and of children. Children themselves are profoundly impacted by gendered constructions of family life. Not only are families powerful creators of children's gender identities, but they are also gendered in part in light of perceived responsibilities to children.

Gender can be understood as one dimension of humanity's diverse creative otherness. It is in part as gendered beings that others both create worlds of relationships and are responded to by others. Part of the reason for this, as I have argued, is that world creativity is embodied: it is through one's brains, eyes, senses, and bodies that one creates worlds of meaning at all. It is in part through bodies and their social construction that family generativity is gendered.

Child-related ethics throughout history have compounded the marginalization of children in families with the further marginalization of mothers and daughters. As the philosopher Luce Irigaray has said, "motherhood—promoted by spiritual leaders as the only worthwhile destiny for women—most often means perpetuating a patriarchal line of descent."[24] Women's generative roles in families have usually been interpreted, in almost every culture in history, from the point of view of how they pass on blood lines and power for men. And, as Irigaray also notes, this means that male sexuality—and I would add male generativity more broadly—has also been systematically distorted in the process. Male power in family relations and elsewhere needs to be fundamentally disrupted and refashioned in order to uncover the deeper humanity that is possible between men, women, and children.

The generative responsibilities of fathers are narrowed in particular ways today. Contemporary fathers may be more likely to attach themselves to children emotionally (though this is debatable), but at the same time they are on the whole less fully attached to them ethically, that is, as a matter of social responsibility. For various reasons, fathers are able to be less engaged in day-to-day family life than, for example, the ancient world's male head of household, the medieval farmer, the Reformation paternal educator, or even the industrial-era breadwinner. Fathers can now relatively easily disengage themselves from child-rearing responsibilities altogether. Male disconnection from family life is not a biological or cultural necessity. Fathers are not inherently incomplete moral beings. What is required is a creative new imagination of fatherhood today as fully engaged in child rearing and family relations—but without, as throughout the past, dominating mothers and children in the process.

The perspective of childhood offers fresh perspectives on why family generativity has historically been imbalanced by gender. Top-down ethics have typically responded to what is seen as children's innate moral unruliness by asserting that families need a strong disciplinary leader. A male rather than female head of household is then justified by men's relative distance from birthing and nursing, which imparts a supposedly greater understanding of the desired higher moral order. Bottom-up ethics tend to interpret family generativity as the nurturing activity of those thought closest to children's natural goodness, namely mothers. But this purported natural closeness of children and mothers is used to argue for fathers' greater power in protecting families from the corruptions of life in public. And developmental approaches have generally viewed child rearing as passing on social skills in phases over time—a process that is often claimed to begin with mothers and gradually transition to fathers. In this case, fathers are easily imagined as embodying the more "fully developed" human ideal. In sum, the history of ethical thought about childhood (written mainly by men) provides a rich diversity of justifications for families to be centered around male prerogatives and power.

It is for this reason, among others, that recent efforts to revive family ethics through what is sometimes called "soft patriarchy" are fundamentally off base. The argument here, made by conservatives and traditionalists across diverse cultures around the globe, is that fathers are less attached to children than mothers by male biological nature, since fathers do not gestate, give birth, or nurse and cannot even be completely sure that the child is "theirs." Therefore, male involvement in the home depends on granting men their own special nonbiological, usually moral and disciplinary, power. This attitude is described as widespread in the contemporary United States by the sociologist W. Bradford Wilcox, in *Soft Patriarchs, New Men*.[25] In Christianity, it involves an ethic of male "servant-leadership" as the best way to "domesticate" fathers into responsibilities in the home. Soft patriarchal fathers overcome their relative biological detachment from parenting by committing themselves to a moral "familism," or attachment to the value of family as such. For this they are both encouraged and recompensed by mothers and communities giving them special family authority. Some even claim that this view accords with feminism, since it is the only realistic way to relieve women's burdens in the home.

The ethical problems with soft patriarchy are manifold and profound. It underestimates the historical depths of male power; mistakes Victorian industrialized gender roles for gender roles throughout history; adopts a biological essentialism; lacks faith in fathers' primordial generative capabilities; and makes an unwholesome trade-off between male attachment and female subordination. In these and other ways, it is a narrow rather than inclusive solution to today's family gender issues.

But the coup de grâce for soft patriarchy—and if for soft patriarchy, then for hard patriarchy too—is its implications for childhood. For patriarchy is and always has justified itself on the grounds that, whatever it means for women, it is what is ultimately best for children—and children's concerns should come first. However, it is here that it proves least morally responsible of all. This is the case regarding motherhood and fatherhood both.

On the one hand, in soft patriarchy motherhood is so closely merged with childhood as to obscure the genuine moral otherness or tension between mother and child. If soft patriarchy affirms a "male problematic," as fathers' biological detachment is sometimes described, this implies that women's family roles are somehow unproblematic. But from a childist point of view, all human relations are "problematic" in the ethical sense that all must strive to create relations responsive to genuine otherness. The core of family generativity is not, from this perspective, the bonds of biology. Rather, it is the more basic relation of other-responsive humanity. It is simply not true that this is only a real problem for fathers.

On the other hand, fatherhood faces the opposite problem, according to soft patriarchy, of being grounded chiefly in difference: the difference of father to child. As we have seen, generativity from a child's point of view involves not only receiving love but also giving it. A father who sees himself only as needing to attach more to his child ignores the fuller circular dynamics of their interdependent relationship. The father does not simply shape the child. The child also needs—and should be encouraged—to shape the father-child bond in turn. A soft patriarchal father falls short of his most important ethical responsibility: to welcome and nurture the expanding other-responsibility of his child. The biological essentialism of the soft patriarchal trade-off undermines the generativity of all parties involved.

GENDER AS GENERATIVE

The childist perspective developed in this book suggests a more fundamentally human connection between gender and generativity. The point of view of childhood does not preclude consideration of gender differences. Modeled in part on third-wave feminism, childism is able to respond to human otherness as socially transformative. The purpose of an inclusive ethical circle is not to erase human differences but to reimagine relations in light of them. Gender can serve the same function as age: to expand historically entrenched assumptions about human relations in order to create a wider sense of moral humanity.

While not all families contain differently gendered parents (nor should they), the conditions and contexts of human procreation should as far as possible be inclusive of parents' gendered otherness. Family generativity is narrowed to the extent that one gender is exploited or more susceptible to violence: such as through sexual abuse, unequal economic power, or one-sided expectations for housework and child rearing. Family generativity is also narrowed along gender lines to the extent that gender differences are obscured: such as when fathers walk away from pregnancies, mothers are not provided adequate prenatal care, or female infants are less valued. In such cases, families are less able to include gender difference in their own larger family generativity.

Gender becomes ethically generative insofar as historically constructed differences between women and men, mothers and fathers, and girls and boys create shared meaning rather than destroy it. For example, boys in the United States are often tempted into a culture of competitive market individualism, so that when they grow up to become fathers they may have difficulty relating to their own children (hence, perhaps, the popularity of soft patriarchy). The real experience of many fathers, however, shows that a broader father-mother-child construction is possible in which boys are encouraged to imagine themselves as future nurturers and caregivers. In this case, other-responsiveness can be a human rather than only female goal. To take another example, girls have historically been assumed to prefer quiet play to the active rough and tumble of sports. Such a construction of gender is destructive for girls as well as for boys. Given the opportunity, many girls enjoy sports as much as boys and often more. In this instance, gender constructions destroy generativity because they narrow the circle of possible human relations rather than expanding it.

Gender difference widens human horizons whenever the lens of gender helps to disrupt and decenter assumed human possibility. As Miller-McLemore has argued, mothers' "biological activities of birthing, giving suck, and rearing hones [the] distinctly human ability to create personhood and community."[26] Such activities as birthing and nursing will never be practiced by men or (prepubescent) children. But they can broaden everyone's sense of humanity insofar as they are valued by family relations and narratives, as well as by societies at large. Similarly, families are enriched by fathers' greater involvement in the same way that the workplace has been enriched by the greater involvement of women: by including in the whole countless other forms of creativity.

In the end, what we learn from childhood about gender relations in families is that they are both historically generated and capable of yet unknown new generativity over time. Gender is at once constructed by history and capable of being reconstructed anew. Just as children can grow in response to others over time, so also can mothers and fathers. Human beings can embrace gender and other kinds of differences as expansions rather than contractions of their moral imaginations.

SOME CONSIDERATIONS OF MARRIAGE

Today's debates about marriage tend to assume a chiefly adult point of view: how marriages are formed, who can enter into them, how to negotiate sex and gender, under what conditions marriages may be dissolved, and so on. Historically, however, the central and fundamental purpose of marriage—as both a religio-cultural and a legal institution, and across the globe—has more than anything else centered on the protection, well-being, and nurturance of children. Augustine influentially stated the three purposes of marriage as *proles* (offspring), *fides* (fidelity), and *sacramentum* (spirituality). It is no accident that *proles* or offspring should come first. Marriage has evolved very differently over the course of history and across diverse cultures, but it has rarely lost sight of its central moral significance for children.

This connection to childhood has taken different forms among the three kinds of childism we have been tracing. Some—and increasingly many today—see marriage as part of how larger communities transmit to children (and, in part, also to adults) higher moral values. Calvin, for example, argues that marriage exists primarily to tie offspring, through their parents, into a larger moral "covenant" with society, legally binding families to extended kin, church, and state, so that the widest possible social resources may be invested in each new generation.[27] Others, for instance Chrysostom and Rousseau, have understood marriage as uniting parents around the essentially private task of nurturing from below children's natural innocence and giftedness. Marriage is the expression of a sexual and procreative single flesh that welcomes children into closely knit bonds. Others, taking their inspiration from figures such as Aristotle and Thomas, argue that marriage invests the natural mother-child relation with moral commitment from the father, creating a private-public social institution that invests both parents in the long process of their children's social development. Marriage should integrate private love with public commitment so as to support the difficult tasks of children's socialization into the world.

Without rehearsing once again the relative strengths and weaknesses of these perspectives on childhood, let us simply note that they provide one way to frame today's highly divisive marriage debates. The fundamental question is not, as some claim, whether to revive traditional marriage or dissolve it. The tradition is itself complex and divided. There is no single marriage ideal in history. Even the Bible offers diverse rationales for marriage, as well as particular practices such as concubinage, child brides, multigenerational households, male-only rights to divorce, the stoning of adulterous women, and almost absolute patriarchy that few today would embrace.[28] Marriage will continue, as it always has and should, to change as a legal and moral institution according to history, culture, and new moral horizons.

One of the most creative new approaches to marriage is developed in an influential book by Don Browning, Bonnie Miller-McLemore, Pamela Couture, K. Brynolf Lyon, and Robert Franklin, aptly titled *From Culture Wars to Common Ground*.[29] It is particularly helpful for our discussion because it explicitly bases marriage on an Eriksonian obligation of generativity.

Marriage can be understood, these authors argue, through an ethics of "progressive familism" (or "critical familism"). "Familism" is defined as the assertion that family and marriage remain both privately and publicly important today for adults, children, and societies. While practices of marriage vary widely across relationships and traditions, it is claimed, overall a culture of nonmarriage, out-of-wedlock parenthood, and high divorce rates in a society undermines human thriving and development, especially for children but also for adults. Social scientific evidence can be drawn upon to show that marriage is on average, though of course not always, correlated with greater physical and mental health for partners, higher family wealth, greater sexual fidelity, increased parental time with children, and children's own elevated psychological, physical, and material well-being.[30]

"Progressive," in the term "progressive familism," means that a stronger family and marriage culture must nevertheless oppose a deeply entrenched historical patriarchy with a full ethics of gender equality. The meaning of marriage today must "progress" in the sense of developing new and truly egalitarian forms. This view is argued to be more fully Christian, since, despite the obvious patriarchy of biblical and theological traditions, the early Jesus movement appeared to promote a trajectory toward gender equality beyond the even more deeply patriarchal Greco-Roman norms of the time. Overall, marriage today should be kept alive as important for human goods, but in a way that is fully responsive to human rights and equality.

The result is a "new family ideal" carving out a middle ground in the culture wars and summarized as "the committed, intact, equal-regard, public-private family."[31] Marriage in particular should bind parents in a public-private institution that offers equal respect and opportunities for both partners. For example, one of the book's signature proposals suggests that, since "it takes time and energy to create an equal-regard family with parents guiding children," there should ideally be, and society should materially support, "a sixty-hour workweek for a mother and father that could be divided between the partners as thirty-thirty or forty-twenty."[32] New interests such as balancing gender and work can be combined with the longstanding benefits of marriage as a social institution. Private relations and public goods can in this way support one another. Marriage is able on the whole, though of course it fails in many instances, to support the simultaneous development of all family members.

Perhaps the chief benefit of this argument is that it resists the privatization of marriage in today's world without reverting to a hierarchically ordered, authoritarian family values moralism. Privatization and moralization need not be locked in mortal combat. The authors of *From Culture Wars to Common Ground* offer a creative new vision of marriage that is more complex and ultimately more helpful for children.

The drawback, however, is that marriage and generativity are still interpreted primarily through the lenses and experiences of adulthood. This is because the book's most significant ethical basis is a developmental one—from Aristotle, Aquinas, and Erikson, as well as more recent evolutionary psychology—that sees children primarily as recipients of adult care rather than as their own generative agents.[33] Marriage is interpreted chiefly through the lens of adult sexuality and parenting. Its major concern, as for Aristotle, is "the male problematic, the tendency of men to drift away from families."[34] Marriage helps fathers resist biological drives to reproduce with many women instead of committing themselves to just one, making it a time-tested strategy for attaching men to their offspring so that the latter stand a greater chance of survival and growth.

Marriage also responds, according to these authors, to "the female problematic, the tendency of females under certain conditions to suppress their own needs and raise children without paternal participation."[35] This represents a progressive acknowledgment of the unique concerns of women. But note that we are still talking only about adults. Both the "male" and "female" problematics involve children as their objects, but from the point of view of parents. Marriage exists to enable the social generativity first of all of parents: fathers through attachment, and mothers through equality and support. But should it not most centrally of all aim to nurture the social generativity of children? And would not the perspective of children change what is meant by family generativity itself?

MARRIAGE IN LIGHT OF CHILDHOOD

Our larger ethical reflections in this book allow us to consider marriage as an institution not just for negotiating adult sexuality and socializing children, but more fundamentally for strengthening the mutual creativity of family relations overall. Sexuality is but one expression of humanity's desire to generate relations in fuller responsiveness to others. Socialization is not the only reason children are in families. From children's own points of view, families are meaningful worlds in and of themselves, in which children and adults share narratives and take on responsibilities. Marriage in particular should be based on these more fully child-inclusive moral grounds. It does not merely cogwheel adults' generativity with children's needs. Rather, it should create conditions that can expand the generativity of all family members at once.

Marriage is both public and private, not just because it serves as a transition between these two worlds, but because such is the nature of human relations. To generate or create relations with others is to draw one's own distinctive experiences of life into broader narratives and responsibilities in the world. Marriage strings together a particularly wide range of private and public practices: from sexuality and love to social and economic ties and to cultural and legal obligations. From a child-centered point of view, marriage draws assistance from society as it brings into society children's and parents' creative energies. Marriage can help stretch human generativity across both the most personal of human connections and the most public of economic and legal supports. Love among parents and offspring can also tie itself into larger kin networks, wider legal accountability, and broader social and cultural meanings.

Of course, marriages are often failures. From a child's point of view, they can fall short in any number of ways, whether in providing a context for support and care, protecting against nonviolence, or nurturing her or his growing otherness. Marriages are rightly dissolved when they become destructive through neglect or abuse. But on the whole, while no marriage is perfect, marriage in general may help in creating a dynamic family world that at once forms enduring narratives over time and responds to its members' irreducible experiences.

The traditional good of marriage of *proles*, or offspring, can then be reinterpreted in a more child-inclusive way. It does not simply mean caring for children, but rather welcoming children into the full dynamics of an interdependent family circle. Parents' legal bondedness to one another may make it easier for children to contribute to an evolving family narrative over time. It may protect children a little more from losing parental connections. And it may help provide a child with a more stable environment in which to make heard her own voice and experiences. Of course, none of this is inevitable—far from it. All families are distinct. Marriage could have the opposite effects. But these are the kinds of ways that marriage should be rethought if it is to include not only adults but also children's growth in generativity.

For these reasons, though I cannot provide a full defense of it here, the point of view of childhood should support the legalization of same-sex marriage. For the particular gender of each parent, while not unimportant, is not as important as the generativity of the family whole. Generativity is more ethically fundamental than gender. Same-sex marriage offers the same public-private environment for children as does opposite-sex marriage.

The usual ethical argument against same-sex marriage is that it is better on the whole for children to be raised by both of their biological parents. However, this argument reduces the relevant differences within families chiefly to the biological, much as in the argument for soft patriarchy. For the world-creating creatures that human beings are, biology is only one part of a larger narrative and social whole. Many children grow up in families today that are headed by two adults of the same sex, whether through adoption, insemination, or a previous relationship. Homosexuality is (or should be) no longer taboo, and gays and lesbians have proven just as good (and bad) at being parents as anyone else. If marriage can in fact bring a wider private-public dynamism to family relations, then it would do a disservice to children with same-sex parents to prevent their being able to form one.

What matters specifically for children is not the sexual orientation of their parents but the degree of their parents' responsive generativity toward them. As the Anglican theologian Adrian Thatcher has argued, "marriage is able to be extended theologically to lesbian and gay couples" because it is at root a "lifelong covenant" linked to caring for children over the long term.[36] The desire to raise and nurture children, while not shared by all, is a characteristic not of any particular sexuality but of humanity. It is one of the most profound ways in which human beings exercise generativity. The base criterion of a morally healthy marriage is the extent to which it supports the creation of other-responsive families, including the growing other-responsive capabilities of any children. Homosexual parents are no less capable of this humanizing aim than any other parent. If anything, in today's world, they may be more easily attuned to the particular struggles of otherness. On the whole, all parents and potential parents should be able to bind themselves legally to one another, should they so desire, so that they and their children may benefit from wider circles of public support.

Contemporary marriage faces tremendous challenges from globalization, clashing cultures, and family worlds' increasing privatization. It is more likely now than at perhaps any other time in history to be understood as a merely private contract between individuals, a "rational choice" of adults in their pursuit of autonomous self-interest.[37] A child-responsive interpretation of marriage offers a dynamic, interdependent, and in the end more fully humanizing alternative. Marriage is neither just an avenue for personal gain nor a buttress for communal tradition, but a cultural and legal means for expanding other-responsibility. It can and should support children in particular as growing members of generative societies.

CONCLUSION

The culture wars over family life prove strangely adult-centered. Either families exist to impose parents' family values or they merely express autonomous individuals' disconnected choices. From the point of view of both actual children and childist ethics, however, families are vital centers of interdependent generativity. Children and adults confront here the most immediate and concrete humanity of others. They are opened up to larger narratives tying them to ancestors, descendents, and immediate others over time. Family members face some of the most complex imaginable responsibilities for creating human relations. Not all families contain children, but all families involve childist aims and obligations.

The ethical purpose of families is to generate human generativity, the capability for creating worlds with others over time and in response to differences. Family generativity falls more expansively on adults and parents because they in principle have wider moral experiences. But exactly the same kind of expanding family responsibility falls also on children. What is more, it is in children that social responsibility is most importantly to be encouraged. Children are not just recipients of family generativity but also its agents. How children generate relations is a lesson to adults. The difference between the responsibilities of parents and those of children is a matter of degree rather than of kind. Families as a whole gain in moral humanity insofar as they include rather than exclude the family creativity of each and every other: male and female, old and young.

Such a view also helps us understand why families are important to larger societies. From a child-centered perspective, families are both ends in themselves and means to larger social capabilities—for children and adults both. This does not mean that families are training grounds for social values, cocoons of social liberty, or pathways toward socialization. It means, more dynamically, that families are crucibles of social responsibility. What children and adults stand to learn in family relations, from a moral point of view, is increasing abilities to create relations responsive over time to others. These abilities, as we saw in previous chapters, are the foundations of a good and just society. No one creates social worlds of a sufficiently other-inclusive kind. But families provide human beings an opportunity to realize moral creativity in uniquely immediate and dynamic ways.

Families can be imagined as ever-expanding moral circles. They are not one circle within other concentric circles of wider society. Rather, they are bound up with the full private-public circularity of all moral life.

Each other who enters a family, whether through birth, adoption, love, marriage, or any other means, should be both welcomed into a responsive family whole and responsible for that family whole themselves. Each enters into a family dynamics that ought to be generated by each family member at once. Family relations become more expansive by protecting, forming, and nurturing their members' different generative capabilities. This includes accountability, among other things, to differences of gender and age. A family's central ethical responsibility is to generate over time more inclusively generative relations. This is why human beings have always created families: not just to continue the species, nor merely for individual satisfaction, but in order to experience the fullness of life lived with others.

Chapter 7

The Art of Ethical Thinking

THE PHILOSOPHER Gareth Matthews has demonstrated that children are complex philosophical, spiritual, and ethical thinkers. Here is one example he gives of an infant, Michael Brown, fifteen months old:

> [Michael] was struggling with his friend, Paul, over a toy. Paul started to cry. Michael appeared concerned and let go of the toy so that Paul would have it, but Paul kept crying. Michael paused, then gave his teddy bear to Paul, but the crying continued. Michael paused again, then ran into the next room, returned with Paul's security blanket, and offered it to Paul, who then stopped crying.[1]

Matthews's argument is not that children possess some kind of superior moral wisdom to adults. It is simply that, contrary to popular understandings of moral development, especially in the West, *"some very young children sometimes act in genuinely moral ways, not just in pre-moral ways."*[2]

In a similar way, Myra Bluebond-Langner has shown that children's ethical and other kinds of thinking and acting are more intricate than often imagined in situations of the child's chronic illness or impending death. A ten-year-old girl, Britt Foster, is in the hospital with an advanced stage of the fatal illness cystic fibrosis (CF). She is talking with her father about her nine-year-old brother Tyler:

> "He worries a lot," Britt replied offhandedly [to her father] while she continued to color. "He worries about me mostly. I don't know why. Here, I'm coloring the shirt in. Sometimes he talks to me about what he worries about. Sometimes, I wouldn't say much, because he doesn't want me to know. He just, well, I can hear it on the phone that he is. At home he says, 'If you don't eat you're going to die.' Or he says, 'You're going to die, BriBri.'

He's, I don't know. He's scared. He's heard a lot of CF patients die. He's really scared. [More discussion of coloring]. I don't get scared. No, I don't get scared. Tyler gets scared because he thinks I'm gonna die. But I don't get scared, because I know I'm not, because I know I'm strong enough. When I was four years old I fought it off, because I was going to die, but I fought it off. I was only twelve months old or something and I did then too. I don't know how, but I did." ... "I'm a fighter," Britt announced. "Tyler just doesn't understand that I am."[3]

Britt is actively thinking through a variety of difficult issues. She is struggling with the possibility of her own death, folding it into her larger story of being a fighter. She is also working out a way to respond to the different feelings of her brother, who is likewise having a difficult time with her illness. Moreover, she is also reassuring her father. In the language of this book, she is recreating her own narrative world and decentering it in response to others.

In fact, we have encountered many examples of children's multifaceted ethical thinking throughout the previous chapters: Ying Ying Fry's concern for abandoned babies, Tony Anderson's articulation of his right to be heard, Ishmael Beah's decision to participate in war and then heal from it, and so on. Examples could be multiplied as many times as there are children. Children's moral thinking capabilities are as complex and diverse as those of adults.

Strangely, this better understanding of children as ethical thinkers has had little to no effect on ideas about ethics itself. On the contrary, what it means to think in an ethical way is, if anything, understood today in an especially adult-centered way. Ethicists tend to assume an adult subject. On the whole, ethical thinking is either rationalistic or traditionalistic. On the one hand, it means exercising autonomy, calculating utilitarian ends, or participating in social argumentation. On the other, it consists in exhibiting good character traits, applying communal virtues, or expressing one's particular culture. The first takes adulthood as its model while the second gives adults all the power. The time has come to ask the difficult question of how the ways in which children think ethically should transform how to understand ethical thinking as such.

This question brings us to a further kind of moral practice—besides enacting social rights and living in families—that is in a sense even more personal. It touches on the innermost recesses of the mind and soul. This chapter is more abstract and experimental than the two previous chapters and does not delve very much into current scholarly debates. My aim is simply to sketch a sense in which ethical thinking is not something that begins at a certain "age of reason," but is a continuous experience all the way from birth to death.

History has often denied full moral thinking capabilities in women, minorities, the poor, the colonized, and most other human groups. Today, however, those most likely to be thought incapable of moral thought are children. What if, however, childhood taught us to think about ethical thinking in a more expansively human way?

WHAT IS ETHICAL THINKING?

The reason it might seem odd to investigate moral thinking in light of childhood is that, historically, it is precisely this capability that has so often been used to define what it means no longer to be a child. From Plato to Paul and Calvin to Kant, adults have been understood as morally rational and children, in contrast, as morally pre-, non-, or irrational. What makes this assumption particularly difficult to overcome is that, on the whole, children are less experienced and powerful than other marginalized groups when it comes to standing up for their particular capabilities in society. Fifteen-month-old Michael Brown is still very new to moral thinking's languages, cultures, and structures. It is easy for adults to assume that he is not yet really a moral thinker.

This problem is compounded by modernity. Despite its many gains, the Enlightenment came to associate moral thinking with the exercise of individual autonomy. The more one is able to free oneself from tradition and community—from habits and dependencies—the more one is thought to be able to think. The mark of ethical wisdom is being able to come to one's own independent judgments. Somehow ethical thinking is the act of a pure and solitary ego liberated from worldly bonds.

This chapter argues, in contrast, that ethical thinking is an art. It creates received historical and social meanings into new worlds of meaning over time and in response to others. It deals in moral tension and disruption as selves confront their own narrative diversity and the otherness of others. The notion of ethical thinking as an art has been actively opposed since Plato's insistence on the censorship of the poets in his ideal moral republic—censorship precisely in order to control the moral education of children. Fixed principles, laws, and virtues have ever since dominated over children in particular and over imagination, interdependence, and change in general.

Ethical thinking, as our reflections in this book suggest, is inherently artful or poetic, not in the sense that it mirrors something else real, but in the sense that it creates more imaginatively expansive relations. Michael Brown extends himself toward his friend by coming up with a new way to comfort him. Britt Foster retells her own story of fatal illness in order to respond to the concerns of her brother and father. To think ethically is always to think more, to think in new ways, to reinterpret oneself and one's relations. No one is an autonomous origin of their own moral beliefs any more than they are autonomous origins of language, culture, or science. In each case, persons join already existing conversations and communities and in the process reshape them over time anew. Thinking itself, to whatever degree, is the reconstruction of already constructed worlds of meaning. Every thought from birth to death is simultaneously old and new, created by a social context and recreative of it. Moral thought is the endless circular art of expanding one's moral horizons.

MORAL EDUCATION

We can begin by considering the notion of moral education. For while the term tends to conjure in the contemporary imagination the training and upbringing of children, it is also obvious that in actual experience moral education is a lifelong pursuit. Everyone young and old is capable of growing morally, whether in the face of changing life experiences or in response to others or problems in society. The notion that moral education applies primarily to children allows adults the comfort of feeling that they have reached some plateau of moral certainty. But this feeling is a dangerous one. It not only separates children into a pre-moral group, but it also makes it easier to demote all others who are not like oneself into a less than fully rational status. If moral education is thought to be something that *ends*, most people will feel that they are the ones who have reached this enlightened point.

The truth, however, is that no adult has ever attained such an Archimedean point of fixed moral wisdom. No adult has ever escaped holding moral beliefs that have turned out to be profoundly flawed, whether about gender, class, race, justice, love, or just about anything else. Often the best among us, the Mohandas Gandhis and Mother Teresas of the world, are the ones most highly attuned to their moral thinking's limitations. From this point of view, children's relative openness to growth—as well as to corruptibility—reveals more about the true nature of moral thinking than any supposed goal of moral maturity. At least it acknowledges that moral education is a continuing struggle over time.

The notion that only children are the subjects of moral education is, if anything, even more common in the West today than in the past. It is advanced from one perspective through the popular psychological idea of moral development. Many assume that moral education is a process by which premoral children increasingly develop adult moral thinking capabilities. For Piaget, as we have seen, it is a movement toward increasing moral autonomy; for Kohlberg, from egoism through conventionalism toward universalism; for Gilligan, from egoism toward relationality. Not everyone reaches the culminating point (indeed for Kohlberg it is relatively few), but everyone must pass through the same sequence of predetermined developmental phases. Even if the aim is different in different cultures, the same developmental logic still applies within a particular cultural path. Childhood, in any case, is the primary concern because it is upon this phase of life that more advanced phases are to be built. By the same token, if adults prove morally deficient, this view suggests it is likely because something went wrong when they were children.

The idea that moral education belongs chiefly to childhood is also characteristic of those who reject this dominant developmental model. As we have seen, ethicists of a more top-down persuasion argue that moral education should consist instead in instilling in children higher moral values. Human nature is unruly and must be infused from early on with coherent moral structures. Moral education is not the stage-specific unfolding of increasing capabilities but the initiation of selves into socially ordered virtues and character. The result, however, is just as adult-centric. For the whole process is imposed by already wise adults upon otherwise morally wayward children. Indeed, ethical thinking is imagined as something to which children *as children* are disinclined.

One might think that a more child-inclusive view could be found in what I have been calling bottom-up approaches. And to a certain extent it is. Children are invested with an original moral goodness or wisdom, perhaps more fully than adults. But the problem with this view throughout history has been that children's moral thinking can still be interpreted through an adult lens. Today, for example, children are sometimes described as having their own moral agency and voice. This is certainly true. Children are much more active moral thinkers than has often been supposed. But the notions of "agency" and "voice" are borrowed in the first place from adulthood. Indeed, as I have argued, they are based in a kind of modernism. The result is that little is finally learned from children's particular experiences and practices about the nature of moral thinking itself. The same kind of agency and voice that has helped liberate previously marginalized adult groups may not so well fit children. As well as examining how children are similar to adults, we should more self-critically examine how adults are similar to children.

MORAL GROWTH

When a fifteen-month-old like Brown, above, decides to help his friend, he is not doing any of the things that traditional views of moral thinking suggest. He is not applying traditional values to this particular case. He is not exercising an unusually developed capacity for moral reason. He is not just expressing his own agency or voice. Rather, even at a very young age, he is responding creatively to otherness. He is expanding his own moral horizons to imagine what is different about his friend's experience that is causing him to cry. In however small a realm—though of course it is not small to him—Brown is inventing, in the thickness of time, a transformed self-narrative and self-other relation. He could have ignored his friend or become angry at him for all the noise, but he chooses to think it through more fully.

Moral education is really a process of moral growth. It is a lifelong effort from birth to death to expand one's narrative and responsive horizons. Such a process of growth does not pass through separate phases of moral being. Nor is it either absent at birth or somehow already fully formed. Rather, moral growth means learning over time to create ever more self- and other-inclusive moral worlds. Each self already belongs at birth to an other-created historical and social environment that he or she is in turn called upon to recreate through the lifelong course of moral experience and reflection.

Children teach this, not because they are somehow morally wiser than adults, but because they face the task of moral growth in the clearest possible terms. We are used to thinking of adults as holding the greater moral responsibilities. This is true from the objective point of view that adults, due to greater experience, are held to wider obligations in their lives. But from a subjective or phenomenological point of view—that of the self's actual experience of its world—the greater responsibilities belong to children. For children are only just beginning to experience what it means to exercise responsibilities. They are more fully called upon to stretch themselves into new stories and relations. Infants face the greatest moral tasks: to learn about others' different experiences, to navigate new relations, and to inhabit the cultural and linguistic systems that make up communities. Adults only experience this degree of ethical thinking in unusual situations such as when they encounter vastly different cultures or deal with moral catastrophes. On the whole, the older one gets, the less one is called upon to think in such profoundly self-transformative ways.

But this is not to say that older children, and then adults and older adults, do not face the same moral educational task. Older children and adolescents are able to stretch their early childhood experiences of themselves and others toward still wider social and public horizons: whether in friendships, school, culture, or politics. Such responsibilities are not different in kind from those of infancy and toddlerhood, but different in degree. They demand more expansive moral imaginations. The moral aim of adolescents is not simply to learn society's moral conventions (as Kohlberg claims) but to stretch out their capacities for creating relations to others in society.

Adulthood does not bring moral education to an end. Rather, if moral thinking consists in responsiveness to others, adulthood only widens the scope of the moral educational task. The aim of a broader moral world is by definition unlimited. The age of eighteen is a convenient social construction, in most contemporary forms of society, for the age at which enough time and experience with others should have prepared one to take on a more or less full range of basic social responsibilities. But "full" here simply means what is minimally required for activities like working, marrying, complete legal culpability, and the like. Some adults, for various reasons, are not capable of taking up such obligations, or not taking them up fully, and some choose not to. But adulthood is not a distinct state of moral being. It is, rather, a socially constructed status of readiness for, in principle, a commonly held range of responsibilities for social creativity. It does not mean that moral horizons are not required to expand still further, even in radical ways. On the contrary, the more experience one has gained in the world, the more one's moral education should continue to grow in diversity and scope.

No adult—like no child—is free of the *human* responsibility of responding to others more widely. Historical experience shows that there has never been a time when even the wisest of persons were not embroiled in too narrow a view of themselves and others around them. Treating oneself and others as fully human always falls short when it comes to their own actual otherness. Even on one's deathbed, one is not suddenly relieved of responsibility for retelling one's own narrative and responding to difference. Arguably, learning from childhood makes possible greater respect for the long experience in time gained by elders. Getting older can be viewed, not as losing moral independence, but as having gained more time to explore the world's moral terrain.

The problem of moral education is a problem of poetics: of renarrating and decentering one's existing moral imagination. The central component of moral thinking is not traditionality or autonomy but expanding relations with others. As for an artist, more experience makes possible still wider possibilities.

Truly listening to children, and critiquing settled assumptions in light of them, teaches that moral education is a lifelong art of moral growth. It is not a straight path from egoism to rationality but an endlessly expanding circle. Human beings enter the world capable of being shaped by, and in turn shaping, how that world is interpreted. This passive-active dynamics of moral thinking begins as soon as one encounters an other in one's life, that is, at birth or even a little earlier. It continues as long as one can create meaning in relation to others in the world, that is, upon brain death. The moral educational aim is the same for all: to grow or expand over time the circumference of one's relations to others. All adults and children surely fall short of this aim. But at least they all can also be affirmed to take this same all-too-human journey.

INTERPRETATION, NARRATION, RESPONSIVENESS

This process of moral thinking can be broken down into three parts along much the same lines as the three elements of ethical life explored in part II. We have seen that moral being, aims, and obligations are distinct but interdependent. Moral thinking necessarily involves all three at once in a continuous cycle of what I will here call interpretation, narration, and responsiveness.

Interpretation refers to the capacity to create a world of meaning for oneself within the larger worlds of meaning into which one is born and socialized.

Consider the kind of thinking undertaken by Britt Foster. Although in many ways she is forced by having CF to respond to new experiences, she cannot help but call upon the constructed meanings already provided to her by her family, culture, society, and history. These create a largely invisible background of social understanding by which her moral thinking has already been shaped. In her case, they include such norms as strong family relations, the value of struggle and fighting, larger cultures of the medical community, a certain faith in science, and even a social milieu that has trouble acknowledging a child's dying. Part of Britt's moral task is to fashion these given ways of thinking, however much they cohere or conflict with one another, into a growing sense of the meaning of her experiences in the here and now.

Selves think morally, in part, by reconstructing their already constructed historical horizons. These horizons are complex, ambiguous, and varied. They are always to some extent morally flawed. Interpreting their meaning for oneself does not involve just passively accepting or receiving them. Neither, however, is it a purely active choice. Rather, it is poetic in the sense that historical conditions must be recreated into one's own sense of being-in-the-world. History, culture, traditions, and mores are handed down to every self from birth onwards as the raw materials of the moral imagination. Yet, they are always also to be interpreted in relation to the self's changing experiences throughout life.

Over the course of a human lifetime, moral interpretation can either narrow or expand. It narrows insofar as the self fails to appropriate its history and conditions into a meaningful understanding of its own experiences. This can include obscuring dimensions of one's personal background, anxiously clinging to one-sided values, mistaking a particular culture for universal principles, excluding the richness and diversity of one's history, destroying relations to other human and non-human beings that are parts of one's world, silencing ancestors, and closing off further moral growth. In other words, interpretation is narrow inevitably.

But moral interpretation can also increasingly expand. To this extent, it fulfills itself as thinking. At any moment in time—including during difficult times such as chronic illness—one's thinking can grow in complexity and breadth to interpret one's historical, cultural, social, familial, psychological, and biological conditions into fuller meaning. As Hans-Georg Gadamer has put it, thinking may achieve a relative "fusion of horizons" between historicity and consciousness. The great and unfathomable multitude of moralities into which each self is already born may be invested with more profound and inclusive wisdom. The first goal of moral thinking is to interpret one's diverse constituting horizons into a growingly meaningful world.

A second ethical thinking capability, relying in part on this first one, is for moral life's *narration* into a larger temporal whole.

Foster, for example, must not only interpret her given moral history but also reconstruct it into a growing narrative or story of her life over the course of time. Facing one's own mortality sets this task in high relief. Doing so as a child is no less difficult and complicated than doing so as an adult. The difference for children is that one must make sense of one's whole life on the basis of relatively less experience with time itself. Nevertheless, as Foster shows, children deal as fully as do adults with the whole arc of life's story, and when faced with death they do so in equally complex narrative ways.

Moral thinking involves forging one's pasts, presents, and possible futures into an increasingly meaningful narrative. Narration, as we saw in chapter 3, is the fashioning of the meaning of time over time. It places the time of experiences in the world into a second constructed time of a story about them. Morally speaking, narration reshapes temporal experience into larger aims and hopes. It stretches the self's various times in the world into a meaningfully whole sense of direction. The story changes as experiences change. But its aim is always an increasingly diverse narrative unity. A human life is a vast complexity of times that can be created into a more or less coherent story over time. Both children and adults must constantly reimagine what their time in the world is all about.

As in reading fiction, narration in this sense is a form of thinking that constructs unfolding possibilities. One's own life story is not simply given in lived experiences but must also constantly be created into new meaning over time. It is time expanded over time. Like interpretation, narration is an ability to create meaning amid the passive-active tensions of the world. But the latter specifically shapes the self's sense of movement through time, including with others, toward an evolving temporal whole. It forges the self's story from birth to death into imaginations of happiness and peace.

The question for moral thinking is whether this narrative capability is able to grow rather than contract, to include the fullness of the self's experiences of time rather than exclude or suppress them. As Søren Kierkegaard has argued, there are many ways in which time in the world can cause despair, but it can always also open up to renewed hope. What is possible is to transform the smallness of time, its narrative fixations and dead-ends, its many incongruities and tragedies, into a larger created story. The cycles of past, present, and future time can always be shaped into more expansive meaning. Time itself can be stretched over time. To narrate oneself is to think time more fully over time, to grow in temporal wholeness.

Finally, moral thinking also involves *responsiveness* toward others (and oneself as an other) in their irreducible otherness.

To take the example of Foster one last time, she does not respond to her younger brother's (and father's) fears simply by exercising her own voice or subordinating her voice to theirs. The moral relation is not exactly between autonomous agents. Nor, as Levinas might say, is it a response made in pure passivity. Her brother does not simply knock her world out of orbit. Rather, she responds to her brother by decentering herself. She disrupts and expands her own horizons of moral understanding. She allows him to become a second center of her own thinking, stretching it along previously untraveled paths.

The self thinks responsibly by opening up its own assumptions and narratives to decentering by others. It learns to think more elliptically. Moral thinking requires stretching oneself toward the ways in which one's understanding may also be created by others. Selves live in relation to others not just as elements in their own stories but also as irreducible to them. To think morally involves reimagining one's life story in growing response to others in their very otherness from oneself.

Growth in moral responsibility rests in part on growth in moral interpretation and narration. One is more likely to be able to stretch oneself toward others the wider and more complex one's moral world is to begin with. In addition, the other is more likely to transform me the more expansively I already tell my own story. However, responding to otherness requires additional capabilities for self-disruption and self-decentering. It stretches the circle of moral thinking into new self-understandings and narratives that only otherness makes imaginable. Responsibility to others, no matter one's age, embraces the endless creative tension of understanding others as far as possible precisely in their concrete experiential difference. Traveling to a foreign country exposes me to the shock of the other and broadens my horizons beyond anticipation.

Ethical thinking in this third dimension is neither self-sacrificial nor self-enclosed. It is the ability to distend one's existing moral horizons in response to others as different from oneself. This decentering may stretch into the past (as in remembering the victims of the Holocaust), the future (leaving our grandchildren a sustainable planet), or the present (being moved by the poor, child soldiers, or family). They may be others to be ethically emulated or others who are examples of what to avoid. In any case, others confront selves with the most complex task of moral growth. They demand not only to be interpreted and narrated but further-more to interpret and narrate me.

The difference between children and adults here is again a matter of degree rather than kind. An infant is capable of responding to otherness in the same sense as an adult. Michael Brown is perfectly able to think in new ways in response to his crying friend. Newborns learn to cope when the breast is unavailable, listen for a sibling's voice, smile at another's smile, and in general both receive and give love. An older child wants to do something for the homeless person on the street, understands her parents more fully, respects the differences of her friends. An ado-lescent learns how societies function as networks of others in response to one an-other. Ethical responsibility is not a capability installed in children that they other-wise lack. It does not appear at some magical age of reason. Rather, it is integral to human thinking throughout life.

If adults are generally held to more expansive responsibilities than children, it is not because only adults are full moral thinkers. It is because adults can be expected to have learned more from experience in the world over time. Whether or not they have actually done so, they are rightly held to broader moral standards. The extent of moral responsibility varies for adults too: by context, culture, and situation. But overall, the older one gets, the wider in principle should be one's ability to extend oneself toward others. As a result, the wider in principle is one's responsibility for doing so further still.

CONCLUSION

What these three dimensions of moral thinking hold in common is that each is a kind of world-creative art. Each stretches the moral imagination to grow. Received history is interpreted into greater meaning, time in the world into a fuller narrative, and relations to others into wider responsiveness. As children teach most vividly, to think morally is always to think more. It is not static but dynamic. It is not un-changing but temporal. It opposes narrowness, fixations, and hubris by opening the mind to creative new horizons. It is the self's constant moral expansion.

If so, then moral thinking also has a religious dimension of stretching the human imagination toward its own beyond. The problem with religious morality, as we have seen, often lies in its self-righteous certitude. Traditions are thought to have provided the timelessly correct moral answer, narrative, or perspective. This fixed-ness is supported by adult-based conceptions of the divine: a Father possessing all moral wisdom; a King with absolute power; a Judge with total authority. At the end of our childist investigations, however, it is more inclusively apt to imagine moral life in the image of a Child, ever newly making the world. In this case, the farthest borderlands of ethical thinking would lie in openness, creativity, and growth. The limits of the moral imagination is where creativity begins.

In the end, we need look no further to understand the depths of moral think-ing than in the very practice itself of childism. For above all, whether for children or adults, childism is an activity of thinking. In light of childhood, human moral thought should always grow and expand into new stories and responsibilities. It is children who most obviously create new meaning with others and demand others' creation of new meaning with them.

Childhood shows that moral thinking is not as simple as has been traditionally thought. Children have been socially marginalized throughout history, not just because adults have failed to think about them, but more profoundly because children have not been considered moral thinkers themselves. Some philosophers and theologians have had their thinking about moral thinking changed in light of childhood in some way, but none particularly fully. If anything has made children second-class moral citizens, it is the idea that children are not moral thinkers. Perhaps this idea is so trenchant because much historical thinking that has been passed on, including about childhood, has been performed by men like Thomas, Locke, Rousseau, and Kant who did not raise any children. Whatever the reason, it is now possible to disentangle being able to think from being or being around children.

The more complex view of ethical thinking that is brought to light by childism is that it creates meaning in an endlessly expanding circle. The circular metaphor pursued throughout these pages is not meant to suggest that moral thinking merely repeats its own premises, or that it takes place within preestablished boundaries. Rather, a full moral circle involves both passively and actively creating new relations over time with others. At the center of this moral circle is a thinking self whose ongoing struggle is to enlarge its moral horizons into wider self-narratives and other-responsibilities.

Ethical thinking is thus in its most fundamental sense creative or poetic. Whether in relation to history, oneself, or others, it is not an act of autonomy or traditionality but rather one of self- and world-transformation. Ethical thinking is an art. It recreates already created relations ever anew. It sets the self and society on a path of endless moral expansion. Every human being is born into already constructed moral relations that they must in turn reconstruct over time for themselves. The great promise of all humanity is to be able to imagine and practice a growing humanity.

Conclusion

THIS BOOK HAS BEEN exploring how the consideration of childhood should transform fundamental ethical understanding. More than just applying ethics to children, it has applied the experiences and perspectives of children to ethics. Since children are fully a third of all humanity, and since they are not morally reducible to adults, this transformation is no small matter. Reimagining ethics in light of childhood—and not just in light of adulthood—is challenging and often surprising. Philosophers and theologians throughout the ages have attempted this task from different angles, but the results of history show that much more work needs to be done. Perhaps more than any other group, children have been persistently marginalized. They call for new horizons of reflection.

To fully consider childhood, ethics needs to become poetic. By "poetic" I do not mean merely self-expressive, as the term has largely been understood since modernity. Nor do I mean an older kind of craftsmanlike fashioning of the world toward useful ends. Nor, finally, is ethical poetics reducible to using literature and art as means for moral purposes. I mean poetics, rather, in the most basic sense of recreating already created worlds of meaning. To be moral, in light of childhood, is to construct and reconstruct social meaning over time and in response to one another.

This is why I have described ethics with the metaphor of a circle. No one stands at moral life's absolute beginning, just as no one will ever bring it to a definitive end. Everyone is born into a particular moral time and place that has already been constructed by others, societies, and histories. As in the arts and sciences, each new self joins an already existing moral conversation. At the same time, and again as in other areas of human life, selves are called upon not just to repeat this given world but to reconstruct it anew for themselves. From birth onwards, moral life is an endless remaking of relations. This poetic ethical circle is deeper than mere freedom, rationality, or historicity. It is what unites humanity, young and old, in the task of forming moral horizons.

If such a moral poetics can be described as broadly postmodern, what this means is that it is critical of modernity's faith in individual autonomy without seeking a return to premodernity's reliance on collective hierarchies. Indeed, the very opposition of premodernity and modernity is brought into question, since both share the same range of top-down, bottom-up, and developmental assumptions about childhood. However, the various ethical projects of postmodernity have themselves also failed to respond adequately to children. Even the ethics of otherness, on which my own work relies to a large extent, has considered the implications of childhood in only the most superficial terms. This means that it has obscured the more profound sense in which others call on selves' and societies' responsive self-creativity.

To be moral is to create more rather than less expansive relations over time in response to each other. It is to transform an always too narrow world toward its own broader possibilities. The ethical demand, in short, is to grow. It is to reconstruct already constructed linguistic, cultural, and social worlds into fuller narrative wholes and wider responses to otherness. Growth! That is the heart of full moral life. That is the poetic imperative. It does not chart a predetermined course but voyages to the horizons of the imagination. Humanity's ethical purpose is the expansion rather than contraction of its own humanity.

I have broken down this poetic ethics into three increasingly complex dynamics. First, moral being is not originally innocent, unruly, or blank, but creative. From birth to death, selves bind themselves up in all manner of narrowness and destruction, but they can also play amid the experiences and possibilities of life to create more meaningful worlds. Second, the ethical aim is to use this capability to grow in narrative wholeness over time. The self's diverse pasts, presents, and possible futures—including with others—should be pressed toward ever more expansively lived stories. Third, the human obligation is to recreate oneself in response to others (including oneself as an other) in their irreducibly diverse otherness. Selves and societies inevitably marginalize differences, but they can also decenter themselves so that others make a difference to them. Each other should be treated as another creator of oneself.

This poetic or creative ethics has helped us formulate new and more child-inclusive perspectives on such practices as human rights, family life, and ethical thinking. Human rights are not just liberties, entitlements, or protections, but social responsibilities. They are society's means for expanding the circle of their self-creativity in response to the diversity of others that constitute them. Likewise, family ethics is less about promoting values, nurturing individuality, or supporting socialization than about cultivating generativity. What children and adults gain morally from families is a close circle of interdependent relations in which to create lasting stories and shared responsibilities. Finally, the practice of ethical thinking is not just applying ordered principles, expressing autonomous freedom, or progressing in social reason, but forging expanding horizons. It is a temporal and other-responsive art that strives against narrowness and complacency to imagine an always more inclusive humanity.

Throughout these discussions, religion has functioned—undoubtedly to the discomfort of some, and too untheologically for others—to describe such a moral poetics' ultimate borderlands. Ethical life can be enhanced by symbolic imaginations of its own beyond. This is another way in which this book has moved beyond modernity: not by returning to premodern traditions, but by acknowledging moral relations' wider liminality. In light of children in particular, ethics hopes for a narrative timefulness and other-responsive love that is ultimately unimaginable. The moral imagination must always stretch beyond itself. Moral creativity is an endlessly new world creation. It is a perpetual coming-of-age ritual. It constantly exceeds its own horizons. However paradoxically, a fully humanized world is always beckoning from humanity's own beyond.

This book also has implications for the emerging field of childhood studies. Childhood studies should pursue, from an ethical point of view, not just children's agency, voices, and participation, but also their distinctiveness, diversities, and otherness. It should examine and promote children's particular creativity, narrativity, and responsiveness to others as these broaden the scope of the creativity, narrativity, and responsiveness of relations and societies overall. This means, furthermore, that childhood studies can best help children by combining both empirical and humanistic inquiry. Actual observations of children need to be informed by self-critical exploration of the assumptions that are brought to doing so; and these assumptions need in turn to be rethought in response to children's actual experiences. Only in this way can childhood studies transcend modernity's subject-object dualism through a fuller phenomenological interpretation of children's lived experiences of being-in-the-world. It would involve, as I have been suggesting, a poetics or hermeneutical circle that fundamentally recreates existing assumptions and practices.

The educator Maria Montessori once said, "I keep pointing at the child; they keep staring at my finger." Ethical reflection and action needs always to consider childhood, not in order simply to note children's presence, but in order to change fundamental understanding. Moral life cannot be practiced fully without attending to its temporal beginnings. Because moral relations exceed anything that is said or thought about them, any response to children must necessarily fall short—including mine in this book. There is no more definitive answer to the meaning of childhood than there is to the meaning of being human. Nevertheless, our gaze should constantly be drawn back to the youngest among us, for in them lies the greatest moral challenge as well as the greatest moral hope. From children is learned the truest depths of moral life. We should not just move away from life's childhood origins but at the same time also toward them. Ethics in light of childhood is ethics in the strongest light of all.

Notes

INTRODUCTION

1. This and the following trends are documented by, among other groups, UNICEF (United Nations Children's Fund) and, for the United States, the Children's Defense Fund.
2. Jonathan Kozol, *Amazing Grace: The Lives of Children and the Conscience of a Nation* (New York: Crown, 1995), 124, 125–26, and 129–31.
3. Ying Ying Fry, with Amy Klatzkin, *Kids Like Me in China* (St. Paul, MN: Yeong & Yeong Book Co., 2001), 2–3.
4. Ishmael Beah, *A Long Way Gone: Memoirs of a Boy Soldier* (New York: Farrar, Straus and Giroux, 2007).
5. Ibid., 126.
6. Ibid., 169.

CHAPTER ONE

1. Philippe Ariès, *Centuries of Childhood*, trans. Robert Baldick (New York: Vintage Books, 1962). Ariès's achievement is to demonstrate that the idea of childhood varies over history, but many have contested his view of what this variation actually consists in; see, for example, Linda Pollack, *Forgotten Children: Parent-Child Relations from 1500–1900* (New York: Cambridge University Press, 1983).
2. Plato, *The Laws*, in *The Collected Dialogues of Plato*, ed. Edith Hamilton and Huntington Cairns, VII, 808d, p. 1379 (Princeton, NJ: Princeton University Press, 1961).
3. This and the following discussions of the Bible in this chapter owe much to Marcia Bunge, ed., *The Child in the Bible* (Grand Rapids, MI: Eerdmans, 2008), and to the perspective of "child theology" found in parts of the Bible in John Collier, ed., *Toddling toward the Kingdom: Child Theology at Work in the Church* (London: Child Theology Movement, 2009).
4. Exodus 20:12.
5. Ephesians 6:1.
6. 1 Corinthians 13:11.

7. Augustine, *Confessions*, trans. R. S. Pine-Coffin (New York: Penguin Books, 1961), I.7, p. 27.

8. Ibid.

9. Ibid., I.7, p. 28.

10. David F. Wright, "How Controversial Was the Development of Infant Baptism in the Early Church?" in *Church, World, and Spirit: Historical and Theological Essays in Honor of Geoffrey W. Bromiley*, ed. James E. Bradley and Richard A. Mueller, 51 (Grand Rapids, MI: Eerdmans, 1987).

11. Qur'an 8:27-28. See also, for example, Qur'an 18:44, 57:19, and 64:15.

12. Martin Luther, *To the Councilmen of All Cities in Germany That They Establish and Maintain Christian Schools*, in *Luther's Works*, ed. Walther I. Brandt, vol. 45, p. 353 (Philadelphia: Muhlenberg Press, 1962).

13. John Calvin, *Institutes of the Christian Religion*, ed. John T. McNeill, trans. Ford Lewis Battles (Philadelphia: Westminster Press, 1960), 4.15.10.

14. Barbara Pitkin, "'The Heritage of the Lord': Children in the Theology of John Calvin," in *The Child in Christian Thought*, ed. Marcia Bunge, 160–93, at 167 (Grand Rapids, MI: Eerdmans, 2001).

15. Calvin, *Institutes of the Christian Religion*, 4.15.11 and 2.8.35.

16. Ibid., 4.6.18; 4.15.11 and 20; 4.16.9, 21, and 32.

17. Anthony Krupp has argued that Descartes holds a particularly dim view of children as the antinomy of his "ideal of cognitive autonomy"; they symbolize for him the merely embodied existence that Enlightened reason must overcome through his method of meditative doubt. Krupp, *Reason's Children: Childhood in Early Modern Philosophy* (Lewisburg, PA: Bucknell University Press, 2009), 28–31.

18. Immanuel Kant, *Education*, trans. Annette Churton (Ann Arbor: The University of Michigan Press, 1960), 11 and 6, respectively.

19. Stanley Hauerwas, *A Community of Character: Toward a Constructive Christian Social Ethic* (Notre Dame, IN: University of Notre Dame Press, 1981), 173.

20. Marcia Bunge, "Introduction," in *The Child in the Bible*, ed. Marcia Bunge, xiv–xxvi, at xxiii.

21. Matthew 18:3-5; see also Mark 9:33–37 and Luke 9:46–48.

22. Judith M. Gundry-Volf, "The Least and the Greatest: Children in the New Testament," in *The Child in Christian Thought*, ed. Marcia Bunge, 29–60, at 40–46.

23. O. M. Bakke, *When Children Became People: The Birth of Childhood in Early Christianity*, trans. Brian McNeil (Minneapolis: Fortress Press, 2005).

24. Clement of Alexandria, *Paedagogus*, Book I, chapter 5, in *The Ante-Nicene Fathers: The Writings of the Fathers Down to A.D. 325*, ed. Alexander Roberts and James Donaldson, rev. A. Cleveland Coxe (Peabody, MA: Hendrickson Publishers, 1994), 2:213–16.

25. John Chrysostom, "Homily LXII" of "Homilies on the Gospel of Saint Matthew," in *Nicene and Post-Nicene Fathers*, First Series, ed. Philip Schaff, trans. W. H. Fremantle (Peabody, MA: Hendrickson Publishers, 1994), 10:385.

26. Qur'an 16:74; see also, for example, Qur'an 26:133, 40:65–69, 42:49, and 60:12.

27. Alfons H. Teipen, "Submission and Dissent: Some Observations on Children's Rights within the Islamic Edifice," in *The Given Child: The Religions' Contribution to Children's Citizenship*, ed. Trygve Wyller and Usha S. Nayar, 51–70, at 56 (Göttingen, Germany: Vandenhoeck & Ruprecht, 2007).

28. See Qur'an 6:74-81 and 21:51-70.

29. Julian of Norwich, *Revelations of Divine Love*, ed. Grace Warrack (London: Methuen, 1901), chap. LX, p. 150.

30. John Amos Comenius, *The School of Infancy*, ed. and intro. Ernest M. Eller (Chapel Hill: The University of North Carolina Press, 1956), 60–62.
31. Jean-Jacques Rousseau, *Emile, or On Education*, trans. Allan Bloom (New York: Basic Books, 1979).
32. Ibid., 37. See also Jean-Jacques Rousseau, *The Social Contract*, trans. Charles Frankel (New York: Hafner, 1947), including its famous opening line (I.1, p. 3): "Man is born free; and everywhere he is in chains."
33. Friedrich Schleiermacher, *Christmas Eve: Dialogues on the Incarnation*, trans. Terrence N. Tice (Lewiston, NY: Edwin Mellon, 1990); *Ausgewählte pädagogische Schriften* [*Aphorisms on Pedagogy*], ed. Ernst Lichtenstein(Paderborn: F. Schöningh, 1959); *The Christian Household: A Sermonic Treatise*, trans. Dietrich Seidel and Terrence N. Tice (Lewiston, NY: Edwin Mellen, 1991); *The Christian Faith*, ed. H. R. Mackintosh and J. S. Stewart (Edinburgh: T & T Clark, 1989). Schleiermacher's other well-known theological treatise, *On Religion: Speeches to Its Cultured Despisers*, trans. Richard Crouter (New York: Cambridge University Press, 1988) is first written early in his career in 1799 but subsequently revised in 1808 and again in 1821.
34. Schleiermacher, *Christmas Eve*, 36, 39, and 45.
35. Ibid., 55 and 62; and Schleiermacher, *The Christian Household*, 42, 69, and 82.
36. Schleiermacher, *The Christian Faith*, 15, 19, 23, 26–27, 488–89, 635–36, etc.
37. Karl Rahner, "Ideas for a Theology of Childhood," in *Theological Investigations*, trans. David Bourke (New York: Seabury Press, 1977), 8:36.
38. Bonnie Miller-McLemore, *Let the Children Come: Reimagining Childhood from a Christian Perspective* (San Francisco: Jossey-Bass, 2003), 144.
39. Aristotle, *Nicomachean Ethics*, trans. W. D. Ross, in Aristotle, *Introduction to Aristotle*, 2nd edition revised and enlarged, ed. Richard McKeon, VIII.1, p. 509, and VIII.12, pp. 527–28 (Chicago: University of Chicago Press, 1947).
40. Aristotle, *Politics*, trans. Benjamin Jowett, in Aristotle, *Introduction to Aristotle*, 2nd edition revised and enlarged, ed. Richard McKeon, I.2, p. 598.
41. Aristotle, *Nicomachean Ethics*, I.9, p. 361.
42. Al-Ghazali, *Revival of Religious Learnings*, trans. Fazlul Karim (Karachi, Pakistan: Darul-Ishaat, 1993), III.II, p. 64.
43. Al-Ghazali, "My Dear Beloved Son or Daughter," trans. Irfan Hasan, in Muslims Internet Directory (Chattanooga, TN: The Islamic Education and Services Institute, www.2muslims.com/directory/Detailed/227111.shtml).
44. Al-Ghazali, *Revival of Religious Learnings*, II.V.2, pp. 101–2.
45. Thomas Aquinas, *Summa Theologica*, trans. Fathers of the English Dominican Province (New York: Benziger Brothers, 1948), II-II, Q. 10, a. 12, and III, Supplement, Q. 43, a. 2. This "developmentalism" is explored in depth in Cristina L. Traina, "A Person in the Making: Thomas Aquinas on Children and Childhood," in *The Child in Christian Thought*, ed. Marcia Bunge, 103–33.
46. Christine De Pizan, *The Treasure of the City of Ladies*, trans. Sarah Lawson (New York: Penguin, 2003), 42.
47. Desiderius Erasmus, *Copia: Foundations of the Abundant Style*, in *Collected Works of Erasmus*, trans. and ann. Betty I. Knott, ed. Craig R. Thompson (Toronto: University of Toronto Press, 1978), 2: 284.
48. Desiderius Erasmus, "On Education for Children," in *The Erasmus Reader*, ed. Erika Rummel (Toronto: University of Toronto Press, 1990), 100.
49. Ibid., 68.

50. John Locke, *Some Thoughts concerning Education*, in *The Clarendon Edition of the Works of John Locke*, ed. J. W. and J. S. Yolton, chap. 1, p. 83 (New York: Oxford University Press, 1989).

51. Ibid., chap. 36, p. 105.

52. John Locke, *Essay concerning Human Understanding* (New York: Oxford University Press, 1975), I.I.27, II.I.6–8 and 20–22, and II.IX.5.

53. John Locke, *Two Treatises of Government*, from *The Works of John Locke*, New Edition, Volume V (London: W. Sharpe and Son, 1823), 126–33, 138, and 179–80.

54. Johann Gottfried von Herder, "Ideas toward a Philosophy of History" in *Against Pure Reason: Writings on Religion, Language, and History*, ed. and trans. Marcia Bunge, 53, 55 (Minneapolis: Fortress Press, 1993).

55. Ibid., 50.

56. John Stuart Mill, *On Liberty* (New York: Penguin, 1985), chaps. 1–5.

57. Ibid., chap. 1.

58. Bacon himself, in 1620, uses the analogy of ants, spiders, and bees to distinguish the methods, respectively, of empiricism, scholasticism, and induction (the last being his own innovation). I am adding also an analogy to flies. See Bacon, *Novum Organum*, ed. Thomas Fowler (Oxford: Clarendon Press, 1889), Book One, Aphorism 95. I have in mind common varieties like the European garden spider, the black garden ant, the housefly, and the honeybee.

CHAPTER TWO

1. Alan Prout and Allison James, "Introduction," in *Constructing and Reconstructing Childhood: Contemporary Issues in the Sociological Study of Childhood*, ed. Alan Prout and Allison James (New York: Falmer Press, 1990), 1–6, at 4.

2. Peter B. Pufall and Richard P. Unsworth, "Introduction: The Imperative and the Process for Rethinking Childhood" in *Rethinking Childhood*, ed. Peter B. Pufall and Richard P. Unsworth (New Brunswick, NJ: Rutgers University Press, 2004), 1–21, at 9 [my emphasis].

3. Myra Bluebond-Langner, *The Private Worlds of Dying Children* (Princeton, NJ: Princeton University Press, 1978), 232.

4. Ibid., 7.

5. See Daniel Thomas Cook, *The Commodification of Childhood: The Children's Clothing Industry and the Rise of the Child Consumer* (Durham, NC: Duke University Press, 2004).

6. Adrian Thatcher, *Marriage after Modernity: Christian Marriage in Postmodern Times* (New York: New York University Press, 1999), 152.

7. Martha Nussbaum, *The Fragility of Goodness: Luck and Ethics in Greek Tragedy and Philosophy*, updated edition (New York: Cambridge University Press, 2001).

8. David Jensen, *Graced Vulnerability: A Theology of Childhood* (Cleveland, OH: Pilgrim Press, 2005), 49.

9. Paul Ricoeur, *Freedom and Nature: The Voluntary and the Involuntary*, trans. Erazin V. Kohák (Evanston, IL: Northwestern University Press, 1966), 484.

10. Kristin Herzog, *Children and Our Global Future: Theological and Social Challenges* (Cleveland, OH: Pilgrim Press, 2005), 164.

11. "The World Congress on 'Giving Children a Voice: The Transforming Role of the Family in a Global Society,'" New Delhi, India, January 3–7, 2009; organized by the Service and Research Foundation of Asia on Family and Culture (SERFAC), Chennai, India.

12. Jacques Derrida, in Jacques Derrida and Jean-Luc Marion, "On the Gift: A Discussion between Jacques Derrida and Jean-Luc Marion," in *God, the Gift, and Postmodernism*, ed. John D. Caputo and Michael J. Scanlon, 54–78, at 59 (Bloomington: Indiana University Press, 1999).

13. Trygve Wyller, "They Owe Us Nothing: The Spirituality of Givenness and the Recognition of Children," in *The Given Child: The Religions' Contribution to Children's Citizenship*, ed. Trygve Wyller and Usha Nayar (Göttingen, Germany: Vandenhoeck & Ruprecht, 2007), 183.

14. Ibid.

15. Jacques Lusseyran, *And There Was Light: Autobiography of Jacques Lusseyran, Blind Hero of the French Resistance* (New York: Parabola Books, 1963).

16. Gabriel Marcel, *Being and Having*, trans. Katherine Farrer (Philadelphia: Westminster, 1949).

17. William Golding, interview with James Keating, in Golding, *Lord of the Flies*, Casebook Edition, 189–95, at 190 (New York: G. P. Putnam's Sons, 1964).

18. Eric Ziolkowski, *Evil Children in Religion, Literature, and Art* (New York: Palgrave, 2001), 163.

19. See Jean M. Baker, *How Homophobia Hurts Children: Nurturing Diversity at Home, at School, and in the Community* (Binghamton, NY: The Haworth Press, 2002), 85–94.

20. Immanuel Kant, *Religion within the Limits of Reason Alone*, trans. Theodore M. Greene and Hoyt H. Hudson (New York: Harper Torchbooks, 1960), 38.

21. John Wall, *Moral Creativity: Paul Ricoeur and the Poetics of Possibility* (New York: Oxford University Press, 2005), 69–75. The ethical discussion of *Antigone* includes figures such as G. W. F. Hegel, Friedrich Nietzsche, Paul Ricoeur, Luce Irigaray, Martha Nussbaum, and Pamela Sue Anderson.

22. Sophocles, *Antigone* in *Sophocles I*, 2nd ed., trans. David Grene (Chicago: University of Chicago Press, 1991).

23. G. W. F. Hegel, *Hegel on Tragedy*, 2nd ed., ed. Anne and Henry Paolucci (Smyrna, DE: Griffon House Publications, 2001), 325.

24. Luce Irigaray, *Speculum of the Other Woman*, trans. Carolyn Burke and Gillian C. Gill (London: Athlone Press, 1993), 119. Pamela Sue Anderson similarly argues that Antigone finds herself in a "double double-bind": "Antigone is, first, marginalized as a woman who remains excluded from the public domain by the ancient *polis*," and "second, she is further marginalized from her family and religious community even as a consequence of her religiously motivated duty to bury her brother, since this involves 'unwomanly' public dissent from a civil religious duty to follow the king's edicts." See Anderson, *A Feminist Philosophy of Religion: The Rationality of Myths of Religious Belief* (Malden, MA: Blackwell Publishers, 1998), 190.

25. Sophocles, *Antigone*, lines 465, 524, 851, 1005, 1175, 1282, 1313, and elsewhere.

26. See, for example, Howard Chudacoff, *Children at Play: An American History* (New York: New York University Press, 2008).

27. Plato, *Laws*, Book I, 643b-c, p. 1243; see also *Laws*, Book VII, 793e-794d, p. 1366; and *Republic*, in *The Collected Dialogues of Plato*, ed. Edith Hamilton and Huntington Cairns (Princeton, NJ: Princeton University Press, 1961), Book VII, 536e, p. 768. This view is to some degree also adopted by the early Christian theologian Jerome, who at once romanticizes play for adults (as seen above) and instrumentalizes it when it comes to actual children, such as when he writes in advice to a friend: "Get for her a set of letters made of boxwood or of ivory and called each by its proper name. Let her play with these, so that

even her play may teach her something." Jerome, Letter 107, "To Laeta," in *Nicene and Post-Nicene Fathers*, Second Series, Volume VI, ed. Philip Schaff and Henry Wace, trans. W. H. Fremantle (Grand Rapids, MI: Eerdmans, 1982–83).

28. Augustine, *Confessions*, Book I, chap. 10, p. 31.
29. John Wesley, *Minutes of the Methodist Conferences* (London: John Mason, 1862), 1:164.
30. John Locke, *Some Thoughts concerning Education*, chap. 130, p.192 (text modernized).
31. Hans-Georg Gadamer, *Truth and Method*, Second Revised Edition, trans. Joel Weinsheimer and Donald G. Marshall (New York: Crossroad, 1989), 104.
32. Ibid., 104–5.
33. Ibid., 110.
34. Jacques Derrida, "Différance," trans. David B. Allison, in *The Continental Philosophy Reader*, ed. Richard Kearney and Mara Rainwater, 441–64, at, respectively, 441, 449, 459, and 449 (New York: Routledge, 1996).
35. Richard Kearney, *On Stories* (New York: Routledge, 2002).
36. Richard Kearney, *Strangers, Gods, and Monsters: Interpreting Otherness* (New York: Routledge, 2003), 188.
37. Ibid., 179.
38. Richard Kearney, *The God Who May Be* (Bloomington: Indiana University Press, 2001), 108; and, for later quotes in this paragraph, respectively, 110, 106, 109, and 109.
39. Matthew 19:26 and 19:15.
40. Jean-Luc Marion, *God without Being*, trans. Thomas A. Carlson (Chicago: University of Chicago Press, 1991), 24.
41. W. Sibley Towner, "Children and the Image of God," in *The Child in the Bible*, ed. Marcia Bunge, 307–23, at 323.
42. I have pursued this general point in my previous book, *Moral Creativity*. Some examples of early Christian readings along these lines include Origin: "Every one who imitates Him according to his ability, does by this very endeavor raise a statue according to the image of the Creator" (*Contra Celsum* [*Against Celsus*], trans. Henry Chadwick [New York: Cambridge University Press, 1953], Book VIII, chapter 18); Mathetes: "Do not wonder that a man may become an imitator of God. He can . . . [who] takes upon himself the burden of his neighbor . . . [and] who, whatever things he has received from God, by distributing these to the needy, becomes a god to those who receive [them]" (*Epistle of Mathetes to Diogenes* in *The Apostolic Fathers* [Grand Rapids, MI: Eerdmans, 1975], chapter 10); Clement of Alexandria: "He is the [true] Gnostic, who is after the image and likeness of God, who imitates God as far as possible, deficient in none of the things which contribute to the likeness as far as compatible, practicing self-restraint and endurance, living righteously, reigning over the passions, bestowing of what he has as far as possible, and doing good both by word and deed" (*Stromateis* [Washington, DC: Catholic University of America Press, 1991], Book II, chapter 19); and Pseudo-Clementine: "Warn and exhort the worshippers, that by good deeds they imitate Him whom they worship, and hasten to return to His image and likeness" (*Recognitions* in *The Apostolic Fathers* [Grand Rapids: Eerdmans, 1975], Book V, chapter 14). In addition, the medieval Jewish theologian Moses Maimonides argues that the perfect human being is "determined to seek loving-kindness, judgment, and righteousness, and thus to imitate the ways of God" (*A Guide for the Perplexed*, trans. Michael Friedländer [New York: E. P. Dutton, 1904], chap. 54). The medieval Christian theologian Nicholas of Cusa claims that "our mind is a certain force that possesses an image of the divine art . . . [so that it] is

created by the creative art, as if this art wanted to create itself" (*Idiota de mente*, II, in Gabriel, *Philosophisch-theologische Schriften*, III, pp. 590–92, quoted in Jean-Louis Chrétien, *Hand to Hand: Listening to the Work of Art*, trans. Stephen E. Lewis [New York: Fordham University Press, 2003], 121–22).

43. William Schweiker, *Responsibility and Christian Ethics* (New York: Cambridge University Press, 1995), 176.
44. John Chrysostom, "An Address on Vainglory and the Right Way for Parents to Bring Up Their Children," in *Christianity and Pagan Culture in the Later Roman Empire*, ed. M. L. W. Laistner (Ithaca, NY: Cornell University Press, 1951), 96.
45. Richard Shweder, *Thinking through Cultures: Expeditions in Cultural Psychology* (Cambridge, MA: Harvard University Press, 1991), 261.
46. See Alma Gottleib, *The Afterlife Is Where We Come From: The Culture of Infancy in West Africa* (Chicago: University of Chicago Press, 2004).
47. Henri Bergson, *Creative Evolution*, trans. Arthur Mitchell (Mineola, NY: Dover Publications, 1998), 7.

CHAPTER THREE

1. Natalie Babbitt, *Tuck Everlasting* (New York: Farrar, Straus, Giroux, 1975), 62–64.
2. Plato, *Laws*, Book II, 653b, p. 1250.
3. Augustine, *Confessions*, Book VIII, chap. 10, p. 175.
4. Clement of Alexandria, *Paedagogus*, Book I, chap. 5, p. 213.
5. Schleiermacher, *The Christian Household*, 63, 64, and 68, respectively.
6. Aristotle, *Nicomachean Ethics*, I.9, p. 361.
7. Locke, *Some Thoughts concerning Education*, chap. 33, p. 103 (text modernized).
8. Immanuel Kant, *Critique of Practical Reason*, trans. Lewis White Beck (New York: Macmillan, 1956), 166.
9. Martin Heidegger, *Being and Time*, trans. John Macquarrie and Edward Robinson (New York: Harper & Row, 1962), II.4, p. 417. See also Edmund Husserl, *The Phenomenology of Internal Time-Consciousness*, trans. James S. Churchill (Bloomington: Indiana University Press, 1964).
10. Dave Eggers, *What Is the What? The Autobiography of Valentino Achak Deng.* (New York: Vintage Books, 2006).
11. See René Descartes, *Meditations on First Philosophy: In Which the Existence of God and the Distinction of the Human Soul from the Body Are Demonstrated*, trans. George Heffernan (Notre Dame, IN: University of Notre Dame Press, 1992). For a somewhat different Enlightenment view, edging a little closer to Heidegger's, see Immanuel Kant, *Critique of Pure Reason*, trans. Norman Kemp Smith (London: Macmillan, 1950), A37, B54, p. 79.
12. Augustine, *Confessions*, Book XI, chap. 14, p. 264.
13. Ibid., Book XI, chap. 28, p. 277 and Book XI, chap. 20, p. 269.
14. Paul Ricoeur, *Time and Narrative, Volume 1*, trans. Kathleen McLaughlin and David Pellauer (Chicago: University of Chicago Press, 1984), 3. See also Paul Ricoeur, *Oneself as Another*, trans. Kathleen Blamey (Chicago: University of Chicago Press, 1992).
15. Birgit Carolin and Pat Milner, "A Medley of Children's Voices," in *Time to Listen to Children: Personal and Professional Communication*, ed. Pat Milner and Birgit Carolin, 19 (New York: Routledge, 1999). Newman's last name is invented.
16. Herbert Anderson and Susan B. W. Johnson, *Regarding Children: A New Respect for Childhood and Families* (Louisville, KY: Westminster John Knox Press, 1994), 9.

17. Sigmund Freud, *New Introductory Lectures on Psycho-Analysis*, trans. James Strachey (New York: W. W. Norton, 1965), 97.
18. Alan Prout, *The Future of Childhood: Towards the Interdisciplinary Study of Children* (New York: RoutledgeFalmer, 2005), 60.
19. Anne Frank, *Anne Frank: The Diary of a Young Girl* (New York: Washington Square Press, 1972), 215.
20. There is also here, of course, the problem of violence; but I am bracketing that for the next chapter.
21. See, for example, Sallie McFague, *Models of God: Theology for an Ecological, Nuclear Age* (Philadelphia: Fortress Press, 1987), 110.
22. Gabriel Marcel, *The Mystery of Being, I. Reflection and Mystery* (Chicago: Henry Regnery Company, 1950), 123–25.
23. Jean Piaget, *The Moral Judgment of the Child*, trans. Marjorie Gabain (New York: Free Press, 1965), 315–17.
24. Lawrence Kohlberg, *Essays on Moral Development* (San Francisco: Harper & Row, 1981).
25. Carol Gilligan, *In a Different Voice: Psychological Theory and Women's Development* (Cambridge, MA: Harvard University Press, 1982).
26. Jürgen Moltmann, *In the End—The Beginning: The Life of Hope* (Minneapolis: Fortress Press, 2004), 17.
27. Karl Rahner, "Ideas for a Theology of Childhood," in *Theological Investigations*, vol. 8, pp. 35–36.
28. Martin Buber, *On the Bible*, ed. Nahum N. Glatzer (New York: Schocken, 1968), 87.

CHAPTER FOUR

1. This true story—though I've invented a last name, since none is given—is told by Barbara Bennett Woodhouse in *Hidden in Plain Sight: The Tragedy of Children's Rights from Ben Franklin to Lionel Tate* (Princeton, NJ: Princeton University Press, 2008), 1–5.
2. The key texts in the background of this discussion are Emmanuel Levinas, *Totality and Infinity: An Essay on Exteriority*, trans. Alphonso Lingis (Pittsburgh: Duquesne University Press, 1969); Paul Ricoeur, *Oneself as Another*; Luce Irigaray, *An Ethics of Sexual Difference*, trans. Carolyn Burke and Gillian Gill (London: The Athlone Press, 1993); and Richard Kearney, *Strangers, Gods, and Monsters* (New York: Routledge, 2003).
3. John Caputo, *Against Ethics: Contributions to a Poetics of Obligation with Constant Reference to Deconstruction* (Indianapolis: Indiana University Press, 1993), 8.
4. Kearney, *Strangers, Gods, and Monsters*, 188.
5. Jürgen Habermas, *Moral Consciousness and Communicative Action*, trans. Christian Lenhardt and Shierry Weber Nicholsen (Cambridge, MA: The MIT Press, 1990), 66 (Habermas's own emphasis).
6. Ibid., 67, revised edition.
7. John Rawls, *A Theory of Justice* (Cambridge, MA: Harvard University Press, 1999), 118.
8. Emmanuel Levinas, *Otherwise than Being, or Beyond Essence*, trans. Alphonso Lingis (Pittsburgh: Duquesne University Press, 1981), 180.
9. Ibid., 141. See also Levinas, *Totality and Infinity*, 305.
10. Levinas, *Otherwise than Being*, 146 and 158. Levinas typically refers to the phrase "here I am" in reference to Abraham in Genesis 22:1 and 11 and Isaiah in Isaiah 6:8. However, other biblical instances of the phrase include Genesis 31:11 and 46:2 (Jacob), Exodus 3:4

(Moses), 1 Samuel 3:4, Psalm 40:7–8, Isaiah 65:1, 2 Esdras 14:2, Luke 1:38, Acts 9:10, and Hebrews 2:11–13.

11. Levinas, *Totality and Infinity*, 215.
12. 1 Samuel 3:4–16.
13. Lisa Guenther, *The Gift of the Other: Levinas and the Politics of Reproduction* (Albany: State University of New York Press, 2006), 3.
14. Enola Aird, "Advertising and Marketing to Children in the United States," in *Rethinking Childhood*, ed. Peter B. Pufall and Richard P. Unsworth, 141–53, at 150 (New Brunswick, NJ: Rutgers University Press, 2004).
15. Levinas, *Otherwise than Being*, 4.
16. Alfred North Whitehead, *Process and Reality*, corrected edition, ed. David Ray Griffin and Donald W. Sherburne (New York: Free Press, 1978), 21.
17. H. R. Niebuhr, *The Responsible Self: An Essay in Christian Moral Philosophy* (New York: Harper & Row, 1963), 71.
18. Bonnie Miller-McLemore, *In the Midst of Chaos: Caring for Children as Spiritual Practice* (San Francisco: Jossey-Bass, 2007), 19–20.
19. Cindi Katz, *Growing Up Global: Economic Restructuring and Children's Everyday Lives* (Minneapolis: University of Minnesota Press, 2004), 8. I have made up the girl's last name (from the last name of an unrelated adult mentioned on p. 3), since no last name is given.
20. Plato, *Republic* III, 414c-415c, pp. 658–59.
21. Aristotle, *Nicomachean Ethics*, VIII. 12, p. 527.
22. Locke, *Some Thoughts concerning Education*, chap. 36, p. 105.
23. Rousseau, *Emile*, Book II, pp. 84–85.
24. Kant, *Education*, 102 and 108.
25. Martin Luther King Jr., "Letter from Birmingham Jail—April 16, 1963," in *Afro-American Religious History: A Documentary Witness*, ed. Milton C. Sernett (Durham, NC: Duke University Press 1985), 433.
26. Luke 6:27–28.
27. Luke 6:31.
28. Jean-Luc Marion, *Prolegomena to Charity*, trans. Stephen E. Lewis (New York: Fordham University Press, 2002), 87.
29. Chrysostom, "An Address on Vainglory and the Right Way for Parents to Bring Up Their Children," 96.
30. Sallie McFague, *Models of God: Theology for an Ecological, Nuclear Age* (Philadelphia: Fortress Press, 1987), 119.

CHAPTER FIVE

1. Lewis Pitts, "The Right to Be Heard: The Child as a Legal Person," in *Children as Equals: Exploring the Rights of the Child*, ed. Kathleen Alaimo and Brian Klug, 165–81, at 174 (New York: University Press of America, 2002).
2. Locke, *Two Treatises of Government*, 107–8, 116–17, 146–47, and 159–61.
3. Ibid., 126–33, 138, and 179–80.
4. Ibid., 127 and 132–33.
5. Rousseau, *The Social Contract*, II.1, pp. 24–25, etc.
6. Ibid., I.2, p. 4 and I.4, p. 9.

7. Immanuel Kant, *Foundations of the Metaphysics of Morals*, 2nd ed., trans. Lewis White Beck (Englewood Cliffs, NJ: Prentice Hall, 1990), 47. See also Immanuel Kant, *The Science of Right*, trans. W. Hastie (Clifton, NJ: A.M. Kelley, 1974; from http://etext.library.adelaide.edu.au/, 2004), Introduction B-C.

8. Kant, *The Science of Right*, para. 28.

9. Ibid., para. 29.

10. Jack Donnelly, *Universal Human Rights in Theory and Practice*, 2nd ed. (Ithaca, NY: Cornell University Press, 2003), 149–50.

11. H. L. A. Hart, "Are There Any Natural Rights?" *Philosophical Review* 64 (1955): 175–91, at 175.

12. Ibid., 175.

13. John Rawls, *A Theory of Justice*, 53.

14. John Finnis, *Natural Law and Natural Rights* (New York: Oxford University Press, 1980).

15. Martha Nussbaum, *Sex and Social Justice* (New York: Oxford University Press, 1999), 40–41.

16. Paul Gordon Lauren, *The Evolution of International Human Rights: Visions Seen*, 2nd ed. (Philadelphia: University of Pennsylvania Press, 2003), 1.

17. Barbara Bennett Woodhouse, *Hidden in Plain Sight: The Tragedy of Children's Rights from Ben Franklin to Lionel Tate* (Princeton, NJ: Princeton University Press, 2008), 309.

18. The one curious exception is that the 1989 CRC drops the child's provision right, present in both previous agreements, to be "brought up in the consciousness that its talents must be devoted to the service of fellow men." From a circular point of view, such a right would seem vital.

19. This and the following analyses are based on UNICEF's classification of the CRC rights, which can be found at www.unicef.org/crc/index_30177.html.

20. Many of the following arguments are found in the large current literature on children's rights. See, for example, Mary John, *Children's Rights and Power: Charging Up for a New Century* (New York: Jessica Kingsley Publishers, 2003); Tom Cockburn, "Children as Participative Citizens: A Radical Pluralist Case for 'Child-Friendly' Public Communication," *Journal of Social Sciences*, Special Issue 9 (2005), 19–29; Ruth Lister, "Why Citizenship: Where, When and How Children?" *Theoretical Inquiries in Law* 8.2 (2007), 693–718; Michael Freeman, "Why It Remains Important to Take Children's Rights Seriously," *International Journal of Children's Rights* 15.1 (2007), 5–23; John Wall, "Human Rights in Light of Childhood," *International Journal of Children's Rights* 16.4 (2008), 523–43; and Barry Percy-Smith and Nigel Thomas, eds., *A Handbook of Children and Young People's Participation: Perspectives from Theory and Practice* (New York: Routledge, 2010).

21. See a discussion of this case—whose full title is *R (Williamson) v. Secretary of State for Education and Employment*—in Michael Freeman, "Why It Remains Important to Take Children's Rights Seriously," *International Journal of Children's Rights* 15 (2007): 5–23, at 6–7.

22. Kathleen Marshall and Paul Purvis, *Honouring Children: The Human Rights of the Child in Christian Perspective* (Edinburgh, Scotland: Saint Andrews Press, 2004), 324.

CHAPTER SIX

1. See Hugh Cunningham, *Children and Childhood in Western Society since 1500* (New York: Longman, 1995), 190.

2. Jean Bethke Elshtain, "The Family and Civic Life," in *Rebuilding the Nest: A New Commitment to the American Family*, ed. David Blankenhorn, Steven Bayme, and Jean Bethke Elshtain, 119–32, at 131 (Milwaukee, WI: Family Service America, 1990). See also

Elshtain, *Public Man, Private Woman: Women in Social and Political Thought* (Princeton, NJ: Princeton University Press, 1981), 326.

3. Gilbert Meilander, "A Christian View of the Family," in *Rebuilding the Nest*, ed. Blankenhorn, et al., 133–48, at 143.

4. Hauerwas, *A Community of Character*, 160.

5. William Doherty, *Take Back Your Kids: Confident Parenting in Turbulent Times* (Notre Dame, IN: Sorin Books, 2000), 15 and 26.

6. The United Nations' 1990 "World Declaration on the Survival, Protection, and Development of Children," article 15.

7. Anderson and Johnson, *Regarding Children*, 9.

8. Kathleen and James McGinnis, *Parenting for Peace and Justice: Ten Years Later* (Maryknoll, NY: Orbis Books, 1990), 143.

9. Sylvia Ann Hewlett and Cornel West, *The War against Parents: What We Can Do for America's Beleaguered Moms and Dads* (New York: Houghton Mifflin Company, 1998), xiii.

10. Anderson and Johnson, *Regarding Children*, 17.

11. Jürgen Habermas, *The Theory of Communicative Action, Volume Two: Lifeworld and System: A Critique of Functionalist Reason*, trans. Thomas McCarthy (Boston: Beacon, 1987), 325–27, 355–58, 367–73.

12. Reinhold Niebuhr, *The Nature and Destiny of Man: A Christian Interpretation. Volume II: Human Destiny* (New York: Charles Scribners, 1943), 124.

13. Diana Baumrind, "Child Care Practices Anteceding Three Patterns of Preschool Behavior," *Genetic Psychology Monographs* 75 (1967): 43–88.

14. The principle of subsidiarity was first applied in official Catholic doctrine to workers, by Pope Pius XI in *Quadragesimo anno* (*Forty Years After [Rerum novarum]*) (1931), based on Pope Leo XIII's encyclical *Rerum novarum* (*On the Condition of Workers*) (1891). See also National Conference of Catholic Bishops, *Economic Justice for All* (Washington, DC: U.S. Catholic Conference, 1986). But it has increasingly come to be applied also to families.

15. Hans Joas, *The Imperative of Responsibility: In Search of an Ethics for the Technological Age* (Chicago: University of Chicago Press, 1984), 134.

16. Erik Erikson, *Childhood and Society* (New York: W. W. Norton, 1950), 231.

17. Miller-McLemore, *Let the Children Come*, 143.

18. Christine Gudorf, "Parenting, Mutual Love, and Sacrifice," in *Women's Consciousness and Woman's Conscience: A Reader in Feminist Ethics*, ed. Barbara Hilkert Andolsen, Christine E. Gudorf, and Mary D. Pellauer, 190 (New York: Harper & Row, 1985).

19. Lisa Sowle Cahill, *Family: A Christian Social Perspective* (Minneapolis: Augsburg Fortress, 2000), 16.

20. Jhumpa Lahiri, *The Namesake* (New York: Houghton Mifflin, 2003).

21. Don S. Browning, Bonnie J. Miller-McLemore, Pamela D. Couture, K. Brynolf Lyon, and Robert M. Franklin, *From Culture Wars to Common Ground: Religion and the American Family Debate*, 2nd ed. (Louisville, KY: Westminster John Knox Press, 2000), 268.

22. Ibid., 47.

23. Pamela Couture, *Seeing Children, Seeing God: A Practical Theology of Children and Poverty* (Nashville: Abingdon Press, 2000), 57.

24. Luce Irigaray, *Thinking the Difference: Towards a Peaceful Revolution*, trans. Alison Martin (London: The Athlone Press, 1994), 99.

25. W. Bradford Wilcox, *Soft Patriarchs, New Men: How Christianity Shapes Fathers and Husbands* (Chicago: University of Chicago Press, 2004).

26. Bonnie Miller-McLemore, *Also a Mother: Work and Family as Theological Dilemma* (Nashville: Abingdon Press, 1994), 150.

27. John Witte, Jr., *From Sacrament to Contract: Marriage, Religion, and Law in the Western Tradition* (Louisville, KY: Westminster John Know Press, 1997), 7.

28. See, for example, Joseph Blenkinsopp, John J. Collins, Carol Myers, and Leo G. Perdue, *Families in Ancient Israel* (Louisville, KY: Westminster John Knox Press, 1997); and David L. Balch and Carolyn Osiek, *Families in the New Testament World* (Louiville, KY: Westminster John Knox Press, 1997).

29. Browning et al., *From Culture Wars to Common Ground*, 268.

30. This evidence is summarized in Linda J. Waite and Maggie Gallagher, *The Case for Marriage: Why Married People Are Happier, Healthier, and Better Off Financially* (New York: Doubleday, 2000).

31. Browning et al., *From Culture Wars to Common Ground*, 2.

32. Ibid., 316–17.

33. I note, however, that in other works, many of them cited for my own argument in this volume, the authors of *From Culture Wars to Common Ground* have separately explored children's agency in family and social contexts.

34. Browning et al., *From Culture Wars to Common Ground*, 106.

35. Ibid.

36. Thatcher, *Marriage after Modernity*, 297–99.

37. This language is endorsed in Gary Becker, *A Treatise on the Family*, enlarged edition (Cambridge, MA: Harvard University Press, 1991).

CHAPTER SEVEN

1. Gareth Matthews, *The Philosophy of Childhood* (Cambridge, MA: Harvard University Press, 1994), 57. Michael Brown's last name is made up by me since it is not given.

2. Ibid., 59–60.

3. Myra Bluebond-Langer, *In the Shadow of Illness: Parents and Siblings of the Chronically Ill Child* (Princeton, NJ: Princeton University Press, 1996), 108.

Index

rights as responsibilities to otherness, 127–32; and ethical poetics, 179; the generative family circle, 146, 148–53, 165; human being-in-the-world and the circle of world creativity, 41
"civil rights" approach to human rights, 120
Clement of Alexandria, 21, 38, 61, 188n42
Comenius, John Amos, 22
Confessions (Augustine), 16–17, 66–68
Convention on the Rights of the Child (CRC), 23, 122–25, 127–30, 192n18; and children's legal right to be heard in court, 114; ethical trajectory of rights, 127–30; participation rights, 123–25, 129; protection rights, 123, 127–28; provision rights, 123, 128–29, 192n18
Cook, Daniel Thomas, 186n5
Couture, Pamela, 156, 161
creation and creativity, 36, 41, 57–58; children's capability for making meaning, 56–57; Creator as symbol for, 56; early Christian theologians and the *imitatio Dei* (imitation of God), 56, 188n42; images of the Creator/ humanity as image of the image, 55–57; and mystery, 53–54; and original innocence of humankind (*adam*), 55–56; and play, 50–53
Cyprian, 21
Cyrus Cylinder, 114

Day, Dorothy, 120
decentering the self: the asymmetrical moral ellipse of self and other, 92–93; and love's hyperbole (ellipse), 108; and self-expansion, 92–95, 108, 110; and self-narration, 94–95
Declaration of Independence (U.S.), 115
Declaration of the Rights of Man and of the Citizen (France), 115
Declaration of the Rights of the Child (1924), 121

Declaration of the Rights of the Child (1959), 122, 123
Deepthi, Kunda, 40
Deng, Valentino Achak (lost boy of Sudan), 64–65, 78
deontological ethics, 9. *See also* ethical obligations in light of childhood (and "the other")
de Pizan, Christine, 26–27
depravity and evil, children's capability for, 18–19, 44–46, 98; Augustine on children's "fallenness" and original sin, 45; and Calvin, 18; and human being as tragic, 48; and Kant, 45; other-dehumanization and failure of responsiveness, 98–100
Derrida, Jacques, 41–42, 51
Descartes, René, 18, 75, 184n17
developmental childism, 14, 25–32; advantages of, 28; Aristotle, 25, 27, 30, 62, 70, 71, 103; contemporary resurgence, 28–29, 79–81; the "end" or aim of moral development, 61–62, 70–71; and ethical narration, 70–72; and family ethics, 141–45, 148–59, 152–53; generative family circle and formation of relationality, 148–49, 152–53; Locke, 27–28, 30, 62, 71, 115, 117, 121; the problem of moral diversity, 28–30; problems with developmental aims and stageism, 79–81; and provision rights, 121; respect for concrete processes of human nature, 29
difference. *See* ethical obligations in light of childhood (and "the other")
disruption, ethical, 90–92
Donnelly, Jack, 118

Edicts of Ashoka, 114
Eggers, Dave, 64
Einstein, Albert, 63
Elshtain, Jean Bethke, 141
Emile, or On Education (Rousseau), 22

human being, the nature of (continued) 53–55; children's capability for making meaning, 56–57; depravity and evil, 19, 44–46, 48, 98; gifts and giftedness, 41–44, 54–55; human being as tragic, 46–48; images of the Creator and humanity as image of the image, 55–57; and phenomenology, 36, 41–44, 50–53; and play, 48–54; vulnerability and agency, 39–41, 43; and Western intellectual tradition, 35–36; and world creativity, 36, 41, 55–58
humanism, 3, 126
human rights in light of childhood, 105, 113–38, 180; adult-centered foundations of rights theory, 114–17; and children's legal right to be heard in court, 114, 117; the circle of human rights and responses to otherness, 127–32; "civil rights" approach, 120; contemporary human rights theory, 117–20; and the CRC (1989), 23, 114, 122–25, 127–30, 192n18; different rights of children and adults, 132–33; and earliest human rights documents, 114; Enlightenment modernity and exclusion of children from human rights, 114–17; and fallacy that rights and responsibilities are opposed, 131–32; and Declaration of the Rights of the Child (1924), 121; global children's rights and agreements of the twentieth century, 121–25; and the horrors of the twentieth century, 125–26; "interest theory," 119–20; and moral "hyperbole" in human rights, 137; nature (nonhuman "others") and rights, 133–35; and necessity of rethinking rationalism, 126; participation rights, 123–25, 129, 130–32, 135; protection rights, 121, 122, 123, 127–28, 130–32, 135; provision rights, 121, 122, 123, 128–29, 130–32, 135, 192n18; religion and rights, 135–38; rights as social

responsibilities to otherness, 125–38; the UN Declaration of the Rights of the Child (1959), 122, 123; "will theory," 118–19
Husserl, Edmund, 36, 189n9

image of God, 20–23, 55, 97, 109, 136, 137
imitatio Dei (imitation of God), 56, 188n42; the Sabbath as, 84–85
infant baptism, 17–18
"interest theory" of human rights, 119–20
interpretation, moral: and narrative expansion, 68–72; and process of ethical thinking, 173–74
Irigaray, Luce, 47, 156–57, 187n21, 190n2
Islam, 17, 21–22, 25–26

James, Allison, 37
Jensen, David, 39
Jerome, 187n27
John Chrysostom, 21, 56, 109, 160
Jonas, Hans, 144–45
Jones, Annabelle (child living in urban poverty), 4–5, 9, 90–91, 94, 100, 117, 119, 130–31
Julian of Norwich, 22
Jung, Carl, 71
justice, 25, 46, 80, 94, 120, 141, 170. *See also* social justice

Kant, Immanuel: on children's moral rationality, 19; and contemporary "will theory," 118–19; definitions of justice on adult grounds, 103; on eternity, 62; and human rights' religious dimensions, 136; on education's moral task, 18; and participation rights, 124; on time, 189n11; top-down childism, 18, 19
Katz, Cindi, 102
Kearney, Richard, 92, 190n2
Kids Like Me in China (Fry), 5
Kierkegaard, Søren, 175
King, Martin Luther, Jr., 104, 120, 136

childism and human original goodness, 22, 29, 38, 103, 115–16, 117; and children's moral agency, 38; and contemporary "civil rights" approach to human rights, 120; definitions of justice on adult grounds, 103; and human rights' religious dimensions, 136; on marriage, 160; and participation rights, 123

Sabbath, 84–85
Sartre, Jean-Paul, 78
Schleiermacher, Friedrich, 22–23, 43, 61
The School of Infancy (Comenius), 22
Schweiker, William, 56
Shweder, Richard, 189n45
Social Contract (Rousseau), 22
social justice, 100, 102–6, 118. *See also* justice
soft patriarchy, 157–58
Some Thoughts concerning Education (Locke), 27
subsidiarity principle, 144

Teipen, Alfons H., 21–22
teleological ethics, 8–9, 59, 64, 78. *See also* ethical aim of human societies in light of childhood
Tertullian, 21
Thatcher, Adrian, 39, 163–64
time: Augustine's discussions of, 61, 66–68, 70, 71; distended (expanded), 65–68; and Enlightenment modernity, 65–66; eternal time of Sabbath, 84–85; growing time as one ages, 63–65; illusion of timeless reason, 60–62; the inner experience of, 62–63; and narrative expansion, 59–60, 68–74, 78–79; neurological experience of, 75–76; and timefulness, 83–85. *See also* ethical aim of human societies in light of childhood
top-down childism, 14, 15–20, 30–32; and Augustine, 16–17, 19; Calvin, 17–18;

and children's capability for doing harm/evil, 18, 19; and moral discipline of children, 18–19; and doctrine of original sin, 16–17; and family ethics, 141–45, 148–49, 151–52; generative family circle and transmission of lifeworlds, 148–49, 151–52; Hebrew Bible, 16; and illusion of escaping time, 61; and infant baptism, 17–18; Islam, 17; and Kant, 18, 19; and narrativity, 69–70; and New Testament, 16; Plato, 15–16, 25, 61; and problem of moral agency, 18–20; Protestant Reformation and Luther, 17
Towner, W. Sibley, 55
tragedy, 46–48; and play, 49, 50–52
Traina, Cristina, 185n45
Treasure of the City of Ladies (de Pizan), 26–27
Tuck Everlasting (Babbitt), 60–61, 78
Turner, Victor, 106
Two Treatises on Government (Locke), 27–28, 115

UNICEF (United Nations Children's Fund), 6, 103, 183n1, 192n19
United Nations (UN), 6, 122, 143. *See also* Convention on the Rights of the Child (CRC), and Declaration of the Rights of the Child (1959)
Universal Declaration of Human Rights (1948), 122
Universal Human Rights in Theory and Practice (Donnelly), 118

voice: children's capabilities for, 36–39, 171, 181; children's own, 10, 23, 46–47, 94–96, 117, 163, 175–76; in society, 88–89, 102–5, 114, 118, 120, 124, 128–32
vulnerability: alternative meanings of, 39–40; bottom-up childism and the problem of, 23–24, 39; and children's